T0259923

Practical Django 2 and Channels 2

Building Projects and Applications with Real-Time Capabilities

Federico Marani

Apress®

Practical Django 2 and Channels 2: Building Projects and Applications with Real-Time Capabilities

Federico Marani
London, UK

ISBN-13 (pbk): 978-1-4842-4098-4   ISBN-13 (electronic): 978-1-4842-4099-1
https://doi.org/10.1007/978-1-4842-4099-1

Library of Congress Control Number: 2018965934

Managing Director, Apress Media LLC: Welmoed Spahr
Acquisitions Editor: Nikhil Karkal
Development Editor: James Markham
Coordinating Editor: Divya Modi

Cover designed by eStudioCalamar

Cover image designed by Freepik (www.freepik.com)

Distributed to the book trade worldwide by Springer Science+Business Media New York, 233 Spring Street, 6th Floor, New York, NY 10013. Phone 1-800-SPRINGER, fax (201) 348-4505, e-mail orders-ny@springer-sbm.com, or visit www.springeronline.com. Apress Media, LLC is a California LLC and the sole member (owner) is Springer Science + Business Media Finance Inc (SSBM Finance Inc). SSBM Finance Inc is a **Delaware** corporation.

For information on translations, please e-mail rights@apress.com, or visit http://www.apress. com/rights-permissions.

Apress titles may be purchased in bulk for academic, corporate, or promotional use. eBook versions and licenses are also available for most titles. For more information, reference our Print and eBook Bulk Sales web page at http://www.apress.com/bulk-sales.

Any source code or other supplementary material referenced by the author in this book is available to readers on GitHub via the book's product page, located at www.apress.com/978-1-4842-4098-4. For more detailed information, please visit http://www.apress.com/source-code.

Printed on acid-free paper

Table of Contents

About the Author

Federico Marani has been a freelance software engineer and DevOps specialist for over 15 years. With a background in computer science and an MSc in Business Psychology, he has worked in companies ranging from e-commerce companies to finance, medical, and banking companies. He started developing web applications with Python 1.5.2 on Red Hat systems and has been using Django since the first 1.x versions, more than 8 years ago. Federico now consults on technology strategy and tech teams with startups, and still is very hands-on with coding. He has open sourced a lot of code online, some of which is part of GNU Social. In his spare time, he enjoys playing drums and running. He can be contacted via `https://federicomarani.me`.

About the Technical Reviewer

Steve Jalim is a senior web developer and consultant who has worked with Django since version 0.9. He has used it to build robust applications for a wide range of clients, from high-growth startups to international charities, across a diverse set of domains, including supply-chain tracking, freelancer marketplaces, environmental campaigns, and even online karaoke. Steve lives with his young family in a hilly part of the UK, where he enjoys trail running. He can be contacted via `https://www.stevejalim.co.uk`.

Introduction

Nowadays, everything can be done through the Web. Ordering food, booking holidays, hailing taxis . . . you name it. Most banking transactions no longer require you to go to the bank. You can make most purchases online.

My intention when writing this book is to cover enough use cases from the real world, without being too focused on a specific business. If you are reading this book, it is because you want to equip yourself with the knowledge to build many of these popular systems.

This book approaches teaching in a very practical way. You will not find much theory in this book, not because it is not useful, but because I believe in understanding the theory by looking at how things work in practice. I am putting emphasis on the word "Practical" by having it in the book title, so be warned!

We are going to build an e-commerce presence for a fictitious company called BookTime, which sells books online. E-commerce is a good paradigm to use because you very likely have experienced it as a user, and it is also where much of my experience comes from.

We will build the online catalog, the checkout process, internal dashboards, integrations with distribution companies, and real-time components that will be used through a mobile application.

This book will put Django at the center of our attention, but it is not possible to do everything in Django. Django is part of a bigger ecosystem of tools, and if some of these are a better fit for our purpose, we will use those instead.

We will use Bootstrap, React, Webpack, and React Native in this book. These tools are needed to reach solutions that will improve the user experience, shorten our time to develop, and follow what most of the Django community does in practice.

We will also integrate Django with some common Django libraries managed by its community: Django-extensions, factory_boy, Django Debug Toolbar, Django-tables2, Django-filter, Django Rest Framework, and, most importantly, Django Channels.

Django Channels is a new piece in the Django ecosystem that allows us to solve a class of problems that standard Django does not solve well: event-driven programming. Event-driven programming is the best paradigm to use when a system has high input/output load, which goes beyond normal HTTP request/response traffic. Chat systems fit in this, because people do not talk by following a request/response pattern.

I encourage you to see these decisions as pragmatic, but not ultimate. Ultimately, you are free to use any libraries you want. I am also conscious that what might be a good decision for me is not necessarily good for you.

This book is for people who already have a basic understanding of Python and want to follow this journey of going from zero to have a good e-commerce platform. Chapters will start simple and build up complexity as you get toward the end of this book.

I hope that the journey we are going to go through will serve you well as a reference in the future when you implement your project in Django.

CHAPTER 1

Introduction to Django

In the last decade, the impact of the Internet on our society has been very deep. It has changed everything from the way we socialize and work to the way we date and go on vacation. The Internet has expanded from the tool that enabled us to virtually travel and be in touch with people from the other side of the ocean, to the tool that enables us to physically travel, with taxi-hailing services, which are a prime example of how impactful it has become.

This trend shows no sign of stopping. What lies ahead might be even more impactful. Nowadays, traditional institutions not only need an online presence, but need an excellent one, giving to their customers the same service both online and offline. Traditional institutions that do not do this will be eventually disrupted by leaner organizations that have the Internet as their backbone.

User-generated data is also becoming pervasive. Online user reviews are now a key factor in making decisions on how to spend our time and money. Online communities are numerous and thriving. Recently there have been lots of advances in machine learning, and without the strong presence of the Web as a way to generate data for those systems, this could not have happened.

© Federico Marani 2019
F. Marani, *Practical Django 2 and Channels 2*,
https://doi.org/10.1007/978-1-4842-4099-1_1

How do we participate in all this exciting activity, as software engineers? Traditional computer science education is only going to give you the fundamentals. Given how quickly user expectations and technology tools evolve, the gap is inevitable. But then, how to bridge this gap is not obvious, given how many tools and tutorials are available online.

If you are reading this book, I assume you are familiar with Python and have made the choice to use it for web development. Python is a very popular programming language. It is an interpreted language with a dynamic, strong type system. In my opinion (and probably yours) it strikes a good balance between speed and safety. Django is written in Python and it is the most widely used Python web framework, although not the only one.

Django has been structured to make the creation of complex, database-driven websites as easy as possible. It offers many components that are battle-tested and ready to be customized for your use case. There are many common patterns in modern websites that could be reused and, in the spirit of practicality, it would be wise to do so.

Book Structure

This book is going to explain Django using a lot of practical examples. I choose e-commerce as a theme throughout the book because nowadays buying online is very common, and therefore you likely know already the terminology and how these sites are structured.

Every chapter in the book will introduce just enough concepts to understand and build a section of an e-commerce site. We will start from the foundations, some presentation pages, to exposing products, a checkout process, and more advanced features. The chapters are a compromise between my personal experience of e-commerce and starting points used to introduce components of Django in an increasingly complex way.

This is not going to be an e-commerce bible; that is not the goal of the book. The goal of the book is for you to learn with the help of familiar concepts. I hope it will be successful in helping you to do so, and I am looking forward to hearing your feedback.

What Is Django

Django is a collection of components that are designed to work together, and they cover many of the common areas of web development. When you browse online, you encounter many different websites that, on the surface, look different, but, in reality, they contain the same patterns.

Every website serves HTML, the language that represents the content of the website, CSS, the language that declares how the content is rendered, images, and so on.

Most websites have the possibility to log in to a private area, where you can see customizations done for the user and data that may not be public. Django supports all this with its components.

An important aspect of Django is that many of its components are independent and, therefore, can be used individually without having to load all of them. That said, some of the more high-level components leverage existing ones.

The Django framework was born at the offices of the *Lawrence Journal-World*, a newspaper published in Lawrence, Kansas. You can see some of the influences of this in the online tutorial on the main Django site. It presents a lot of views on the content that are filtered by date and time. While it is true that, in the first versions, the designers (Adrian Holovaty and Simon Willison) probably focused on solving the problems specific to a newspaper, nowadays the framework is able to tackle any domain.

I have personally been involved many years with Django. I have used it in many fields—from visualizing finance data, creating online medical questionnaires, building e-commerce stores, to scraping dashboards, online directories and business intelligence tools—and have always found its value unquestionable. Every time I have used it, it has allowed me to focus on the business problem, rather than reinventing the wheel.

Django is not a micro-framework; it comes with baggage. If your online presence is growing to the point that you have multiple engineering teams working on different areas of the software that have very specific requirements, Django may not be lean enough for you anymore. But for the majority of sites, it works quite nicely.

Django is a framework that follows the model-template-view pattern, which is very similar to the model-view-controller pattern that many other frameworks have. The model layer represents the database layer, used for data storage. Django abstracts you from writing SQL queries. Instead of SQL, you use Python objects, and the load/save operations are handled for you.

The template layer is responsible for composing the HTML responses. It allows you to divide the HTML in sections, incorporate these sections in multiple pages, do on-the-fly transformations and generation of data, and many other operations.

The view layer is the layer that sits in between the database and HTML, and normally is the biggest layer in an application. It is where most business logic is located. It is responsible for telling the template layer what output to generate, to pass the data that needs to be returned to the user, to handle form submissions, and to interface with the model layer for persisting data.

Domain-Driven Design

Domain-driven design (DDD) is a technique to write software. It focuses on the domain, which is the knowledge or the activity that the software needs to model and support. During the development, concepts from the domain will be incorporated with the help of business experts and engineers.

What Django can bring to this is focus. Due to the fact that engineers can leverage existing code for many of the functionalities that are not domain-specific, delivering features is usually faster.

Some of the concepts of DDD are present in Django. Entities, Repositories, Aggregates, Value Objects, are somehow resembling the abstractions of ORM models, managers, or HTTP request objects. The code that is missing from Django is the code specific to your business, and that is where DDD can help.

What You Need Before Starting

Before jumping into Django, you need to make sure you have a few tools installed, including Python, a database, and Pipenv.

Python

Django 2.0 and all following versions will require Python 3. Django 2.0 specifically requires at least Python 3.4 installed. Therefore, the first thing you need to check is whether Python is installed and is the right version. If you have not already done so, please go to the downloads page of the Python main site (`www.python.org/downloads`) and download the latest 3.x version. At the time of writing, Python 3.7 is available and it is supported by Django 2.

If you are using Linux or macOS, instead of downloading from the official site, you can use your OS package manager to download Python. If a recent version of Python is available in the OS repository, I suggest you install it via this method. It is cleaner because it will check for conflicts, and, if required, it makes uninstalling Python easier.

If you are not sure, I suggest you search online for tutorials on how to install Python 3, preferably using your distribution tools, such as `brew`, `apt`, or `yum`.

Database

Although not strictly essential, the second thing that I recommend to install is a database. Django is able to use SQLite, which is an embedded database engine, but it is not suggested for production environments because that is not its purpose. I suggest you start from the beginning with the same tools that you will use when you publish your work online. By using the same tools, you will lower the chances of having bugs that only appear in production.

You have a few options available when it comes to databases. The most commonly used ones are both open source: PostgreSQL and MySQL. Historically, they have had a different evolution. While PostgreSQL has focused more on delivering many features, MySQL has focused more on performance of the core functionalities. Nowadays, there is no clear winner between the two.

In the Django community, however, there is a preference for PostgreSQL. Some of the core committers have created Django `contrib` packages (which are not considered core, although they are included) that rely on PostgreSQL extensions on standard SQL. In addition to that, Heroku, which is the hosting provider that will be used in the chapter about production deployment (Chapter 10), offers a PostgreSQL free tier that will be handy for us.

Pipenv

Pipenv is a new tool for managing Python packages, and is the latest in a long series of them. Unlike its predecessor, Pip, Pipenv has a much closer integration with Python `virtualenv`. It also keeps track automatically of what you install, and locks the versions for you, so you always know what Python libraries are running.

To do the tracking, Pipenv generates two files. `Pipfile` is the file where you list all the direct dependencies of your project. It also generates another file called `Pipfile.lock` in which all the versions and hashes of all the dependencies are listed. The latter file is used to produce deterministic builds, which means Pipenv is able to replicate environments exactly every time. It is also not meant to be edited manually.

You can install Pipenv using your OS package manager, or use Pip. Personally, I always prefer the OS package manager, but given that Pipenv is a young project, at this point I advise to use Pip.

If you prefer to stick with the standard `pip`, there is no reason for you to not use it. Python package formats are the same. I am going to use `pipenv` as reference in this book, but the same can be done with `pip`.

Getting Started

The first step is to install Django. We are going to keep using this project in the following chapters, so we need a good project name. Because we are going to sell books, we will name the project BookTime. Go to your home folder (or any folder you want) and type the following:

```
$ mkdir booktime
$ cd booktime
$ pipenv --three install Django
```

We now have an environment with Django installed. Because virtualenvs need to be activated before being used, we have to do so:

```
$ pipenv shell
```

Now that it is active, we will create the initial skeleton of the project. We will reuse the name we picked before because it is the name we will use in the configuration files and in the folder structure:

```
$ django-admin startproject booktime .
```

At this point we should have an initial folder structure (in the current folder) that looks like this:

- `manage.py`: The command-line utility that allows you to interact with the Django project. You will use this very frequently throughout the book.

- `booktime`: A Python package that contains the files every Django project needs, which are

  - `booktime/__init__.py`: This is an empty file that is only needed to make the other files importable.

  - `booktime/settings.py`: This file contains all the configuration of our project, and can be customized at will.

  - `booktime/urls.py`: This file contains all the URL mappings to Python functions. Any URL that needs to be handled by the project must have an entry here.

  - `booktime/wsgi.py`: This is the entry point that will be used when deploying our site to production.

- `Pipfile`: The list of Python libraries the project is using. At this point it is only Django.

- `Pipfile.lock`: The internal Pipenv file.

Starting the Development Server

At this point, we should be able to see the Django initial web page. To do so, we need to start the development server, as follows. This is how we will see the results of any coding presented in this book.

```
$ ./manage.py runserver
```

If everything worked correctly, the output you will see is similar to the following:

```
Performing system checks...

System check identified no issues (0 silenced).

You have 14 unapplied migration(s). Your project may not ...
Run 'python manage.py migrate' to apply them.

March 19, 2018 - 18:16:54
Django version 2.0.3, using settings 'booktime.settings'
Starting development server at http://127.0.0.1:8000/
Quit the server with CONTROL-C.
```

You will use and reuse this command extensively when developing in Django, so do not forget it!

If you navigate to the link that is shown in the output, you will see an initial page similar to that shown in Figure 1-1. This is a temporary page. Our aim will be to change this to be our project.

django   View release notes for Django 2.0

The install worked successfully! Congratulations!

You are seeing this page because DEBUG=True is in
your settings file and you have not configured any
URLs.

 Django Documentation    Tutorial: A Polling App    Django Community
Topics, references, & how-to's   Get started with Django   Connect, get help, or contribute

Figure 1-1. *Django initial page*

Django Projects vs. Apps

If you have read any decent introduction about Django online, you will
have seen these two concepts already. A Django project is the thing we just
created. It is an entire website, for instance.

A Django app represents a section of the website that is self-contained.
For example, when considering e-commerce, order management can be
thought as reasonably self-contained. In reality, though, due to changing
requirements, it is hard to foresee what divisions are going to be helpful in
the future and what divisions are going to slow down the development due
to cognitive overhead.

For now, we will start creating a "main" app, as follows, which will contain everything we build. During the development, it will become clear if there are contexts that are bounded enough to deserve a clearer separation.

```
$ ./manage.py startapp main
```

This following will create an additional folder called main along with all the existing files that were listed in the previous section.

```
main/:
admin.py  apps.py  __init__.py  migrations  models.py  tests.py
views.py
main/migrations:
__init__.py
```

Each file listed above is using the corresponding Django component with the same name. Throughout the book we will introduce each one of them. In addition to this, most edits that we will do in the book will be done in this folder; therefore, when only the file name is mentioned, the file will be in this main folder.

Settings

Many parts of Django can be configured, or need to be, depending on the component. When you created the Django project a bit earlier, a file called settings.py was initialized. This is a Python file with many constants defined. Everything here that is UPPERCASE is considered configuration and will be available in every part of the project by simply importing django.conf.settings.

Please be careful when adding Python code to this file. This is not the place to add functions or complex code. Loading of this file needs to stay fast, so remember to limit the complexity of your code to not much more than assignments.

11

Another thing to stay away from is changing any content of this at runtime. Every time you change anything inside `settings.py`, the application should be redeployed (or at least restarted).

Here is a run-through of the most important configuration variables that you should know before proceeding. Consider these to be like a few basic words that you should know before speaking Django.

DEBUG

This is a Boolean that turns on/off debug mode. Debug mode offers a lot of extra information during development. As we compose our final product, we will inevitably write some code that does not work. There will be bugs in our code, and debug mode is very useful in telling us at what point in the code the error condition was triggered.

When an error occurs, instead of the output that we would expect in the browser, a debug page will appear. This page will visualize the code that failed, and provide a lot of context information, such as current variables, the HTTP request information, current databases, session information, and so on.

Figure 1-2 shown an example of the debug page after I wrote some code that tries to divide an integer by zero.

ZeroDivisionError at /

division by zero

Request Method:	GET
Request URL:	http://localhost:8000/?g=2
Django Version:	2.0.3
Exception Type:	ZeroDivisionError
Exception Value:	division by zero
Exception Location:	/home/flagz/workspace/django-book/booktime/main/views.py in home, line 4
Python Executable:	/home/flagz/.local/share/virtualenvs/booktime-8-1qP2a4/bin/python
Python Version:	3.6.3
Python Path:	['/home/flagz/workspace/django-book/booktime', '/home/flagz/.local/share/virtualenvs/booktime-8-1qP2a4/lib/python36.zip', '/home/flagz/.local/share/virtualenvs/booktime-8-1qP2a4/lib/python3.6', '/home/flagz/.local/share/virtualenvs/booktime-8-1qP2a4/lib/python3.6/lib-dynload', '/usr/lib/python3.6', '/home/flagz/.local/share/virtualenvs/booktime-8-1qP2a4/lib/python3.6/site-packages']
Server time:	Thu, 22 Mar 2018 16:28:07 +0000

Traceback Switch to copy-and-paste view

/home/flagz/.local/share/virtualenvs/booktime-8-1qP2a4/lib/python3.6/site-packages/django/core/handlers/exception.py in inner

```
35.          response = get_response(request)
```
▶ Local vars

/home/flagz/.local/share/virtualenvs/booktime-8-1qP2a4/lib/python3.6/site-packages/django/core/handlers/base.py in _get_response

```
128.             response = self.process_exception_by_middleware(e, request)
```
▶ Local vars

/home/flagz/.local/share/virtualenvs/booktime-8-1qP2a4/lib/python3.6/site-packages/django/core/handlers/base.py in _get_response

```
126.             response = wrapped_callback(request, *callback_args, **callback_kwargs)
```
▶ Local vars

/home/flagz/workspace/django-book/booktime/main/views.py in home

```
4.      result = 33 / 0
```
▶ Local vars

Request information

USER	AnonymousUser
GET	Variable Value g '2'
POST	No POST data
FILES	No FILES data

Figure 1-2. *Django debug page*

As you can see, the first thing at the top of the debug page is the exception type, ZeroDivisionError, followed by some basic information. The second and most useful section is the Traceback section.

In addition to what you see with a `traceback` from the command line, as you would when you use Python from the command line, on the debug page you can also click and see all the local variables of all frames.

After the Traceback section, there is a long section containing all the HTTP request variables, all the META information (environment variables of the shell that is running the development server), and all the current Django settings.

INSTALLED_APPS

This is the list of apps, both internal to Django and from external libraries, that are loaded on startup. Django will initialize them, load and manage their models, and make them available in the application registry.

For our Django project with only one "main" app, this is the way it should appear:

```
INSTALLED_APPS = [
    'django.contrib.admin',
    'django.contrib.auth',
    'django.contrib.contenttypes',
    'django.contrib.sessions',
    'django.contrib.messages',
    'django.contrib.staticfiles',
    'main.apps.MainConfig',
]
```

Whereas in the past you could just type `main`, now you should specify the `AppConfig` subclass. Typically there is only one and it is already created for you by the `startapp` command, and it is located in the `apps.py` file of the Django app.

As we can see, Django has itself some apps that may be enabled and disabled at will. If, for instance, we are not interested in the Messages framework, we could disable it by removing the entry from the list.

LOGGING

Logging is a fundamental part of applications. The goal of logging is to save time when problems happen, and to do so you need to be able to track what is happening during runtime. Logging is important both for development and for production sites.

If you are not familiar with the concepts of logging in Python, I suggest you review the logging module documentation. Throughout the book, we will use logger objects to log what is happening, and we will use the appropriate log levels.

To start with, this LOGGING Django setting is about configuring the logging system using `logging.config.dictConfig()`. If you want to understand how this is composed, consider this example:

```python
LOGGING = {
    'version': 1,
    'disable_existing_loggers': False,
    'formatters': {
        'simple': {
            'format': '%(levelname)s %(message)s'
        },
    },
    'handlers': {
        'console': {
            'level': 'DEBUG',
            'class': 'logging.StreamHandler',
            'formatter': 'simple'
        },
    },
    'loggers': {
        'main': {
            'handlers': ['console'],
```

```
            'level': 'DEBUG',
            'propagate': True,
        },
        'booktime': {
            'handlers': ['console'],
            'level': 'DEBUG',
            'propagate': True,
        },
    },
}
```

This will print any logging statement coming from the loggers named booktime and main. It is common practice to name loggers after the Python module name, and that is the convention we will use.

Regardless of the configuration, which can be changed quickly, it is harder to retrofit logging practices to an existing project. We will add logging as we add code to the project.

STATIC_ROOT/STATIC_URL

Every site needs a way to serve static content, whether this is images, CSS, JavaScript, and so on. The way this works is different between development and production environments. In development mode, everything you put inside the static folder in your Django application (in our case, main) will be automatically available under STATIC_URL. This is the only configuration variable that matters for that environment.

For production environments, where performance and security are much more important, Django will not serve static assets. Instead, Django will support a more efficient HTTP server (like Nginx) or similar by collecting all static files in a unique directory. This unique directory is the one specified in STATIC_ROOT.

16

MEDIA_ROOT/MEDIA_URL

Django makes a distinction between static content that comes bundled with the Django project and content that is uploaded by the website users. The user-generated content is managed separately, and the configuration for it is similar to the one for static files. MEDIA_ROOT is the location on the local drive where all the user files will be uploaded. All these files will also be automatically available for download and their URL will be prefixed with MEDIA_URL.

The same reasoning from the previous section applies here: the development server will serve the media files back at you if you configure it to do so, but in production environments this is not recommended. More on this later.

From now forward, we will use this configuration:

```
MEDIA_ROOT = os.path.join(BASE_DIR, 'media')
MEDIA_URL = '/media/'
```

MIDDLEWARE

Middleware is a powerful feature of Django. It allows you to plug in extra code that will be executed at specific points of the HTTP request/response cycle. An example of this is the SessionMiddleware, which is used to associate sessions to users.

The order of which middleware components are specified matters. Some middleware components depend on the result of some others, and they would work only in one direction.

Examples of middleware components will be presented later in the book. For now, it is enough to learn what are the most important ones.

SessionMiddleware and AuthenticationMiddleware provide the basic functionalities for a project that has the concept of user. If you do not have user customizations on the site, you may remove them.

17

If you want to use caching on the view layer, you may want to look at the cache middleware. If you will serve content in multiple languages, the LocaleMiddleware class will do the language negotiation between the client and the server. There are many others; look at the Django middleware documentation for more details.

TEMPLATES

This variable is used to configure the template engine of Django. If you do not have specific interoperability requirements, you are likely to keep using the Django template system. In that case, there are a few things you can configure. The setting I normally change the most is context_processors.

Context processors are a way to inject additional variables in the scope of templates. By doing so, you would not have to do it in every view that requires these variables.

A good example would be to have some values defined as constants in settings.py and used in the templates. In that case, a convenient way would be to define a context processor that reads them from the global configuration and pushes them to the template. An example of this will be presented in Chapter 10 of the book.

DATABASES

Your project will likely use a database to store data. One of the major benefits in using Django instead of a smaller framework is that this aspect is entirely managed for you. This is an initial configuration that uses PostgreSQL for storage:

```
DATABASES = {
    'default': {
        'ENGINE': 'django.db.backends.postgresql',
        'NAME': 'mydatabase',
        'USER': 'mydatabaseuser',
```

```
        'PASSWORD': 'mypassword',
        'HOST': '127.0.0.1',
        'PORT': '5432',
    }
}
```

Remember to substitute the details above with the ones you picked when you configured your database. If you proceed with this configuration, it is important to install the PostgreSQL drivers. In the same directory of Pipfile, you would need to run pipenv install psycopg2, sample output of which is shown here:

```
Installing psycopg2...
Collecting psycopg2
  Downloading psycopg2-2.7.4-cp36-cp36m-manylinux1_x86_64.whl(2.7MB)
Installing collected packages: psycopg2
Successfully installed psycopg2-2.7.4

Adding psycopg2 to Pipfile's [packages]...
Pipfile.lock (374a8f) out of date, updating to (843434)...
Locking [dev-packages] dependencies...
Locking [packages] dependencies...
Updated Pipfile.lock (843434)!
Installing dependencies from Pipfile.lock (843434)...
```

If you do not want to install PostgreSQL now, you can always use SQLite. In that case, you would not need to install additional drivers:

```
DATABASES = {
    'default': {
        'ENGINE': 'django.db.backends.sqlite3',
        'NAME': 'mydatabase',
    }
}
```

But again, as noted before, SQLite is not recommended for production use.

EMAIL_BACKEND

Django has a library to send e-mails. It supplies several backends, and this is the configuration for it. As a general rule, I use the console backend for development purposes and the SMTP backend for production.

During development, using the console backend allows you to see the e-mails without worrying about the e-mails being received by whoever you specified as receiver. In production, that would be the behavior you want.

SECRET_KEY

This is a random string that is used in security-sensitive contexts. For now it is sufficient to know that this needs to stay private.

Class- and Function-Based Views

Historically Django represented views using functions. A function-based view (FBV) would just be a Python function that takes as an argument a request object and returns a response object. This function would be called when a request for a specific URL happens.

For a long time, while other Python frameworks were using classes, Django kept using functions. The beauty of functions is that they are minimal. There is no hidden behavior—what you see is what you get. Additional behavior can be added with decorators, but the code still stays quite readable.

Class-based views (CBVs) were introduced in Django 1.7. The reason behind this addition was that with a documented structure and inheritance, the developer would be able to customize a class-based view more than a function-based view.

While with a function-based view, you would have to add code that handles all the behaviors you want, with a class-based view the approach would be different. Django offers many CBVs as starting points for further customization, and you would do so using inheritance.

As you can imagine, the approach is fundamentally different. Functions are purely additive. You need to add code to add behavior. With CBVs, on the other hand, you may have to add code to change default behavior, or code to disable extensions.

There are no clear winners between function-based views and class-based views. If you want to code a view that does not resemble what is available as a CBV in Django, go for a function-based view. If the view code you are modifying is morphing into something that goes beyond the purpose of the CBV, perhaps it is time to reconsider writing it in a function-based view.

Always use your judgment whether you should write a function or a class. In the book I will present both cases. If at any point you realize that you structured your code with CBVs that are making the code hard to read, please remember that having automated tests is going to enable you to change the view to an FBV with limited risks.

Testing

After having finished the development, we should be eager to present our work to the world, and if we care about others using our software, it needs to work. To make sure it works, in web development you would just open your browser and check it. If you are happy with the interactions, you will mark it as done.

Automated testing is what sits in between "it works" and "it always works." If you want people to rely on your software, you need to make sure any new modification does not break existing functionality. While in theory you could do that manually, in practice you rarely test everything manually every time you do a release.

Automated testing is the only way to have the confidence that your new version is, besides adding features, not breaking critical sections of the site. Similarly, automated testing is the only way to make sure that your refactoring has not gone wrong.

Testing is very easy to do, but for it to work it needs to be part of our coding routine. It is important that our tests cover as much code as possible, and that they are granular enough to be able to tell us where exactly our problem is, if one happens.

In this book we will use the standard `unittest` package. Tests written using this package work with every test runner. There are other test runners besides the Python default, such as `pytest`, but they will not be covered in this book. For our purposes, the standard way is good enough for us.

Summary

This chapter illustrated the fundamentals of Django: what it is and what you need to install and use it. It is recommended for this project to have Python 3.7 installed and PostgreSQL 10.5.

We have covered the most important settings of Django and how to configure them, and some other miscellaneous topics such as different types of views and the approach on testing that we will keep throughout the book.

In the next chapter we will start with a use case, a fictitious company website that sells books.

CHAPTER 2

Getting Started with a Simple Company Site

In this chapter we will start to build the first pages of the site. These pages will offer the base functionality that is expected from a site, such as presentation pages and forms to gather leads.

We are going to discuss

- Basic templates

- Serving templates

- Serving CSS and JS

- How to add URLs

- Creating a form that sends e-mails

Starting with the Homepage

The very first step that we will do is write the homepage for our site. It will give us something tangible to start with, and we will use this opportunity to introduce a few Django concepts.

© Federico Marani 2019
F. Marani, *Practical Django 2 and Channels 2,*
https://doi.org/10.1007/978-1-4842-4099-1_2

23

To serve the homepage, we will start by writing the HTML in a template. We will use the application we created in Chapter 1. We need to add the templates folder to it:

```
$ mkdir main/templates/
```

In order to start with something a bit more stylish than bare-bones HTML, we will implement a base template with Bootstrap. Bootstrap is a frontend framework that gives us a good set of styles and components to start with. Feel free to ignore this if you do not care, but in the spirit of using frameworks, we will use it as an example.

Let's add some HTML to main/templates/home.html:

```
<!doctype html>
<html lang="en">
  <head>
    <!-- Required meta tags -->
    <meta charset="utf-8">
    <meta
      name="viewport"
      content="width=device-width, initial-scale=1, shrink-to-
      fit=no">

    <!-- Bootstrap CSS -->
    <link
      rel="stylesheet"
      href="https://maxcdn.bootstrapcdn.com/bootstrap/4.0.0/
      css/bootstrap.min.css">
    <title>Hello, world!</title>
  </head>
  <body>
    <h1>Hello, world!</h1>
```

```
<script
  src="https://code.jquery.com/jquery-3.2.1.slim.min.js">
</script>
<script
  src="https://cdnjs.cloudflare.com/ajax/libs/popper.js/
  1.12.9/umd/popper.min.js">
</script>
<script
  src="https://maxcdn.bootstrapcdn.com/bootstrap/4.0.0/js/
  bootstrap.min.js">
</script>
</body>
</html>
```

This is just a "Hello world" example from the Bootstrap documentation. Its content does not really matter, as we are going to change it soon, but it is a start!

This page is not visible yet, though, because it needs a URL. Given that this is the homepage, we want this page to be served for any requests coming to /. To do so, we need to configure the URL routing layer by adding this to booktime/urls.py:

```
from django.contrib import admin
from django.urls import path
from django.views.generic import TemplateView

urlpatterns = [
    path('admin/', admin.site.urls),
    path(", TemplateView.as_view(template_name="home.html")),
]
```

Now we finally can go to the browser and see our results, as you can see in Figure 2-1.

Hello, world!

Figure 2-1. *Hello, world! example*

This is enough to see the page, but we still have two problems to solve:

- Files are loaded from an external content delivery network (CDN), which may be good for production sites, but in development we want the ability to work completely offline.

- It does not have an automatic test.

We need a copy of Bootstrap inside our repository. To do this quickly, we can download that from the link that we already have in the HTML. We can use curl (or wget) for this task:

```
$ mkdir main/static/
$ mkdir main/static/css/
$ mkdir main/static/js/
$ curl -o main/static/css/bootstrap.min.css \
  https://maxcdn.bootstrapcdn.com/bootstrap/4.0.0/css/
  bootstrap.min.css
...

$ curl -o main/static/js/jquery.min.js \
  https://code.jquery.com/jquery-3.2.1.slim.min.js
...
```

```
$ curl -o main/static/js/popper.min.js \
  https://cdnjs.cloudflare.com/ajax/libs/popper.js/1.12.9/umd/
  popper.min.js
...

$ curl -o main/static/js/bootstrap.min.js \
  https://maxcdn.bootstrapcdn.com/bootstrap/4.0.0/js/bootstrap.
  min.js
...
```

All the assets linked are now available offline. The last thing to do to finish this is replace the links to external sites with links to local links. To do so we will change main/templates/home.html to use the static template tag:

```
{% load static %}
<!doctype html>
<html lang="en">
  <head>
    <!-- Required meta tags -->
    <meta charset="utf-8">
    <meta
      name="viewport"
      content="width=device-width, initial-scale=1, shrink-to-
      fit=no">
    <!-- Bootstrap CSS -->
    <link rel="stylesheet"href="{% static "css/bootstrap.min.
    css" %}">

    <title>Hello, world!</title>
  </head>
  <body>
    <h1>Hello, world!</h1>
```

```html
    <script src="{% static "js/jquery.min.js" %}"></script>
    <script src="{% static "js/popper.min.js" %}"></script>
    <script src="{% static "js/bootstrap.min.js" %}"></script>
  </body>
</html>
```

Testing

The only thing now missing is the test. We want to make sure that our homepage works all the time.

One key concept to remember when writing tests is that you want to test the behavior rather than the internal implementation. In this specific case, though, we will focus on testing the behavior at the HTTP level rather than at the browser level.

We want to make sure that

- The HTTP status code for this page is 200.

- The template home.html has been used.

- The response contains the name of our shop.

Our tests in Django will be initially stored inside main/tests.py. This will get us started quickly, but we will change it once we have written more code.

```python
from django.test import TestCase

class TestPage(TestCase):
    def test_home_page_works(self):
        response = self.client.get("/")
        self.assertEqual(response.status_code, 200)
        self.assertTemplateUsed(response, 'home.html')
        self.assertContains(response, 'BookTime')
```

In Django, automated tests are similar to standard Python unittests, but they inherit from a different set of base classes. There are quite a few base classes, each one adding a bit more functionality to the base unittest.TestCase. For now, we will stick with django.test.TestCase.

You can now run this test with the command ./manage.py test, which produces the following output:

```
Creating test database for alias 'default'...
System check identified no issues (0 silenced).
F
================================================================
FAIL: test_home_page_works (main.tests.TestPage)
----------------------------------------------------------------
Traceback (most recent call last):
  File "/home/flagz/workspace/django-book/booktime/main/
  tests.py",...
    self.assertContains(response, 'Booktime')
  File "/home/flagz/.local/share/virtualenvs/booktime-8-1qP2a4/
  lib/...
    self.assertTrue(real_count != 0, msg_prefix + "Couldn't
    find %s...
AssertionError: False is not true : Couldn't find 'BookTime' in
response
----------------------------------------------------------------
Ran 1 test in 0.011s

FAILED (failures=1)
Destroying test database for alias 'default'...
```

Oops, we have a failure. The test expects to find the word "BookTime," which was not included in the previous HTML file. That needs to be changed.

This sort of activity loop—writing code, writing tests, running tests, failure, and fixing—will be a very common routine if you follow the examples in this book. For developers who are not used to this approach, it may seem slow at first. However, once you are familiar with the mechanics, you will likely discover that the cognitive effort you put forth while coding will reduce and you will go faster.

After having changed the content of main/templates/home.html, your test will succeed:

```
Creating test database for alias 'default'...
System check identified no issues (0 silenced).

.
----------------------------------------------------------------
Ran 1 test in 0.010s

OK
Destroying test database for alias 'default'...
```

Before we proceed to create the next website page, let's review the areas we've touched upon thus far.

Templates

The following is the default Django configuration for templates, which you can see in booktime/settings.py:

```
TEMPLATES = [
    {
        'BACKEND': 'django.template.backends.django.DjangoTemplates',
        'DIRS': [],
        'APP_DIRS': True,
        'OPTIONS': {
            'context_processors': [
                'django.template.context_processors.debug',
```

```
                'django.template.context_processors.request',
                'django.contrib.auth.context_processors.auth',
                'django.contrib.messages.context_processors.
                messages',
            ],
        },
    },
]
```

Template loading in this configuration works by looking for a templates directory inside all the apps listed in INSTALLED_APPS, and trying to find home.html in it. This is because APP_DIRS is True.

By using the default DjangoTemplates backend, you will have available a list of "tags", words surrounded by {% and %}, that you can use in templates. Some of these tags are built in, while some others are only available after loading external modules.

In the previous section we saw two tags: {% load %} and {% static %}. In our case, we had to compose URLs to the CSS files we had in our main/static/ folder. To do so, the correct way is to use the static tag. This tag however is not loaded by default, which is why we had to use load. Later in the book we will see that we can define our own tags, and they will be loadable as well.

TemplateView

TemplateView is the first class-based view that we see in this project. It is very simple: it renders a template. It can take a few keyword arguments, but the most important one is template_name. That argument specifies the path of the template to render. Other possible keyword arguments could be extra_content or content_type.

There is a degree of customization that we can do to this view without subclassing it. This is the beauty of using CBVs: in certain cases, it allows you to write even less code than FBVs.

For the sake of completeness, if you wanted to implement this in a function, you would not have to write much more than this:

```
def home(request):
    return render(request, "home.html", {})
```

This is effectively what TemplateView does.

URLs

The URL-matching mechanism in Django starts by loading the file referenced in the ROOT_URLCONF variable in settings.py. Once loaded, it will traverse all the entries listed in a variable called urlpatterns.

Following the contents of the file displayed before, there are two entries in urlpatterns: admin/ is for using the built-in Django admin, which will be introduced later in the book, and the second one is an empty entry. An empty entry represents no path, therefore the homepage.

Every entry in urlpatterns is an instance of django.urls.path(), or django.urls.re_path() in case the pattern that needs to be expressed is more complex than what the first function allows.

Django will traverse the patterns trying to match the requested path in the HTTP request with what is there and, in our case, the first match will be accepted. Once matched, the traversal is finished.

This could allow us to do some priority-based matching if we wanted:

```
urlpatterns = [
    path('product/95/', views.product_95),
    path('product/<int:id>/', views.product),
    re_path(r'^product/(?P<id>[^/]+)/$', views.product_unknown),
]
```

The first path would only match with product 95. The second path would match with any product with an integer as an identifier. The third path would match with anything that is at least one character long, because of what the regular expression requires. If you do not know what regular expressions are, do not worry, because we will not use them in this book.

Adding an About Us Page

The site we want to build will be an e-commerce site, but before we get to any of that, we need to add a web page to describe the company. Every respectable company has an About us page, and that is what we will talk about here.

It is the second page of our website, an important step, because it will allow us to introduce a bit more structure. Starting with the template, we want the new page and the existing one to have the initial bits in common, and only the core content to be different.

In order to achieve this goal, we will start using template inheritance. Templates can inherit from a base template, and override some of the sections with new data. These sections are called "blocks" in Django terms. We need to change the existing template before working on the new page.

This will be the new structure, a new file called main/templates/base. html:

```
{% load static %}
<!doctype html>
<html lang="en">
  <head>
    <!-- Required meta tags -->
    <meta charset="utf-8">
    <meta
      name="viewport"
      content="width=device-width, initial-scale=1, shrink-to-
      fit=no">
```

```
<!-- Bootstrap CSS -->
<link  rel="stylesheet" href="{% static "css/bootstrap.min.
css" %}">

<title>BookTime</title>
</head>
<body>
  <h1>BookTime</h1>
  {% block content %}
  {% endblock content %}

  <script src="{% static "js/jquery.min.js" %}"></script>
  <script src="{% static "js/popper.min.js" %}"></script>
  <script src="{% static "js/bootstrap.min.js" %}"></script>
</body>
</html>
```

This file will contain most of the HTML that used to be in main/
templates/home.html. main/templates/home.html will be using the file
above and extend it:

```
{% extends"base.html" %}

{% block content %}
  <h2>Home</h2>
  <p>this will be the content of home</p>
{% endblock content %}
```

And the new main/templates/about_us.html file will look like this:

```
{% extends"base.html" %}

{% block content %}
  <h2>About us</h2>
  <p>BookTime is a company that sells books online.</p>
{% endblock content %}
```

This is a good enough start, but there is still something missing: a navigation bar. We are going to use the Bootstrap navbar here, but the concept is pretty common in any frontend framework. Insert this HTML code in main/templates/base.html, replacing the h1 header:

```html
<nav class="navbar navbar-expand-lg navbar-light bg-light">
  <a class="navbar-brand" href="/">BookTime</a>
  <button
    class="navbar-toggler"
    type="button"
    data-toggle="collapse"
    data-target="#navbarSupportedContent">
    <span class="navbar-toggler-icon"></span>
  </button>
  <div
    class="collapse navbar-collapse"
    id="navbarSupportedContent">
    <ul class="navbar-nav mr-auto">
      <li
        class="nav-item">
        <a class="nav-link" href="/">Home</a>
      </li>
      <li
        class="nav-item">
        <a class="nav-link" href="/about-us/">About us</a>
      </li>
    </ul>
  </div>
</nav>
```

This will give us a navigation bar, which brings our site a lot closer to the average site. Now, we want to highlight the current page in the navbar. There are many ways to do so. We will pick one that allows us to explore yet another concept of Django, the context processors:

```
...
<li
  class="nav-item {% if request.path == "/" %}active{% endif %}">
  <a class="nav-link" href="/">Home</a>
</li>
<li
  class="nav-item {% if request.path =="/about-us/" %}active
  {% endif %}">
  <a class="nav-link" href="/about-us/">About us</a>
</li>
...
```

Because we have `django.template.context_processors.request` in our `context_processors`, the variable `request` is available to be used in templates. It is an instance of `django.http.HttpRequest` that represents the current HTTP request. It has many attributes, such as the HTTP method used, the path requested, GET parameters, and so on.

Another thing we have not seen before is the `{% if %}` template tag. It behaves exactly like the `if` statement in Python.

Please note that the previous snippet is using a lot of hard-coded URLs. There is a better way to do this, as you will see in the next chapter.

Now we need to wire up the URL /about-us/ with the new template. While doing so, we will see yet another new feature of Django. As we have done with templates, we will do some restructuring. Here is the new booktime/urls.py:

```
from django.contrib import admin
from django.urls import path, include
```

```
urlpatterns = [
    path('admin/', admin.site.urls),
    path(", include('main.urls')),
]
```

The include() function allows various URL patterns to be nested. In our case, we want to separate Django URLs from our application URLs. While doing that, we also add a new URL for our newly created template. The argument of the function is the path of the following file, which will be main/urls.py.

```
from django.urls import path
from django.views.generic import TemplateView

urlpatterns = [
    path(
        "about-us/",
        TemplateView.as_view(template_name="about_us.html")),
    path(
        "",
        TemplateView.as_view(template_name="home.html")),
]
```

That is enough to see our new creation, shown in Figure 2-2.

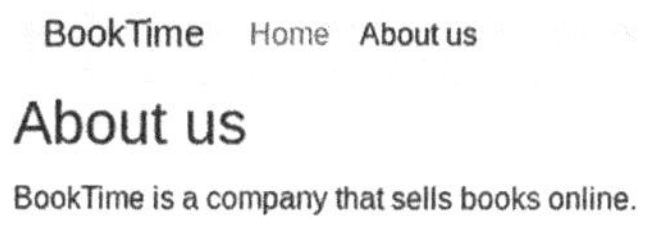

BookTime   Home   About us

About us

BookTime is a company that sells books online.

Figure 2-2. *About us page*

Now it is time to make sure it will always work, and we do so with a test to add to the existing test class. The test is similar to the last one:

...

```
    def test_about_us_page_works(self):
        response = self.client.get("/about-us/")
        self.assertEqual(response.status_code,200)
        self.assertTemplateUsed(response, 'about_us.html')
        self.assertContains(response, 'BookTime')
```

As a last thing, it is worth introducing a better way to manage URLs, instead of hard-coding them, a way that will give us more freedom later to change the URLs structure. To do so, we will have to name all the URLs in the urls.py file:

```
from django.urls import path
from django.views.generic import TemplateView

urlpatterns = [
    path(
        "about-us/",
        TemplateView.as_view(template_name="about_us.html"),
        name="about_us",
    ),
    path(
        "",
        TemplateView.as_view(template_name="home.html"),
        name="home",
    ),
]
```

This will allow us to use a function called reverse() that maps the names we just inserted to the actual URL paths. This is useful in case in the future you want to tweak the URLs, without changing the information that the page contains.

We need to remove the hard-coded URLs inside the tests. This would be the final version of main/tests.py:

```python
from django.test import TestCase
from django.urls import reverse

class TestPage(TestCase):
    def test_home_page_works(self):
        response = self.client.get(reverse("home"))
        self.assertEqual(response.status_code, 200)
        self.assertTemplateUsed(response, 'home.html')
        self.assertContains(response, 'BookTime')

    def test_about_us_page_works(self):
        response = self.client.get(reverse("about_us"))
        self.assertEqual(response.status_code, 200)
        self.assertTemplateUsed(response, 'about_us.html')
        self.assertContains(response, 'BookTime')
```

Creating a Contact Us Form

At this point, we have two pages already on the site, and we would like to add a bit of interactivity. Many companies have a contact form, and we would like to add one to the site.

In Django, forms are managed by the forms library, which is a set of functions to manage rendering and processing of HTML forms. To use this library, the first step is to declare the fields of the form in a class that inherits from the base form. We will do so in a new file main/forms.py:

```python
from django import forms

class ContactForm(forms.Form):
    name = forms.CharField(label='Your name', max_length=100)
```

```
    message = forms.CharField(
        max_length=600, widget=forms.Textarea
    )
```

This class declares a form with two text fields named name and message. When this form is rendered into HTML, it will generate two input widgets. In our case, it will be one <input type="text"> and one <textarea>.

We want this form to be responsible for handling the communication, and using e-mail is the simplest way to do so in this case. There are other ways, like triggering a message to the internal chat system, but e-mail is omnipresent and very well supported by Django. To do so, we need to add an additional method to the class above:

```
from django.core.mail import send_mail
import logging

logger = logging.getLogger(__name__)

class ContactForm(forms.Form):
    ...

    def send_mail(self):
        logger.info("Sending email to customer service")
        message = "From: {0}\n{1}".format(
            self.cleaned_data["name"],
            self.cleaned_data["message"],
        )
        send_mail(
            "Site message",
            message,
            "site@booktime.domain",
            ["customerservice@booktime.domain"],
            fail_silently=False,
        )
```

There are two new functionalities here: the Django e-mail library and logging. As explained before, logging is a practice that, if done correctly, dramatically reduces the recovery time in case failures happen. Here we are triggering an e-mail send, which potentially can lead to a crash. We want to be logging enough information to pinpoint this quickly.

Django offers a function called send_mail() (and some others) to send e-mails. This is tightly integrated with Django and I suggest using this instead of using other Python mail functions. One of the main advantages of this is that it is integrated into the Django test library.

Testing

As is necessary for any other pieces of code, the contact form needs to have an integration test. Before proceeding here, we must do some restructuring. We will split the main/tests.py file into multiple files, one per Django layer.

Please do the following:

- Create a main/tests/__init__.py empty file to indicate it is a package.

- Move the current file main/tests.py to main/tests/test_views.py.

- Add a new file called main/tests/test_forms.py inside the main app.

This new file structure will still be discovered by Django and run, and it will be a bit clearer.

Before proceeding, also note that there are some rules on how to name tests:

- Test files need to be named with the test_ prefix.

- Test methods appearing in classes inheriting from TestCase need the test_ prefix.

Having noted this, it is time to write the form test. The form test, which will be in main/tests/test_forms.py, needs to test both for valid and invalid data:

```python
from django.test import TestCase
from django.core import mail
from main import forms

class TestForm(TestCase):
    def test_valid_contact_us_form_sends_email(self):
        form = forms.ContactForm({
            'name': "Luke Skywalker",
            'message': "Hi there"})

        self.assertTrue(form.is_valid())

        with self.assertLogs('main.forms', level='INFO') as cm:
            form.send_mail()

        self.assertEqual(len(mail.outbox), 1)
        self.assertEqual(mail.outbox[0].subject, 'Site message')

        self.assertGreaterEqual(len(cm.output), 1)

    def test_invalid_contact_us_form(self):
        form = forms.ContactForm({
            'message': "Hi there"})

        self.assertFalse(form.is_valid())
```

Running the test suite with ./manage.py test -v 2 should now show that the test discovery built in Django is finding both the views tests and the form test:

```
Creating test database for alias 'default' ('test_booktime')...
...
```

```
System check identified no issues (0 silenced).
test_invalid_contact_us_form (main.tests.test_forms.
TestForm) ... ok
test_valid_contact_us_form_sends_email (main.tests.
test_f...) ... ok
test_about_us_page_works (main.tests.test_views.TestPage)
... ok
test_home_page_works (main.tests.test_views.TestPage) ... ok

----------------------------------------------------------------
Ran 4 tests in 0.028s

OK
Destroying test database for alias 'default' ('test_booktime')...
```

This concludes the work we had to do on the contact form. Before proceeding to making this form visible in the site, we are going to review the concepts we have seen in a bit more detail.

Test Discovery

By default Django finds the tests to run using some customizations over the unittest discovery functionality. It will traverse all subfolders from the current folder, looking for files named test*.py. Of those files, all the subclasses of unittest.TestCase contained in them will be included.

The test suite can be run in several ways. By default it runs all the tests, which is not ideal when we want to have quick feedback on some specific refactoring. Here are some examples:

```
$ # Run all the views tests
$ ./manage.py test main.tests.test_views.TestPage

$ # Run the homepage test
```

```
$ ./manage.py test main.tests.test_views.TestPage.test_home_
page_works

$ # Run all tests
$ ./manage.py test
```

Besides positional arguments, there are a few options that you can pass: `--failfast` if you want the test suite to stop as soon as there is a fail, and `--keepdb` if you want to preserve the test database between runs. They are both very helpful to speed up the execution of the previously listed test commands.

Form and Fields

Django forms can be quite complex and intimidating. In this section we will talk about them in a bit more detail.

As you saw earlier, to create a form you inherit from `django.forms.Form` and you add instances of `django.forms.fields.Field`. These fields represent a single piece of information. In a typical HTML form there are many inputs, and therefore it is typical to find many fields in a Django form.

Some of the most common fields in a Django form are as follows:

- `BooleanField`: Typically a check box

- `CharField`: A text input box (typically `<input type="text">` or `<textarea>`)

- `ChoiceField`: A selector between a set of options

- `DecimalField`: A decimal

- `EmailField`: A text input that uses a special widget to only accept e-mail addresses

- `FileField`: A file input

- `ImageField`: Like FileField, but only validates image formats

- `IntegerField`: An integer

There are other fields, but these give us enough options for the most common cases. If you need one or more fields that are not listed here, check the Django documentation, which is more comprehensive than this list.

Every field has a set of core arguments that are accepted. The arguments that are worth remembering are

- `required` (True/False): Is the value required or optional?

- `label` (string): A friendly name for input.

- `help_text` (string): A longer description.

- `widget`: The `django.forms.Widget` subclass that is used to render the field. Some fields can be rendered in multiple ways.

In addition to this list of arguments, there are a few methods that you can add in your form subclass:

- `clean_<fieldname>()`: These functions, if defined, will be called to run custom validation on the corresponding field. If, for instance, you have to check that fieldname is a valid VAT number, you would do it here.

- `clean()`: This is the only place you can do cross-field validation rules, which are rules that validate the form across multiple fields.

There are many more options you can specify when declaring the form; again, if you are interested, there is a lot of Django documentation online.

After data submission, the following are a few standard methods that you use to interact with forms from the view layer. Depending on whether you use function-based views or class-based views, some of this may be done implicitly by Django.

- is_valid(): Run all validators and clean functions, to check everything correctly validates.

- errors: If the form is not valid, this array will contain all the errors.

You can use these methods in templates as well, along with all declared fields. Sometimes you need to do this in order to control exactly how the template is rendered. More on this later.

Sending E-mails

We already introduced the function send_mail(). This function can be used to send common e-mails, to one or more recipients, with a text body and an optional HTML version. For anything more complex than that, such as attaching files, the class django.core.mail.EmailMessage is available.

E-mails can be sent in several ways, the most common being SMTP. Most of the time, this is the backend you will want to use, although sending e-mails while you run the development server may not be desirable. You will end up spamming people.

During development, it is better to use the console backend. Alternatively, you can keep using SMTP but with a service dedicated to testing, such as MailHog or others.

A snippet of configuration that works for me is to select the backend based on the value of DEBUG:

```
if not DEBUG:
    EMAIL_BACKEND = 'django.core.mail.backends.smtp.EmailBackend'
    EMAIL_HOST_USER = "username"
```

```
    EMAIL_HOST = 'smtp.domain.com'
    EMAIL_PORT = 587
    EMAIL_USE_TLS = True
    EMAIL_HOST_PASSWORD = "password"
else:
    EMAIL_BACKEND = (

        "django.core.mail.backends.console.EmailBackend"
    )
```

Please add the preceding code to your booktime/settings.py.

Adding the Form to the Contact Us Page

Having declared this form, now we need to create a template for the Contact us page, and a URL mapping.

The Contact us template will be named main/templates/contact_form.html, with its content as shown next. We will rely on the default rendering method of forms by just adding {{ form }}.

```
{% extends "base.html" %}

{% block content %}
  <h2>Contact us</h2>
  <p>Please fill the form below to contact us</p>
  <form method="POST">
    {% csrf_token %}
    {{ form }}
    <button type="submit" class="btn btn-primary">Submit
    </button>
  </form>
{% endblock content %}
```

The {% csrf_token %} tag helps to protect against Cross-Site Request Forgery (CSRF) attacks, attacks in which the user is misled onto a site with a form that submits to an external site, site that could be ours. This tag is required with the default Django configuration. I encourage you to read more about it in the Django documentation online.

Now we need a URL mapping. We will add another entry in main/urls.py, but before getting to that there is a bit more groundwork to cover than in the previous case. This page not only needs to render a form, but also needs to handle the form submission.

We can use a class-based view called FormView for this, but Django requires us to specify a few too many arguments to use it directly in the URLs file. Let's create our first customized view in main/views.py:

```python
from django.views.generic.edit import FormView
from main import forms

class ContactUsView(FormView):
    template_name = "contact_form.html"
    form_class = forms.ContactForm
    success_url = "/"

    def form_valid(self, form):
        form.send_mail()
        return super().form_valid(form)
```

Having done this, it is time to add the URLs entry. We will import our main/views.py file in the file with urlpatterns. For the sake of brevity, only the sections that have changed are shown here:

```python
...
from main import views

urlpatterns = [
    path(
        "contact-us/",
```

```
      views.ContactUsView.as_view(),
      name="contact_us",
  ),
  ...
]
```

At this point, we have a working page with a form that submits. You can see this yourself by opening your browser to `http://localhost:8000/contact-us/`.

To finish this part, the last thing we need is a test. The form itself has a test already. What is left to test is that the view is rendered when hitting the URL, and the page contains the contact form.

```
from main import forms
...

    def test_contact_us_page_works(self):
        response = self.client.get(reverse("contact_us"))
        self.assertEqual(response.status_code, 200)
        self.assertTemplateUsed(response, 'main/contact_form.html')
        self.assertContains(response, 'BookTime')
        self.assertIsInstance(
            response.context["form"], forms.ContactForm
        )
```

Now we should be able to navigate to the contact form through its URL. Alternatively, we could add it to the navigation bar in the base template, and that link would be present in all pages. See Figure 2-3.

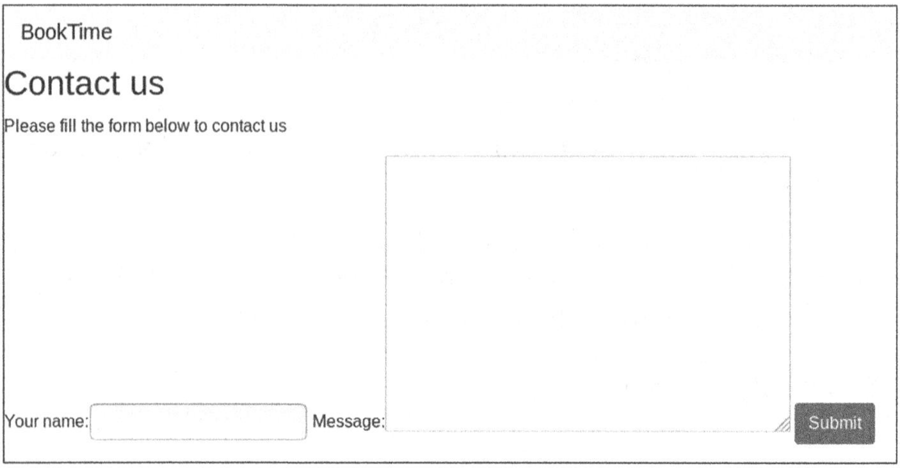

Figure 2-3. *Contact us page*

Filling out the form on the site and clicking Submit will trigger the e-mail as expected. You can see it in the logs:

```
INFO Sending email to customer service
Content-Type: text/plain; charset="utf-8"

MIME-Version: 1.0
Content-Transfer-Encoding: 7bit
Subject: Site message
From: site@booktime.domain
To: customerservice@booktime.domain
Date: Sat, 07 Apr 2018 17:37:14 -0000
Message-ID: <152312263451.9182.16061866787963579063@computer>

From: hello
just want to say hello world.
------------------------------------------------------------
```

We have seen a number of new Django functions in this section. They are described next in turn.

FormView

FormView is a very important class-based view, and it also is the base for more advanced views that interact with models, which will be presented later.

Besides initially rendering the template, FormView handles the submission using the Post/Redirect/Get pattern.[1] As soon as the POST request comes in, the validation is run and then a couple of functions are called: form_valid() is called if the form validates, and form_invalid() is called for the opposite case. By default form_valid() redirects to the success_url.

This class also implements the same functionality as TemplateView, which is template rendering. It can take the same keyword argument. template_name specifies the path of the template to render.

For the sake of completeness, if you wanted to implement the Contact us view in a function, you would have to write a bit more:

```
def contact_us(request):
    if request.method == 'POST':
        form = forms.ContactForm(request.POST)
        if form.is_valid():
            form.send_mail()
            return HttpResponseRedirect('/')
    else:
        form = forms.ContactForm()

    return render(request, 'contact_form.html', {'form': form})
```

---

[1]https://en.wikipedia.org/wiki/Post/Redirect/Get

Form Rendering

Historically, forms offered only a few ways to render themselves in HTML; {{ form.as_p }} and {{ form.as_ul }} are good examples, besides the default.

Nowadays, many websites enhance the forms with JavaScript and CSS that require a rendering that is more focused on semantics than on layout. What this means is that sometimes you might need to render fields individually.

Given that we use Bootstrap as a CSS framework, the previous example can be customized a bit more with the styles of Bootstrap forms:

```
<form method="POST">
  {% csrf_token %}
  <div class="form-group">
    {{ form.name.label_tag }}
    <input
      type="text"
      class="form-control {% if form.name.errors %}is-invalid{%
      endif %}"
      id="id_name"
      name="name"
      placeholder="Your name"
      value="{{ form.name.value|default:"" }}" >
    {% if form.name.errors %}
      <div class="invalid-feedback">
        {{ form.name.errors }}
      </div>
    {% endif %}
  </div>
```

```
<div class="form-group">
  {{ form.message.label_tag }}
  <textarea
    class="form-control {% if form.message.errors %}
    is-invalid{% endif %}"
    id="id_message"
    name="message"
    rows="3">
    {{ form.message.value|default:""}}
  </textarea>
  {% if form.message.errors %}
    <div class="invalid-feedback">
      {{ form.message.errors }}
    </div>
  {% endif %}
</div>
<button type="submit" class="btn btn-primary">Submit</button>
</form>
```

There is a lot of flexibility when rendering forms in Django. You could access and render fields directly with {{ form.name }}, or render specific things such as the label tag with {{ form.name.label_tag }}.

When a form is submitted and is invalid, Django will render the original page with a form that contains information about the invalid state. In Bootstrap there are conventions to display error states, and you can see in the previous listing how to structure those.

Summary

In this chapter we started creating the basic pages that everyone would expect on a company website: a homepage, an About us page, a contact form, and so on. To create these, we adopted a step-by-step process.

This chapter illustrated the basic class-based views, such as TemplateView and FormView, the URL routing system, and the e-mail sending function of Django.

Most times we also added tests to the features we added to the project, because it is an important step in good software development.

For the Contact us page, we introduced Django forms and how they can be used to manage data submission and e-mail sending.

In the next chapter we will talk about databases and how we can leverage them to build a more complex web application.

CHAPTER 3

Adding the Product Catalog to the Site

In this chapter we will start building product pages for our BookTime website, and these will be driven by data contained in databases. We will also see how to operate on the data and how to import it from CSV files.

This chapter introduces

- The Django ORM

- Migrations

- Management commands

- Signals

- `ListView` and `DetailView`

- Uploaded file management

Creating the First Models

Django has a layer called the ORM, which stands for Object Relational Mapper. It is a known pattern in software and it has been around for years. It consists of wrapping all rows loaded from the database into a series of models. Models are Python objects that have attributes that correspond to columns in a database row.

© Federico Marani 2019
F. Marani, *Practical Django 2 and Channels 2,*
https://doi.org/10.1007/978-1-4842-4099-1_3

A model has methods to interact with the underlying database row: save() writes any change of attributes of the model back into the database, and delete() deletes the database row.

These models are declared as Python classes first, inheriting from django.db.models.Model. In order for Django to detect any new models added to the system, they must be contained in the file models.py (or in a models package, like we did for tests in Chapter 2).

Product

Our company needs to visualize data about its products, so we will start with a Product model. To create this, write the following in the empty file models.py:

```
from django.db import models

class Product(models.Model):
    name = models.CharField(max_length=32)
    description = models.TextField(blank=True)
    price = models.DecimalField(max_digits=6, decimal_places=2)
    slug = models.SlugField(max_length=48)
    active = models.BooleanField(default=True)
    in_stock = models.BooleanField(default=True)
    date_updated = models.DateTimeField(auto_now=True)
```

Analyzing the preceding model, you will notice that it is a class with many attributes. All the attributes there are ultimately inheriting from django.db.models.fields.Field, and they map roughly to database types. CharField, for example, maps to the SQL type VARCHAR, IntegerField maps to SQL integers, BooleanField maps to SQL booleans, and so on.

Many of the attributes passed to field constructors represent further SQL specifiers. Taking CharField as reference, max_length is the maximum number of characters allowed, and it is passed as an argument to VARCHAR: this maximum is enforced at the database level.

There are also attributes that are used by other parts of Django. blank is used by Django admin, for instance. auto_now (available for only date/datetime fields) is managed by Django: it automatically updates the field with the time the model was last modified. Each field has its own possible configurations.

Once we have declared the model in the file, it is still not working. We would need to create a migration first. Migrations are special files that contain a list of database directives to create tables, add columns, remove them, and so on. All data definition language (DLL) commands (those to create and change schemas) are wrapped in a Python API that is used in migration files.

Although these migration files can be created manually, Django offers the makemigrations command to create them automatically. For most cases, it works as expected, as shown next. For some particularly difficult cases, the automatic creation may not create the correct migration. In those cases, it must be corrected manually.

```
$ ./manage.py makemigrations
Migrations for 'main':
  main/migrations/0001_initial.py
    - Create model Product
```

To illustrate the point I made earlier about migrations containing DDL commands, here is the one we just ran:

```
from django.db import migrations, models

class Migration(migrations.Migration):

    initial = True

    dependencies = [
    ]
```

```
operations = [
    migrations.CreateModel(
        name='Product',
        fields=[
            ('id', models.AutoField(auto_created=True,
                                    primary_key=True,
                                    serialize=False,
                                    verbose_name='ID')),
            ('name', models.CharField(max_length=32)),
            ('description', models.TextField(blank=True)),
            ('price', models.DecimalField(decimal_places=2,
                                    max_digits=6)),
            ('slug', models.SlugField(max_length=48)),
            ('active', models.BooleanField(default=True)),
            ('in_stock', models.BooleanField(default=True)),
            ('date_updated', models.DateTimeField
            (auto_now=True)),
        ],
    ),
]
```

Notice in the file that there is an extra id field. This is automatically added by Django when no field in your model explicitly has the attribute primary_key=True. A primary key is needed by the ORM to be able to map Python objects to database rows.

ProductImage

As for any product catalog, having an image for every product is a must. In our case, we want the possibility to have any number of images per product. To accomplish this, the information about the image needs to be in a separate table that we can link back to the Product model via a foreign key relationship:

```
class ProductImage(models.Model):
    product = models.ForeignKey(
        Product, on_delete=models.CASCADE
    )
    image = models.ImageField(upload_to="product-images")
```

There are a couple of more-complex fields here, compared to the previous model. ForeignKey is a field that stores the primary key of the linked Product model. It is used by the ORM to run JOIN operations automatically when accessed.

ImageField is a subclass of FileField, and it offers a few additional functionalities specifically for uploaded images. These extra functions require an additional library called Pillow. To install it, you need to run pipenv install Pillow.

At this point, we can run the Django ./manage.py makemigrations command again. It will generate a new migration for this model. The migration will contain a CreateModel directive along with three fields, the two just introduced and the id field.

ProductTag

The last model that we are going to introduce is the concept of "tag" as a generalization of categories: one product may have one or many tags, and one tag may contain one or more products.

```
class ProductTag(models.Model):
    products = models.ManyToManyField(Product, blank=True)
    name = models.CharField(max_length=32)
    slug = models.SlugField(max_length=48)
    description = models.TextField(blank=True)
    active = models.BooleanField(default=True)
```

Django offers a special type of field called ManyToManyField, which automatically creates a linking table between two tables, in this case Product Tags and Products. This linking table allows you to create relationships where any tags can be associated to any products and vice versa.

This was the last model for now. Remember to generate the migration for this, and then you can run all of them by running the migrate command:

```
$ ./manage.py migrate
Operations to perform:
  Apply all migrations: admin, auth, contenttypes, main, sessions
Running migrations:
  ...
  Applying main.0001_initial... OK
  Applying main.0002_productimage... OK
  Applying main.0003_producttag... OK
```

Subsequent chapters will introduce more models, but for the remainder of this chapter we will focus on implementing functionalities on top of these initial three models.

Thumbnail Generation

At this stage we already have enough to build new web pages, but before doing that we will add some extra functionality to the ProductImage model: thumbnails.

We do not want to serve to web clients images that are too big, because the loading time will be too high and customers will leave because of our unresponsive website.

We need to add a new `ImageField` field to the model, and that will hold the thumbnail image:

```
class ProductImage(models.Model):
    ...
    thumbnail = models.ImageField(
        upload_to="product-thumbnails", null=True
    )
```

Running the `makemigrations` command on it will generate a new migration with an `AddField` directive:

```
from django.db import migrations, models

class Migration(migrations.Migration):

    dependencies = [
        ('main', '0003_producttag'),
    ]

    operations = [
        migrations.AddField(
            model_name='productimage',
            name='thumbnail',
            field=models.ImageField(null=True,
                                    upload_to='product-
                                    thumbnails'),
        ),
    ]
```

Once added, the content of this field needs to be populated automatically, and to do so, we will use Django signals. Signals are a way to run code when specific events happen, and Django offers many hooks to connect them to ORM operations.

Signals are very useful in certain cases, but you should used them sparingly. An application that uses a lot of signals may become harder to debug, because the order in which they are executed is not deterministic.

The convention when writing signal handlers is to place them in a file called signals.py inside the relevant Django application, main in our case. Here we will put the code that generates the thumbnail:

```python
from io import BytesIO
import logging
from PIL import Image
from django.core.files.base import ContentFile
from django.db.models.signals import pre_save
from django.dispatch import receiver
from .models import ProductImage

THUMBNAIL_SIZE = (300, 300)

logger = logging.getLogger(__name__)

@receiver(pre_save, sender=ProductImage)
def generate_thumbnail(sender, instance, **kwargs):
    logger.info(
        "Generating thumbnail for product %d",
        instance.product.id,
    )
    image = Image.open(instance.image)
    image = image.convert("RGB")
    image.thumbnail(THUMBNAIL_SIZE, Image.ANTIALIAS)

    temp_thumb = BytesIO()
    image.save(temp_thumb, "JPEG")
    temp_thumb.seek(0)
```

```
# set save=False, otherwise it will run in an infinite loop
instance.thumbnail.save(
    instance.image.name,
    ContentFile(temp_thumb.read()),
    save=False,
)
temp_thumb.close()
```

Once we have done this, we need to make sure this file is initialized when the Django application is launched by the internal Django application registry. The suggested way to do this is to add a method called ready() in the application config inside main/apps.py:

```
from django.apps import AppConfig
class MainConfig(AppConfig):
    name = 'main'

    def ready(self):
        from . import signals
```

This is enough to make sure that signals are registered. Handlers will now be called for every new product image uploaded to the site.

Given that this is the first time we are managing user-uploaded files, we need to make sure Django knows where to store these files, and where to serve them from. These two values need to be specified in booktime/settings.py:

```
...

MEDIA_ROOT = os.path.join(BASE_DIR, "media")
MEDIA_URL = "/media/"
```

To test the signal, we are going to write a Django test. We will put this test in a file called main/tests/test_signals.py.

The following test, and many in this chapter, will rely on some bootstrapping data (images and CSVs). This data is included in this book's code repository.

```python
from django.test import TestCase
from main import models
from django.core.files.images import ImageFile
from decimal import Decimal

class TestSignal(TestCase):
    def test_thumbnails_are_generated_on_save(self):
        product = models.Product(
            name="The cathedral and the bazaar",
            price=Decimal("10.00"),
        )
        product.save()

        with open(
            "main/fixtures/the-cathedral-the-bazaar.jpg", "rb"
        ) as f:
            image = models.ProductImage(
                product=product,
                image=ImageFile(f, name="tctb.jpg"),
            )
            with self.assertLogs("main", level="INFO") as cm:
                image.save()

        self.assertGreaterEqual(len(cm.output), 1)
        image.refresh_from_db()

        with open(
            "main/fixtures/the-cathedral-the-bazaar.thumb.jpg",
            "rb",
        ) as f:
```

```
    expected_content = f.read()
    assert image.thumbnail.read() == expected_content

image.thumbnail.delete(save=False)
image.image.delete(save=False)
```

In the test, we are creating some database content and, given that the test base class inherits from `TransactionTestCase`, any model created is reset at the end of the test. The same thing cannot be said of the files, which need to be deleted manually.

QuerySets and Managers

In the last section we talked about models, including how we define them and how we create database rows with them. The next set of SQL operations that we will examine includes SELECTs and UPDATEs, which rely on QuerySets and Managers.

A Manager is a class responsible for building queries against a model. Every model needs to have at least one manager. By default, an instance of `django.db.models.Manager` is connected to every model through an attribute in the model called `objects`. All the standard methods of a Manager return querysets.

A QuerySet is a collection of models loaded from the database. QuerySets are constructed and populated by Manager instances. QuerySets also have methods that can be used to further filter the models, such as `filter()` or `exclude()`. QuerySets are similar to Python lists: they can be sliced, and they can be iterated with a `for` loop.

These two methods accept keyword arguments that represent field lookups, which Django converts to WHERE clauses at query time. Field lookups are expressed in the form of `field__lookuptype=value`. If you omit the `lookuptype` section, it is assumed you want to check for equality.

Here are some examples of queries using the default manager for the models created earlier:

- `Product.objects.all()`: Returns all products

- `Product.objects.filter(price__gt=Decimal("2.00"))`: Returns products with a price greater than 2.00

- `Product.objects.filter(price__lte=Decimal("2.00"))`: Returns products with a price less than (or equal to) 2.00

- `Product.objects.exclude(price__gt=Decimal("12.00"))`: Returns products with a price greater than 12.00

- `Product.objects.filter(price=Decimal("2.00"))`: Returns products with a price of exactly 2.00

- `Product.objects.filter(name__icontains="cathedral")`: Returns products with names that contain the word "cathedral" (case insensitive)

- `...filter(name__startswith="The", price__gt=Decimal("9.00"))`: Returns a combination of two clauses with an AND

All the preceding queries are limited to one table. If you need to match on fields that are in other tables, Django offer you a way to build JOINs while querying. `Product.objects.filter(producttag__name="sci-fi")` is an example of this. It will return products that have the tag "sci-fi" associated, and to calculate this it builds two extra JOINs: one with the linking table and another to the tag table.

If you want to build more advanced queries, like OR queries or queries that refer to other fields, you need to use `django.db.models.Q` objects or `django.db.models.F` objects. Here are some examples:

- `...filter(Q(name__startswith="The") | Q(price__gt=Decimal("9.00")))`: Returns products whose name starts with "The" OR price is greater than 9.00.

- `...filter(price__gt=F("price") - 1)`: Returns products with a price greater than the price itself minus 1. This is a silly example to prove how it works.

Now that we know how managers work, we are going to create one. The reason why you would do that is to add extra methods that return filtered QuerySets. Given that we have an `active` field in the `Product` model, we are going to add a manager with a filter on that:

```
class ActiveManager(models.Manager):
    def active(self):
        return self.filter(active=True)
```

After having declared this, we will connect it to the model by overriding an attribute called by convention `objects`:

```
class Product(models.Model):
    ...

    objects = ActiveManager()
```

This method will then be available to use as in the previous examples: `Product.objects.active()` to return only active products. To finish this functionality, we need to write the test. Here is one that works:

```
from decimal import Decimal
from django.test import TestCase
from main import models
```

```python
class TestModel(TestCase):
    def test_active_manager_works(self):
        models.Product.objects.create(
            name="The cathedral and the bazaar",
            price=Decimal("10.00"))
        models.Product.objects.create(
            name="Pride and Prejudice",
            price=Decimal("2.00"))
        models.Product.objects.create(
            name="A Tale of Two Cities",
            price=Decimal("2.00"),
            active=False)
        self.assertEqual(len(models.Product.objects.active()), 2)
```

Migrations

Given how impactful database schema management is, it deserves its own section. We already saw that migrations are the way Django applies database changes following model changes. These migration files, once generated, are part of the project. They need to be put under source control and shared between everyone working on the project.

When performing migrations, there are a few commands to know:

- makemigrations: Generate migration files (in Python) that can be modified later

- migrate: Run migration files that have not been applied in order

- showmigrations: List migrations that have been applied or not

- sqlmigrate: Display the SQL of a migration

With these commands in mind, it is worth taking another look at the migration file we have generated so far and talk about migration dependencies. If you open any migration file, you will notice an attribute called dependencies. This is used to build a dependency graph. Ours is displayed in Figure 3-1.

Figure 3-1. *Migrations*

Directionality

With the command migrate, migrations can be run either forward or backward, which means applying changes or reverting changes that have been applied already. In order for this bidirectionality to work, when creating migrations, they should be structured in a reversible way. Some examples of reverse operations are

- When adding a field, the reverse is removing the field.

- When adding a table, the reverse is removing the table.

- When removing a nullable field, the reverse is adding it back.

There are, however, some situations that are not clearly reversible. Some examples are non-nullable field removal and casting text data back to number. When making migrations, we should avoid making migrations that are not reversible.

As an overview of the possibilities bidirectionality gives us, we will start by analyzing what the current database state is:

```
$ ./manage.py showmigrations main
main
 [X] 0001_initial
 [X] 0002_productimage
```

```
[X] 0003_producttag
[X] 0004_productimage_thumbnail
```

We have all migrations applied already, but we can revert them if we wish. Reverting them, or applying them backward, can be done using the migrate command:

```
$ ./manage.py migrate main 0003_producttag
Operations to perform:
  Target specific migration: 0003_producttag, from main
Running migrations:
  Rendering model states... DONE
  Unapplying main.0004_productimage_thumbnail... OK
```

Reverting/applying migrations is useful when working on multiple branches. If different versions of code require a different database state, this allows you to switch it. To reapply, we simply use the migrate command without specifying the migration:

```
$ ./manage.py migrate main
Operations to perform:
  Apply all migrations: main
Running migrations:
  Applying main.0004_productimage_thumbnail... OK
```

Merging Migrations

When working with version control systems such as Git, it is very easy to create branches and work on copies of the same code base independently. Given that database structure in Django is managed through Python code, it is possible that two branches contain two different sets of models.

Both source control systems have a way of merging code, but after having done so, we might have a situation where multiple migrations are at the top of the dependency graph. An example is the best way to illustrate this. Let's assume that on branch "A" someone edits the name field of product to be 40 characters long, instead of the current 32. The result of makemigrations would be

```
./manage.py makemigrations -n productname_40
Migrations for 'main':
  main/migrations/0005_productname_40.py
    - Alter field name on product
```

But on another branch, "B," someone else edits the models of the same Django application (in our case, main). That person changes the name of tags to be 40 characters long:

```
$ ./manage.py makemigrations -n producttagname_40
Migrations for 'main':
  main/migrations/0005_producttagname_40.py
    - Alter field name on producttag
```

When it is time to merge this to branches, we will have two "0005" migrations that both depend on the same base. If we try to run migrate in this situation, we would get an error:

```
$ ./manage.py migrate
CommandError: Conflicting migrations detected;...
...multiple leaf nodes in the migration graph:
(0005_productname_40, 0005_producttagname_40 in main).

To fix them run 'python manage.py makemigrations --merge'
```

This is happening because Django does not allow the migration graph to have two heads, which would be the current state (illustrated in Figure 3-2).

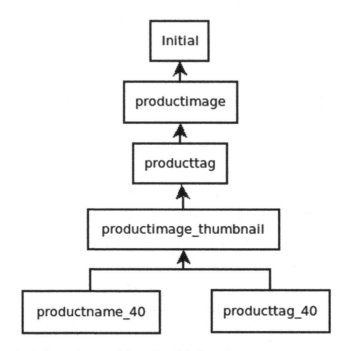

Figure 3-2. *Migrations with a double head*

If we run the recommended makemigrations --merge command, we will rectify this issue by having a special, empty migration that depends on each of the migrations that we created in branches A and B (see Figure 3-3).

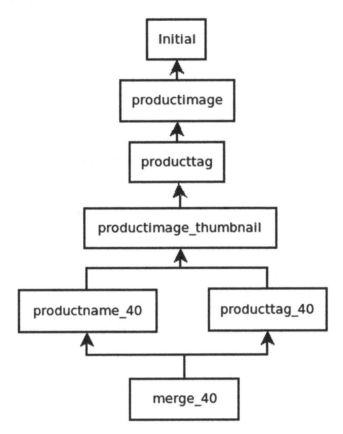

Figure 3-3. *Migrations after merge*

Data Migrations

Besides schema changes, it is possible to use migrations to load data, or transform existing data. It is common, for example, to do type conversions when changing a field type with a three-step process:

1. Schema migration to add the destination field.

2. Data migration to cast and save data to the new field.

3. Schema migration to remove the original field.

In order to illustrate their usage, we will focus on a simpler use case. Let's create a data migration that capitalizes names of products. To do so, we start with an empty migration:

```
$ ./manage.py makemigrations main --empty -n productname_capitalize
```

The resulting file needs to be filled with our code:

```
from django.db import migrations

def capitalize(apps, schema_editor):
    Product = apps.get_model('main', 'Product')
    for product in Product.objects.all():
        product.name = product.name.capitalize()
        product.save()

class Migration(migrations.Migration):
    ...

    operations = [
        migrations.RunPython(
            capitalize,
            migrations.RunPython.noop
        ),
    ]
```

Instead of using operations like `CreateModel` or `AlterField`, we are using a lower-level operation called `RunPython`, which takes a forward function and a backward function. In our case, we specify a `noop` backward function, which will allow us to go backward doing nothing instead of raising an exception.

Once we apply this, all current products will have their name capitalized. It is important to realize that this migration will only be applied once. If we have data transformations that have to be applied independently from database changes, migrations may not be the best means for that.

One thing to notice is that in the forward/backward functions, we must use that special way to import models. That is because at the point of execution of the migration, the database schema will be different than the schema declared in the models file. The `apps.get_model()` method will return the old model, stripped from its custom methods.

Managing Data Through Django admin

One of the often-cited killer features of Django is its admin interface. It is a UI to create, update, and delete any model in the system. It also offers an authentication and permission system, used to assign different level of privileges to different users.

Admin is a really useful tool that comes for free; it just needs to be activated. To do so, we will start by creating a file called `main/admin.py`:

```
from django.contrib import admin
from . import models

admin.site.register(models.Product)
admin.site.register(models.ProductTag)
admin.site.register(models.ProductImage)
```

Once we have done this, we need to create the first user of our Django project. It will be the admin user. Django does not come with any initial data, therefore this step needs to be done manually. There is a Django command called `createsuperuser` for this:

```
$ ./manage.py createsuperuser
Username (leave blank to use 'flagz'): admin
Email address: me@site.domain
Password:
Password (again):
Superuser created successfully.
```

This should be enough to start using it. By default, the admin interface is accessible at `http://localhost:8000/admin/`.

When using the admin interface, a user will land on its login page and, once logged in, will see a list of models divided by Django apps, as shown in Figure 3-4. Each of the model names can be clicked, which leads to a view that lists all instances of the model.

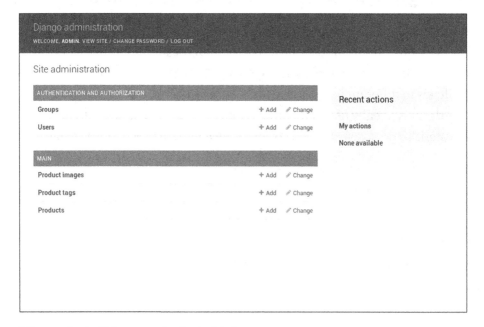

Figure 3-4. *Django admin initial page*

At this stage, you do not have any data yet. To fully try the admin interface, you should at least insert one product. Go ahead and insert the title of your favorite book. You can do so in the product list view. Click Products and then click the add button in the top-right corner.

For any model list view there are a few things on the page. In the top-right corner, there is a button to add new instances of the selected model. On the left, there is a list of models, along with a check box for each. After you click a check box, you can apply an action to the selected model.

Admin actions are operations that can be applied to a group of models (of the same kind). Available actions are listed in the drop-down box above the models list. By default, the only action available is deletion.

Simple Customizations

At this point, with a little more effort, we could make the admin interface more useful to us. Here are some simple customizations for list views:

- `list_display` is a list of fields that, if specified, will be used to create columns in the model list view. Besides fields, these can also be functions.

- `list_filter` is a list of fields that will be used as filters for this list. When selected, only a subset of all models will be visualized.

- `search_fields` is an option that, when present, will instruct Django to add a search box, which can be used to search on the fields specified.

- `list_editable` is a list of fields that will make some of the columns specified in `list_display` editable.

When visualizing single items instead of a list of items, use the following:

- `autocomplete_fields` is useful in case you have a field that refers to another table with many entities. This could make it difficult to use standard select boxes, because of the number of options.

- `prepopulated_fields` is useful for slug fields. It tells the admin interface to create the slug from another field automatically.

- `readonly_fields` is a list of fields that will not be made editable.

Using all of these customizations, we can put together something friendlier than the default configuration, the result of which is shown in Figure 3-5:

```
from django.contrib import admin
from django.utils.html import format_html

from . import models

class ProductAdmin(admin.ModelAdmin):
    list_display = ('name', 'slug', 'in_stock', 'price')
    list_filter = ('active', 'in_stock', 'date_updated')
    list_editable = ('in_stock', )
    search_fields = ('name',)
    prepopulated_fields = {"slug": ("name",)}

admin.site.register(models.Product, ProductAdmin)
```

```python
class ProductTagAdmin(admin.ModelAdmin):
    list_display = ('name', 'slug')
    list_filter = ('active',)
    search_fields = ('name',)
    prepopulated_fields = {"slug": ("name",)}
    autocomplete_fields = ('products',)

admin.site.register(models.ProductTag, ProductTagAdmin)

class ProductImageAdmin(admin.ModelAdmin):
    list_display = ('thumbnail_tag', 'product_name')
    readonly_fields = ('thumbnail',)
    search_fields = ('product__name',)

    def thumbnail_tag(self, obj):
        if obj.thumbnail:
            return format_html(
                '<img src="%s"/>' % obj.thumbnail.url
            )
        return "-"
    thumbnail_tag.short_description = "Thumbnail"
    def product_name(self, obj):
        return obj.product.name

admin.site.register(models.ProductImage, ProductImageAdmin)
```

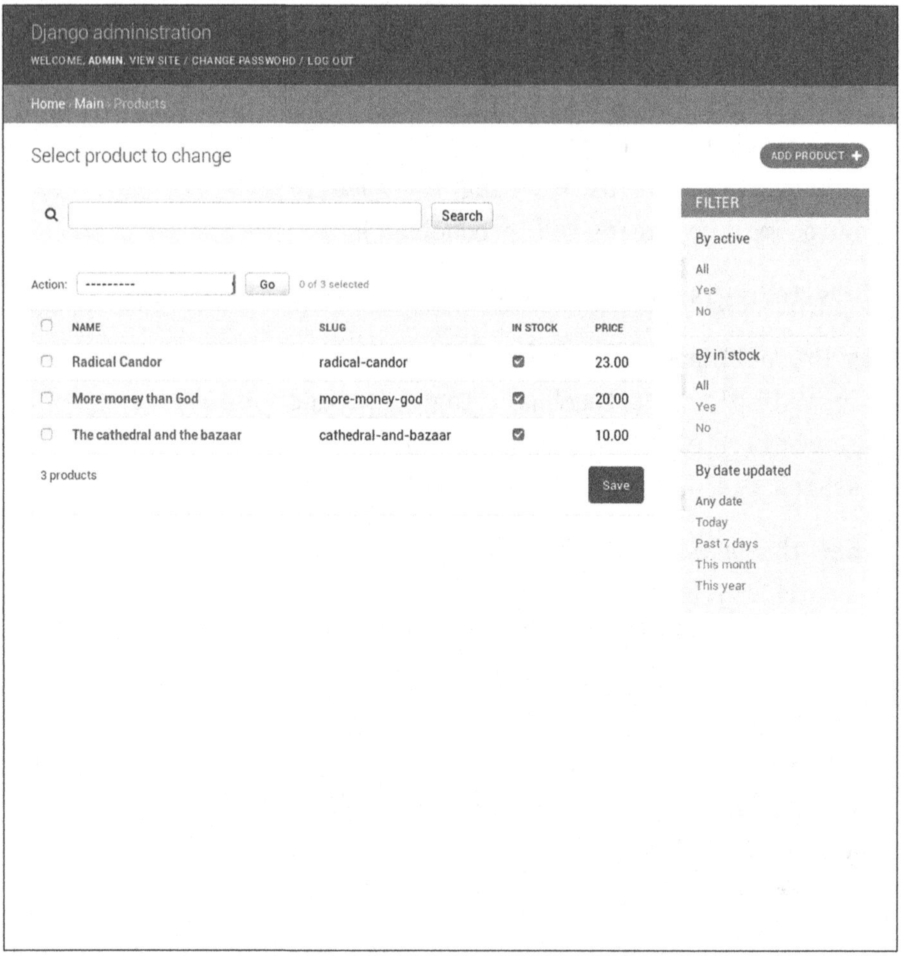

Figure 3-5. *Our Product admin*

This configuration will

- When listing products, display the columns `name`, `slug`, `in_stock`, and `price`. Of these four columns, `in_stock` will be editable. After changing what product is in stock or not, clicking the Save button saves the changes.

- Make the products filterable on the fields specified. These filters are listed on the right.

- Add a search box above the products table. Whatever you search for, Django will look for that string to be contained in the fields specified, ignoring the case of the letters.

- When adding a product, compute the slug on-the-fly as the product name is being typed.

- While working on the product tags, provide a similar configuration to the one of products (see Figure 3-6).

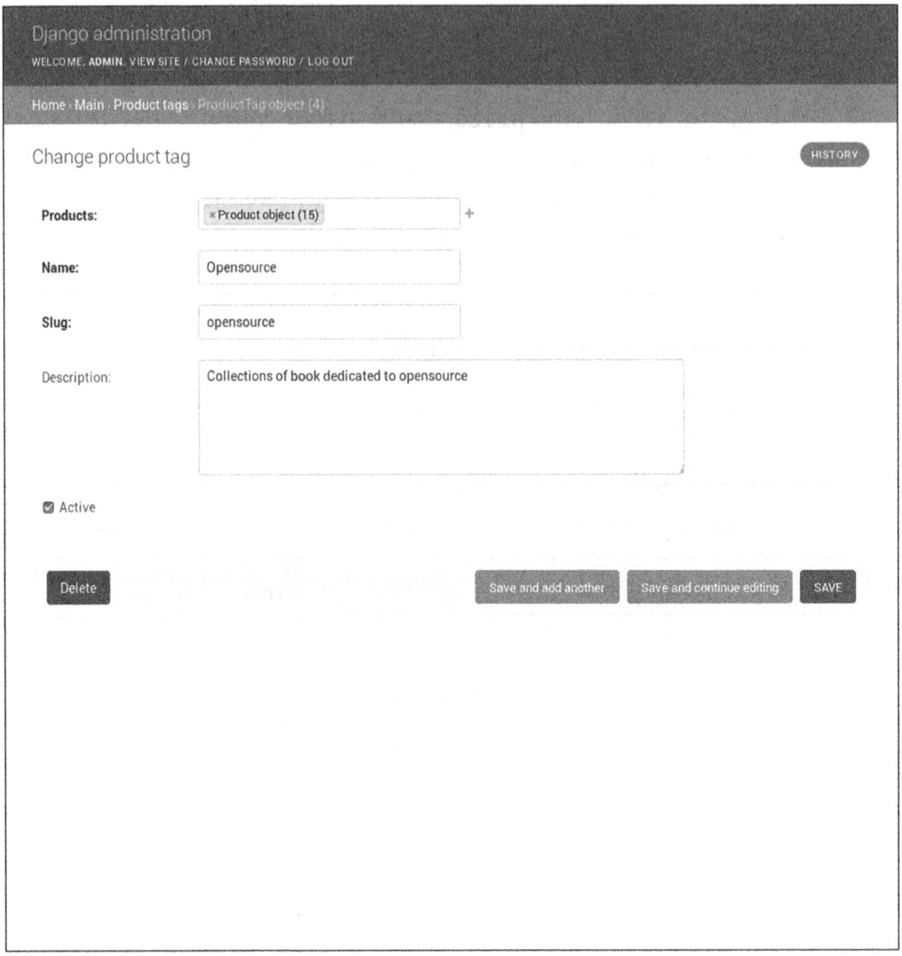

Figure 3-6. *Tags admin*

- Add an autocomplete while selecting products belonging to a specific tag.

- Display the images in two columns, the content of which will be the returned values of the two functions specified in the admin class, one of which is returning HTML.

- Add a search box in the images list view. This search will be applied on the linked product table (using a JOIN) rather than the productimage table (see Figure 3-7).

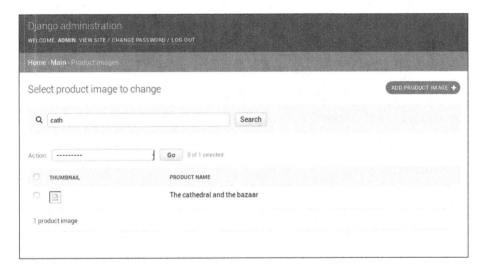

Figure 3-7. *Images management*

At this point, there are a couple of things to fix. Django admin, when building selectors or generally visualizing items, relies on its string representation. In our case, the autocomplete needs a good string representation. To fix this, we need to add methods to all models. Here is an example:

```
class Product(models.Model):
    ...

    def __str__(self):
        return self.name
```

The last thing to fix is serving user-uploaded images. At the moment, although the correct image and thumbnail URLs are served, those URLs return 404s. We need to fix this inside the main URLs file booktime/urls.py.

```
from django.contrib import admin
from django.urls import path, include
from django.conf import settings
from django.conf.urls.static import static

urlpatterns = [
    path('admin/', admin.site.urls),
    path('', include('main.urls')),
] + static(settings.MEDIA_URL, document_root=settings.MEDIA_ROOT)
```

This is all we are going to customize for now. In the following chapters we will talk about the more advanced features.

Management Commands

Thus far in the book you have seen several commands such as ./manage.py runserver or ./manage.py migrate. In Django those utilities are called *management commands*. These can be added at will, but there are a number of these included and ready to be used. You can print the full list of available commands with ./manage.py.

makemessages and compilemessages are used to manage translation files in Django. You would use these if the user interface of your project needs to support multiple languages.

check is an interface to the Django system check framework, which is used when starting any Django command to ensure that all the conditions required for the project to work are met. It is useful in case your project depends on some configuration variables being specified in the environment, for example.

dbshell and shell are interactive command-line prompts. dbshell will launch the database command-line client, while shell will launch a Python interpreter, with the Django project initialized already.

loaddata and dumpdata are very useful as a simple data loading mechanism. They are used to bootstrap a database with data from *fixtures*, which are simple data files in a format that Django understands. They can be JSON or XML and, as long as the structure is what Django dictates, they will be managed without any extra code.

We are going to leverage the loaddata and dumpdata commands to manage tags. Tags will be a fixed set and managed by developers, and the fixture will be committed to the repository. We will also introduce another Django functionality called *natural keys*.

We can use Django admin to create those initially. After adding six tags (see Figure 3-8), we will export them with the dumpdata command.

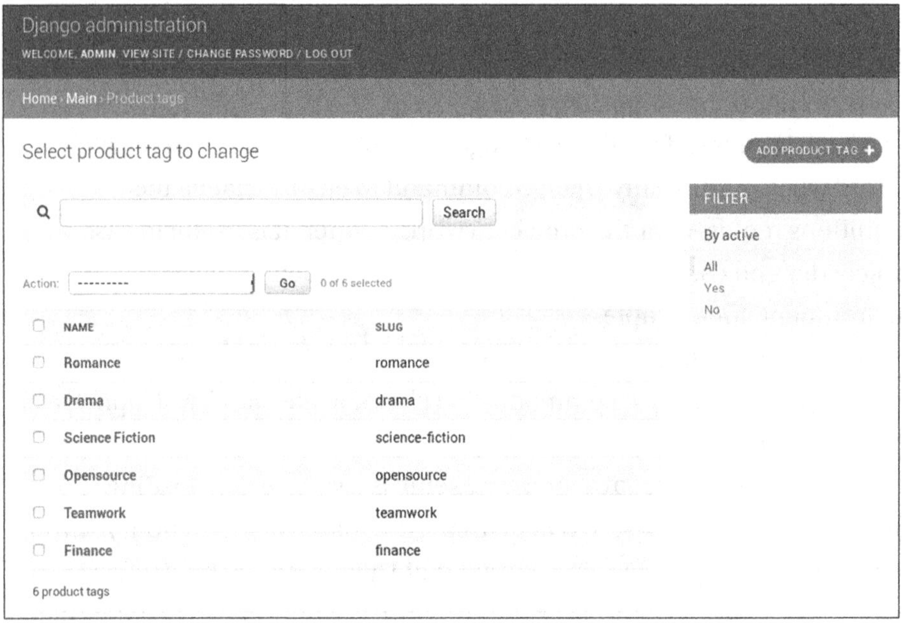

Figure 3-8. Tags list

Serialization and Natural Keys

Serialization, in Django, means converting data stored in a database table to something that can be written to a file. Django supports XML, JSON, and YAML file formats. *Deserialization* is the opposite operation, going from files to a populated database table.

Django offers serialization and deserialization facilities through both helper functions and management commands. We will focus on management commands for now. The following is an example of how to use the dumpdata command:

```
$ ./manage.py dumpdata --indent 2 main.ProductTag
[{
  "model": "main.producttag",
  "pk": 2,
```

```
  "fields": {
    "name": "Finance",
    "slug": "finance",
    "description": "",
    "active": true,
    "products": [
      16
    ]
  }
},
...
```

Unfortunately for us, this is not suitable for distribution with our repository. It contains many internal IDs that are specific to a database instance.

One way to solve this would be to use independent IDs, such as UUIDs, but they are not very human-friendly. Instead we will use natural keys, and therefore we will need to do a few things to the current models:

- Move ManyToManyField out of tags and into the Product model

- Make sure the __str__() method for tags is defined

- Define tags natural_key() method

The first bullet point is easily done by removing the products field in the ProductTag model and re-adding it to the Product model:

```
class Product(models.Model):
    ...
    tags = models.ManyToManyField(ProductTag, blank=True)
    ...
```

At the database level, not much has changed: we still have a linking table. The difference now is that this link is more easily traversable from the products. This change impacts the Django admin, specifically the autocomplete_fields setting, which needs to be moved as well:

```
class ProductAdmin(admin.ModelAdmin):
    ...
    autocomplete_fields = ('tags',)
```

The second tweak is to add the __str__() method and we do it for the same reason we have done it already, which is usability.

As a last step, we will add a method called natural_key(), which will return the tag natural key. In our case, we will use the slug as a natural key. The rationale behind this is that slugs, used as part of URLs, are unlikely to change (simplifying a bit here).

Following all the changes suggested, this is how the class would look like now:

```
class ProductTag(models.Model):
    name = models.CharField(max_length=40)
    slug = models.SlugField(max_length=48)
    description = models.TextField(blank=True)
    active = models.BooleanField(default=True)

    def __str__(self):
        return self.name

    def natural_key(self):
        return (self.slug,)
```

With this model, it is possible to run dumpdata using natural keys instead of internal database keys. We will also output the following to a file for later use. The resulting file will be independent from internal identifiers and, therefore, more portable between different database environments.

```
$ ./manage.py dumpdata --indent 2 --natural-primary main.ProductTag
[
{
  "model": "main.producttag",
  "fields": {
    "name": "Finance",
    "slug": "finance",
    "description": "",
    "active": true
  }
},
...

$ ./manage.py dumpdata --indent 2 --natural-primary main.
ProductTag \
    > main/fixtures/producttags.json
```

How to Load Using Natural Keys

When loading data using natural keys, Django cannot use the natural_
key() method we defined already, because model loading happens
through managers, not models themselves. To be able to load tags back in,
we need to create a Manager for that model and implement the get_by_
natural_key() method:

```
class ProductTagManager(models.Manager):
    def get_by_natural_key(self, slug):
        return self.get(slug=slug)

class ProductTag(models.Model):
    ...
    objects = ProductTagManager()
    ...
```

If you followed all the preceding steps, loading it (or reloading it) should just be a one-command operation. To test this, we can add some descriptions of tags in the file and reload them. If the data exists already in the database, it will be updated.

```
$ ./manage.py loaddata main/fixtures/producttags.json
Installed 6 object(s) from 1 fixture(s)
```

Importing Data with a Management Command

Besides the management commands that are already included, the project can also define new commands. Once created, they are available to be launched using the manage.py script.

We are going to create an ad hoc command to import products data.

In order to create a management command, you need to add a file inside main/management/commands/. The file name you choose will be the command name. There will be one management command per file; if you want to create multiple commands, you will need multiple files.

Every management command can take options: these are parsed with argparse, and Django has some conventions on specifying these as well.

To start the task of creating a management command, we first need to set up some basic folders:

```
$ mkdir main/management
$ touch main/management/__init__.py
$ mkdir main/management/commands
$ touch main/management/commands/__init__.py
```

These commands will make these folders Python modules, enabling Django to inspect and execute the content of them. Next we will create main/management/commands/import_data.py, which will contain the importer:

```python
from django.core.management.base import BaseCommand

class Command(BaseCommand):
    help = 'Import products in BookTime'

    def handle(self, *args, **options):
        self.stdout.write("Importing products")
```

This is enough for the command to execute, and the conventions here are clearly visible. These files need to contain a Python class that inherits from django.core.management.base.BaseCommand and implements the handle() function. This will also make it discoverable by Django.

Here are some example interactions:

```
$ ./manage.py
Type 'manage.py help <subcommand>' for help on a specific
subcommand.

Available subcommands:

...
[main]
    import_data
...

$ ./manage.py import_data
Importing products
```

The body of the handle() method is where the import logic will be. Let's assume we need to populate the data from a CSV file like this one:

```
name,description,tags,image_filename,price
The cathedral and the bazaar,A book about open source
methodologies,Open source|Programming,cathedral-Siddhartha,A
novel by Hermann Hesse,Religion|Narrative,siddhartha.jpg,6.00
Backgammon for dummies,How to start playing Backgammon,Games
|Manual,backgammon.jpg,13.00
```

To test the command later in this section, save the preceding data in a file.

This file contains fields that in our database structure are spread over separate tables. We cannot use the loaddata command here, for that reason. Another reason is that CSV is not one of the serialization formats that Django handles. This is an implementation that imports the preceding file:

```
from collections import Counter
import csv
import os.path
from django.core.files.images import ImageFile
from django.core.management.base import BaseCommand
from django.template.defaultfilters import slugify
from main import models

class Command(BaseCommand):
    help = "Import products in BookTime"

    def add_arguments(self, parser):
        parser.add_argument("csvfile", type=open)
        parser.add_argument("image_basedir", type=str)

    def handle(self, *args, **options):
        self.stdout.write("Importing products")
        c = Counter()
        reader = csv.DictReader(options.pop("csvfile"))
        for row in reader:
            product, created = models.Product.objects.get_or_
            create(
                name=row["name"], price=row["price"]
            )
            product.description = row["description"]
            product.slug = slugify(row["name"])
            for import_tag in row["tags"].split("|"):
```

```python
            tag, tag_created = models.ProductTag.objects.
            get_or_create(
                name=import_tag
            )
            product.tags.add(tag)
            c["tags"] += 1
            if tag_created:
                c["tags_created"] += 1
        with open(
            os.path.join(
                options["image_basedir"],
                row["image_filename"],
            ),
            "rb",
        ) as f:
            image = models.ProductImage(
                product=product,
                image=ImageFile(
                    f, name=row["image_filename"]
                ),
            )
            image.save()
            c["images"] += 1
        product.save()
        c["products"] += 1
        if created:
            c["products_created"] += 1

    self.stdout.write(
        "Products processed=%d (created=%d)"
        % (c["products"], c["products_created"])
    )
```

```
self.stdout.write(
    "Tags processed=%d (created=%d)"
    % (c["tags"], c["tags_created"])
)
self.stdout.write("Images processed=%d" % c["images"])
```

There is much to explain in the code of this new import_data command. First of all, the add_arguments function: management commands can accept command-line options, and Django offers some options that are available to all commands (verbosity, for example), but this list can be extended.

We also added two positional arguments on top of all Django options. The first positional argument is the path to the CSV file to import, and the second is the path to the images directory. The syntax of add_argument is explained in the argparse module documentation, which is the Python module that Django is using.

The use of script arguments, instead of hard-coded variables, gives to this script flexibility. When running these imports in environments different than your machine's environment, you may be using this in conjunction with other commands like wget or gunzip to download and decompress archives in temporary folders with dynamically generated names.

After opening the CSV file, the script cycles over the rows and tries to load (or generate) a product with the same name/price combination. The get_or_create function returns two values: a model and a boolean flag to indicate whether it is a new model.

Once we have a product loaded, we update its tag list by cycling through all the tags in the tags field in the CSV file. Given that CSVs are a flat format, this list need to be expanded from its contracted form (pipe-separated list).

Once tags are inserted, the script tries to open the image by joining the basedir and the specified file name, with os.path.join(). A new instance of the ProductImage model is created by passing the product and the opened file wrapped in an ImageFile object, which adds extra information about the file.

In the command, there are several calls to `self.stdout.write`. This writes to standard output. In a similar vein, `self.stderr.write` is also available, if standard error is preferable.

As for all the sizeable procedural code presented so far, this code needs a test, to make sure it never breaks:

```
from io import StringIO
import tempfile
from django.conf import settings
from django.core.management import call_command
from django.test import TestCase, override_settings
from main import models

class TestImport(TestCase):
    @override_settings(MEDIA_ROOT=tempfile.gettempdir())
    def test_import_data(self):
        out = StringIO()
        args = ['main/fixtures/product-sample.csv',
                'main/fixtures/product-sampleimages/']

        call_command('import_data', *args, stdout=out)

        expected_out = ("Importing products\n"
                        "Products processed=3 (created=3)\n"
                        "Tags processed=6 (created=6)\n"
                        "Images processed=3\n")

        self.assertEqual(out.getvalue(), expected_out)
        self.assertEqual(models.Product.objects.count(), 3)
        self.assertEqual(models.ProductTag.objects.count(), 6)
        self.assertEqual(models.ProductImage.objects.count(), 3)
```

As you can see, Django offers the function `call_command()` to invoke management commands from Python itself, which is very convenient in tests.

After we put the sample CSV file (along with some images) in the locations specified, it will be possible to run this test. The test asserts that the stdout is equal to what is expected, and the number of models present after the import is what it should be.

In the test, the decorator override_settings is used. Its purpose is to override Django settings for a specific test. In this case, we are creating a new temporary folder as MEDIA_ROOT because we are dealing with potentially many uploaded files. Django, unlike the database, does not clean these files. Using a temporary folder makes sure this will be eventually cleaned by the operating system.

For all tests involving databases, Django, before running these, creates a test database that will be temporarily used. At the end of test runs, this test database is dropped. In our case, the test database would be a new PostgreSQL database with the same name as the specified name with a test_ prefix added. Management of this is automatic.

This test is not exhaustive: it does not test for the csv file to exist, images to be present in the basedir, and so on. This is left as an exercise for you.

Adding a Product List Page

In this chapter so far we have not done any website work, only data foundations. It is time now to create our first database-driven web page, starting from listing the products. We can leverage another class-based view for this called ListView. Django has a lot of CBVs that help with building database-driven views, and we will use those when appropriate. Here is the view that we are going to use:

```
from django.views.generic.list import ListView
from django.shortcuts import get_object_or_404
from main import models
```

```
class ProductListView(ListView):
    template_name = "main/product_list.html"
    paginate_by = 4

    def get_queryset(self):
        tag = self.kwargs['tag']
        self.tag = None
        if tag != "all":
            self.tag = get_object_or_404(
                models.ProductTag, slug=tag
            )
        if self.tag:
            products = models.Product.objects.active().filter(
                tags=self.tag
            )
        else:
            products = models.Product.objects.active()

        return products.order_by("name")
```

Our view leverages ListView but adds a customization: an extra filtering parameter (tag). Depending on the content of kwargs, it returns a list of active products belonging to that tag, or simply all active ones if the tag all is specified.

ListView, like the CBVs we have seen so far, uses template_name for rendering. It will look for that template when rendering the view. Please note that, unlike in the initial views, we put an extra main. This is a convention that we will start using to mirror what other database views do.

This view also transparently manages pagination, with the paginate_by parameter.

When an instance of this view is created, the attributes args and kwargs are populated with information from the URL route. In our case, this view is expecting to be called with the tag specified in the URL path, rather than in a GET parameter. If, on the other hand, the tag were a GET parameter, it could be accessed using the self.request.GET dictionary.

The function get_object_or_404 is a very useful shortcut: it returns an object that corresponds to the filters specified, or raises a 404 exception (django.http.Http404). Django will then catch this and create an HTML response for a 404 status (404 is the "not found" HTTP status code), using the 404.html template if available.

To use this new view, it needs an entry in the urlpatterns:

```
from main import views

...

urlpatterns = [
    path(
        "products/<slug:tag>/",
        views.ProductListView.as_view(),
        name="products",
    ),
    ...
]
```

This is the first URL in the project that has a variable path. Django will try to convert whatever is written in the section surrounded by < and > with the slug converter, which accepts letters, numbers, hyphens, and underscores.

The last thing that the product list page needs in order to work is a template, which will be stored in main/templates/main/product_list.html:

```
{% extends "base.html" %}

{% block content %}
  <h1>products</h1>
  {% for product in page_obj %}
    <p>{{ product.name }}</p>
    <p>
      <a href="{% url "product" product.slug %}">See it here</a>
    </p>
    {% if not forloop.last %}
      <hr>
    {% endif %}
  {% endfor %}
  <nav>
    <ul class="pagination">
      {% if page_obj.has_previous %}
        <li class="page-item">
          <a
            class="page-link"
            href="?page={{page_obj.previous_page_number}}">
            Previous</a>
        </li>
      {% else %}
        <li class="page-item disabled">
          <a class="page-link" href="#">Previous</a>
        </li>
      {% endif %}
      {% for pagenum in page_obj.paginator.page_range %}
```

```
    <li
      class="page-item{% if page_obj.number == pagenum %}
      active{% endif %}">
      <a class="page-link" href="?page={{pagenum}}">{{pagenum}}
      </a>
    </li>
  {% endfor %}
  {% if page_obj.has_next %}
    <li class="page-item">
      <a class="page-link" href="?page={{page_obj.next_
      page_number}}">Next</a>
    </li>
  {% else %}
    <li class="page-item disabled">
      <a class="page-link" href="#">Next</a>
    </li>
  {% endif %}
  </ul>
 </nav>
{% endblock content %}
```

There are a few new things in this template that are worth explaining.
We are building on top of the existing base template and tags seen already,
and using a new for tag. This tag does what the equivalent in Python does:
it repeats a section. We will generate as many HTML sections as elements
in that list.

Inside the for loop, we can use a variable called forloop that contains
a series of dynamic values that we can use. This variable is automatically
set by Django. In our case we print an horizontal separator for every cycle
except the last one.

The last section in the template prints the pagination section. The
page_obj variable that is populated by the view contains a slice of the
results that needs to be visualized, along with some page information, like
what the current page is and whether there is a next page. Figure 3-9 shows
how the template above looks when rendered.

Figure 3-9. *Products list view*

As a last step for the product list view, we will add its tests. We can add
those in the test_views.py file:

```
...
from decimal import Decimal
from main import models

class TestPage(TestCase):
    ...

    def test_products_page_returns_active(self):
        models.Product.objects.create(
            name="The cathedral and the bazaar",
```

```python
            slug="cathedral-bazaar",
            price=Decimal("10.00"),
        )
        models.Product.objects.create(
            name="A Tale of Two Cities",
            slug="tale-two-cities",
            price=Decimal("2.00"),
            active=False,
        )
        response = self.client.get(
            reverse("products", kwargs={"tag": "all"})
        )
        self.assertEqual(response.status_code, 200)
        self.assertContains(response, "BookTime")

        product_list = models.Product.objects.active().order_by(
            "name"
        )
        self.assertEqual(
            list(response.context["object_list"]),
            list(product_list),
        )

    def test_products_page_filters_by_tags_and_active(self):
        cb = models.Product.objects.create(
            name="The cathedral and the bazaar",
            slug="cathedral-bazaar",
            price=Decimal("10.00"),
        )
        cb.tags.create(name="Open source", slug="opensource")
        models.Product.objects.create(
            name="Microsoft Windows guide",
```

```
        slug="microsoft-windows-guide",
        price=Decimal("12.00"),
    )
    response = self.client.get(
        reverse("products", kwargs={"tag": "opensource"})
    )
    self.assertEqual(response.status_code, 200)
    self.assertContains(response, "BookTime")

    product_list = (
        models.Product.objects.active()
        .filter(tags__slug="opensource")
        .order_by("name")
    )

    self.assertEqual(
        list(response.context["object_list"]),
        list(product_list),
    )
```

Given that the product list page always returns database data, every test will need to populate these tables. The two main execution paths are whether there is a query with tags or without, and there is a test for each.

The last assertion of both tests is the assertion that tests whether the right products are passed to the template for rendering. Here we use object_list instead of page_obj, but the principle is similar.

We use product_list as the expected result for the last assertion. When creating that, as you can see, all the methods that return querysets are chainable. That is why it is possible to use active() along with filter() and order_by().

Path Converters

I briefly mentioned earlier URL paths and converters, with the slug converter. Path converters, along with the path() function, are a recent addition to Django, with version 2.0. They are a very convenient shortcut instead of repeatedly specifying long and hard-to-read regular expressions.

The format is <type:name>. Django has some path converters already included:

- str matches any non-empty string excluding the character /.

- int matches any integer greater than or equal to zero.

- slug matches letters, numbers, hyphens, and underscore.

- uuid matches UUIDs.

- path is like str but also matches /.

It is possible to create your own converters, in case you have some identifiers that appear frequently in the project and do not belong to any of the listed classes. The online documentation explains how to create these in case you need to do so.

Adding a Single Product Page

To round out this chapter, we are going to create a visualization for a single product, with more detail than the product list page. Similarly to ListView, we can leverage another view called DetailView.

Unlike the previous view, our version of the detail view will not require many customizations. We will customize only the template and wire up the URL. We will rely on its conventions, including its way to compose template names. In our case it is main/templates/main/product_detail.html.

```
{% extends "base.html" %}

{% block content %}
  <h1>products</h1>
  <table class="table">
    <tr>
      <th>Name</th>
      <td>{{ object.name }}</td>
    </tr>
    <tr>
      <th>Cover images</th>
      <td>
        {% for image in object.productimage_set.all %}
          <img src="{{ image.thumbnail.url }}" alt="cover"/>
        {% endfor %}
      </td>
    </tr>
    <tr>
      <th>Price</th>
      <td>{{ object.price }}</td>
    </tr>
    <tr>
      <th>Description</th>
      <td>{{ object.description|linebreaks }}</td>
    </tr>
    <tr>
      <th>Tags</th>
      <td>{{ object.tags.all|join:","|default:"No tags
      available" }}</td>
    </tr>
```

```
<tr>
  <th>In stock</th>
  <td>{{ object.in_stock|yesno|capfirst }}</td>
</tr>
<tr>
  <th>Updated</th>
  <td>{{ object.date_updated|date:"F Y" }}</td>
</tr>
</table>
<a href="{% url "add_to_basket" %}?product_id={{ object.id }}">
Add to basket</a>
{% endblock content %}
```

The template itself is quite simple: it just displays some attributes
of the variable object, which is what DetailView defines for the model
instance. This template, however, shows a good sample of template filters.

Template filters are operations that transform some value into another,
which is helpful in case data has some visualization requirements that are
not met in its original form.

linebreaks takes the content of the description field and generates a
<p> tag for every new line that is in the field. join joins a list of strings with
the specified separator. default outputs its argument in case the current
output is None.

yesno converts true/false to the strings yes/no. capfirst capitalizes
the first word. date is useful when converting date objects into a string,
and it is possible to specify a format. The format in this case is month and
year only.

The common format for using filters is variable|filtername:arg1,
arg2.... Some filters take arguments, and some do not.

Another thing worth mentioning in the template is how related models are traversed. If a model has a foreign key to another table, it is possible to call the methods of the related managers by just specifying their names. object.tags.all in templates, for example, is equivalent to object.tags.all() in Python.

There are many other filters in Django. There are also ways to create our own filters, and we will see that later in the book.

To wire this up, here is the right urlpattern:

```
from django.views.generic.detail import DetailView
from main import models

urlpatterns = [
    path(
        "product/<slug:slug>/",
        DetailView.as_view(model=models.Product),
        name="product",
    ),
    ...
```

Using the DetailView without subclassing is good enough for our use case. Because of this, we avoided writing any Python code and, therefore, there is no need to write an automated test for it. Figure 3-10 shows how this page looks like.

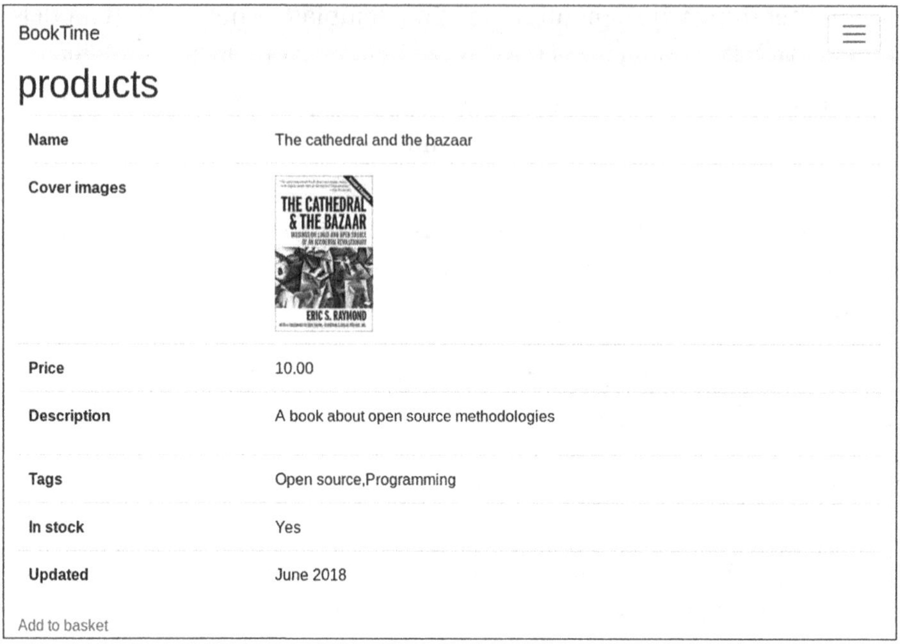
BookTime
products
Name
The cathedral and the bazaar
Cover images
THE CATHEDRAL
& THE BAZAAR
ERIC S. RAYMOND
Price
10.00
Description
A book about open source methodologies
Tags
Open source,Programming
In stock
Yes
Updated
June 2018
Add to basket

Figure 3-10. *Product detail view*

Summary

In this chapter we defined our first models. We modeled the products that our fictitious company sells online, including descriptive tags and all the imagery that is linked to specific products. Besides models, we also included views and URLs to display this data to the website user.

We talked about migrations. Migrations is an important part of how a database is managed in Django. It used to be a separate library, but it has been integrated in the framework in recent versions.

This chapter also introduced Django admin, a management dashboard for internal users to manage the database content. In our case, we created panels to add, change, and delete data about our products.

We also talked about management commands, what they are and how they work, along with model serialization and deserialization. We leveraged these two concepts to create an product importer from CSV files.

In the next chapter we will talk about how to list these products for sale online, so that orders could be placed directly via the Web.

CHAPTER 4

A Checkout System for Receiving Orders Online

Having laid down the database foundations of our project in Chapter 3, in this chapter we are going to build the remaining models on top of that, to store user-generated data. In our case it is a checkout system, which is very important for e-commerce sites.

We are going to cover the following topics:

- Customizing the User model

- Registration and login flows

- CRUD[1] views in Django

- Middleware components

- Django widgets

- Displaying complex data in the admin interface

---

[1]https://en.wikipedia.org/wiki/Create,_read,_update_and_delete

© Federico Marani 2019
F. Marani, *Practical Django 2 and Channels 2*,
https://doi.org/10.1007/978-1-4842-4099-1_4

The User Model

Whatever model we are going to create for storing user-generated data will most likely be connected to the User model. The User model is the model that contains all the necessary data for a website user to log in. This model is also the model that is usually created at the registration stage.

Django has a built-in User model, located in `django.contrib.auth. models.User`. There are several fields available:

- username and password are used as credentials to log in to the system.

- first_name, last_name, and email are all optional and they are descriptive fields.

- groups is a relationship to all the Group models that the user belongs to.

- user_permissions is a relationship to all the Permission models that the user has.

- is_staff is a flag representing whether the user can use the Django admin.

- is_superuser is a flag that, if True, gives the user permission to do anything.

- is_active represents, in the simplest case, whether a user can log in.

The User model also has some commonly used methods:

- set_password() and check_password() are used to set and check passwords.

- has_perm() and has_perms() are used to check permissions.

- objects.create_user() creates users.

There are many other methods, properties, and attributes of this model, but those will suffice for the most common operations. In the Django documentation you will find all the specifics.

Django also provides the option to override the built-in User model with one you specify in your Django project, as long as it inherits from the base User class and implements some required functionality. We are going to do this now before going any further because

- Our products' data can be easily reimported.

- None of our existing models are linked to the User model yet.

- The Django default of having a username field is not what we need. We want the email field to be our user identifier for everyone, with no exception.

Given that our intention is to remove the username field, besides redefining the User model, we need to redefine the built-in UserManager as well. Here is the code that we are going to use:

```
from django.contrib.auth.models import (
    AbstractUser,
    BaseUserManager,
)
...


...


class UserManager(BaseUserManager):
    use_in_migrations = True

    def _create_user(self, email, password,**extra_fields):
        if not email:
            raise ValueError("The given email must be set")
        email = self.normalize_email(email)
        user = self.model(email=email, **extra_fields)
```

```
        user.set_password(password)
        user.save(using=self._db)
        return user

    def create_user(self, email, password=None, **extra_fields):
        extra_fields.setdefault("is_staff", False)
        extra_fields.setdefault("is_superuser", False)
        return self._create_user(email, password, **extra_fields)

    def create_superuser(self, email, password, **extra_fields):
        extra_fields.setdefault("is_staff", True)
        extra_fields.setdefault("is_superuser", True)

        if extra_fields.get("is_staff") is not True:
            raise ValueError(
                "Superuser must have is_staff=True."
            )
        if extra_fields.get("is_superuser") is not True:
            raise ValueError(
                "Superuser must have is_superuser=True."
            )

        return self._create_user(email, password, **extra_fields)

class User(AbstractUser):
    username = None
    email = models.EmailField('email address', unique=True)

    USERNAME_FIELD = 'email'
    REQUIRED_FIELDS = []

    objects = UserManager()
```

By adding this in the models.py file, we are able to use our own version of the User model and make sure Django can operate on it. As a last thing, we need to add a configuration directive to settings.py:

```
AUTH_USER_MODEL = "main.User"
```

This is enough for all the basic systems to work. Django admin, however, will not work, because the standard configuration requires the presence of the username field. To fix this, we need to define a Django admin handler for our custom User. Add this to your main/admin.py file:

```python
from django.contrib.auth.admin import UserAdmin as
DjangoUserAdmin

...


...


@admin.register(models.User)

class UserAdmin(DjangoUserAdmin):
    fieldsets = (
        (None, {"fields": ("email", "password")}),
        (
            "Personal info",
            {"fields": ("first_name", "last_name")},
        ),
        (
            "Permissions",
            {
                "fields": (
                    "is_active",
                    "is_staff",
                    "is_superuser",
```

```python
                    "groups",
                    "user_permissions",
                )
            },
        ),
        (
            "Important dates",
            {"fields": ("last_login", "date_joined")},
        ),
    )
    add_fieldsets = (
        (
            None,
            {
                "classes": ("wide",),
                "fields": ("email", "password1", "password2"),
            },
        ),
    )
    list_display = (
        "email",
        "first_name",
        "last_name",
        "is_staff",
    )
    search_fields = ("email", "first_name", "last_name")
    ordering = ("email",)
```

Here we have redefined the configuration for the Django admin to suit our custom User model. Specifically, we have modified the contents of some class variables. We are already familiar with some of these variables, from the previous chapter, but fieldsets and add_fieldsets are new.

Those two tuples specify what fields to present in the "change model" page and in the "add model" page, along with the names of the page sections. If these were not present, for any other model, Django would make every field changeable. The built-in DjangoUserAdmin, however, introduces some customizations to the default behavior that need to be undone.

At the end of all this, we will need to reset our database and migrations. This is a destructive operation, but, unfortunately, changing the User model requires us to apply these irreversible changes. If you work in a team, this will impact everyone, and therefore it is important to find agreement before doing this.

What we are going to do is remove all the migrations:

```
$ rm main/migrations/0*
rm 'booktime/main/migrations/0001_initial.py'
rm 'booktime/main/migrations/0002_productimage.py'
rm 'booktime/main/migrations/0003_producttag.py'
rm 'booktime/main/migrations/0004_productimage_thumbnail.py'
rm 'booktime/main/migrations/0005_productname_40.py'
rm 'booktime/main/migrations/0005_producttagname_40.py'
rm 'booktime/main/migrations/0006_merge_40.py'
rm 'booktime/main/migrations/0007_productname_capitalize.py'
rm 'booktime/main/migrations/0008_move_m2m.py'
```

Reset the database by using the psql client directly, as follows. If you are using another database, use the appropriate command-line client. If you are using SQLite, deleting the database file will do the job. Substitute the word booktime with your database name before running the following commands.

```
$ psql postgres
psql (9.6.8)
Type "help" for help.
```

```
postgres=# DROP DATABASE booktime;
DROP DATABASE
postgres=# CREATE DATABASE booktime;
CREATE DATABASE
postgres=# \q
```

Re-create the initial migration and then apply it:

```
$ ./manage.py makemigrations
Migrations for 'main':
  main/migrations/0001_initial.py
    - Create  model  User
    - Create model Product
    - Create model ProductImage
    - Create model ProductTag
    - Add field tags to product
$ ./manage.py migrate
Operations to perform:
  Apply all migrations: admin, auth, contenttypes, main, sessions
Running migrations:
  Applying contenttypes.0001_initial... OK
  Applying contenttypes.0002_remove_content_type_name... OK
  Applying auth.0001_initial... OK
  Applying auth.0002_alter_permission_name_max_length... OK
  Applying auth.0003_alter_user_email_max_length... OK
  Applying auth.0004_alter_user_username_opts... OK
  Applying auth.0005_alter_user_last_login_null... OK
  Applying auth.0006_require_contenttypes_0002... OK
  Applying auth.0007_alter_validators_add_error_messages... OK
  Applying auth.0008_alter_user_username_max_length... OK
  Applying auth.0009_alter_user_last_name_max_length... OK
  Applying main.0001_initial... OK
```

```
Applying admin.0001_initial... OK
Applying admin.0002_logentry_remove_auto_add... OK
Applying sessions.0001_initial... OK
```

To test that all the preceding steps have worked, and to be able to use Django admin again, you need to create a superuser again. Please note that, unlike in Chapter 3, the username is not requested.

```
$ ./manage.py createsuperuser
Email address: admin@admin.com
Password:
Password (again):
Superuser created successfully.
```

Creating a Registration Page

Now that we have the type of user model that we want, it is time to expose it to the world. Externally, the functionality we want to build is similar to the contact form we saw in Chapter 2: a bunch of fields will be filled and submitted, and an e-mail will be sent. There will be a bit more to it:

- Validate the submission

- Create a new user in our user table

- Send a "welcome" e-mail

- Log in the user

- Display on the page a success message

For the first three actions in the list we will create a form. These three actions do not need to be performed at view level because they do not interact with the request object. Using only the form layer will make this functionality more reusable by other views.

119

As a general rule, having reusable code is a good thing. Please bear in mind that Django exists in the wider context of Python. Using plain Python functions is sometimes the only thing you need to encapsulate your code.

Add the following code to main/forms.py:

```
...
from django.contrib.auth.forms import (
    UserCreationForm as DjangoUserCreationForm
)
from django.contrib.auth.forms import UsernameField
from . import models

...

class UserCreationForm(DjangoUserCreationForm):
    class Meta(DjangoUserCreationForm.Meta):
        model = models.User
        fields = ("email",)
        field_classes = {"email": UsernameField}

    def send_mail(self):
        logger.info(
            "Sending signup email for email=%s",
            self.cleaned_data["email"],
        )
        message = "Welcome{}".format(self.cleaned_data["email"])
        send_mail(
            "Welcome to BookTime",
            message,
            "site@booktime.domain",
            [self.cleaned_data["email"]],
            fail_silently=True,
        )
```

To this form we have just added a method to send e-mails. This is going to be very similar to the method we already used in the ContactForm form we saw in Chapter 2.

For the registration, we can reuse a Django class called UserCreationForm. It provides us with a basic registration form, where the password is asked twice (second time for confirmation). In the latest Django 2.0 release, the inner Meta class needs to be overridden when there is a custom User model. Django 2.1 will change that.

After we create the form, some higher-level functionality is required. Let's create a class-based view in our main/views.py file:

```
...
import logging
from django.contrib.auth import login, authenticate
from django.contrib import messages

...

logger = logging.getLogger(__name__)

class SignupView(FormView):
    template_name = "signup.html"
    form_class = forms.UserCreationForm

    def get_success_url(self):
        redirect_to = self.request.GET.get("next", "/")
        return redirect_to

    def form_valid(self, form):
        response = super().form_valid(form)
        form.save()
```

```
        email = form.cleaned_data.get("email")
        raw_password = form.cleaned_data.get("password1")
        logger.info(
            "New signup for email=%s through SignupView", email
        )

        user = authenticate(email=email, password=raw_password)
        login(self.request, user)

        form.send_mail()

        messages.info(
            self.request, "You signed up successfully."
        )

        return response
```

This view is reusing FormView, a class that we already used for the contact form. The difference is that we do a few more things in the method form_valid().

First of all, the registration form we created is a special type of form called ModelForm. In Django parlance, that is a specialization of Form where the data submitted can be automatically stored in a model, and the fields for the form default to those on the relevant model. The act of storing happens when the method save() on the form is called.

Later there are a couple of functions called: authenticate() and login(). These methods are used to interact with the Django authentication system. Django authentication can be database based, if the user information is stored in the application database, or in some other way (e.g., LDAP/Active Directory). Whatever abstraction is used under the hood, these two methods will work always in the same way.

authenticate() makes sure that the credentials passed are valid according to the authentication backend. If they are, it returns an instance of the User model. If they are not, it returns None. The result of this is then passed to login(), which associates a User with the current request and future ones, via a session.

Before the method form_valid() ends, there is a call to messages.info(), a method from the Django messages framework. It is very useful for displaying "flash" messages to the user upon their browser's next HTTP request.

This method returns a response object obtained from the superclass form_valid() method, which is normally a redirect to the URL either specified in the class variable success_url or returned by the method get_success_url(). We implemented get_success_url() here to mirror what the built-in Django login view does: if a parameter called next is passed in the GET request, it uses that to redirect.

This view now needs a template (main/templates/signup.html):

```
{% extends"base.html" %}

{% block content %}
<h2>Sign up</h2>
<p>Please fill the form below.</p>
<form method="POST">
  {% csrf_token %}
  <div class="form-group">
    {{ form.email.label_tag }}
    <input
      type="email"
      class="form-control {% if form.email.errors %}
      is-invalid{% endif %}"
      id="id_email"
      name="email"
      placeholder="Your email"
      value="{{ form.email.value|default:"" }}" >
```

```
    {% if form.email.errors %}
      <div class="invalid-feedback">
        {{ form.email.errors }}
      </div>
    {% endif %}
</div>
<div class="form-group">
  {{ form.password1.label_tag }}
  <input
    type="password"
    class="form-control {% if form.password1.errors %}
    is-invalid{% endif %}"
    id="id_password1"
    name="password1"
    value="{{ form.password1.value|default:"" }}">
  {% if form.password1.errors %}
    <div class="invalid-feedback">
      {{ form.password1.errors }}
    </div>
  {% endif %}
</div>
<div class="form-group">
  {{ form.password2.label_tag }}
  <input
    type="password"
    class="form-control{% if form.password2.errors %}
    is-invalid{% endif %}"
    id="id_password2"
    name="password2"
    value="{{ form.password2.value|default:"" }}">
```

```
  {% if form.password2.errors %}
    <div class="invalid-feedback">
      {{ form.password2.errors }}
    </div>
  {% endif %}
</div>
<button type="submit" class="btn btn-primary">Submit</button>
</form>
{% endblock content %}
```

Again, this template is similar to the template for the Contact us page. It renders a different set of fields given that the form fields are different.

After we have mapped the view to an URL, we will be able to see the result:

```
urlpatterns = [
    path('signup/', views.SignupView.as_view(), name="signup"),
    ...
]
```

What we have done so far is enough to get a working page, as shown in Figure 4-1. To finalize this code, we need tests for both the view and the form.

BookTime	≡

Sign up

Please fill the form below.

Email address:

Your email	🔳

Password:

	🎤

Password confirmation:

	🎤

Submit

Figure 4-1. Signup page

```python
class TestForm(TestCase):
    ...

    def test_valid_signup_form_sends_email(self):
        form = forms.UserCreationForm(
            {
                "email": "user@domain.com",
                "password1": "abcabcabc",
                "password2": "abcabcabc",
            }
        )

        self.assertTrue(form.is_valid())

        with self.assertLogs("main.forms", level="INFO") as cm:
            form.send_mail()

        self.assertEqual(len(mail.outbox), 1)
        self.assertEqual(
            mail.outbox[0].subject, "Welcome to BookTime"
        )

        self.assertGreaterEqual(len(cm.output), 1)
```

The code above is going to test_forms.py, while the following in test_views.py.

```
from unittest.mock import patch
from django.contrib import auth
...

class TestPage(TestCase):
    ...

    def test_user_signup_page_loads_correctly(self):
        response = self.client.get(reverse("signup"))
        self.assertEqual(response.status_code, 200)
        self.assertTemplateUsed(response, "signup.html")
        self.assertContains(response, "BookTime")
        self.assertIsInstance(
            response.context["form"], forms.UserCreationForm
        )

    def test_user_signup_page_submission_works(self):
        post_data = {
            "email": "user@domain.com",
            "password1": "abcabcabc",
            "password2": "abcabcabc",
        }
        with patch.object(
            forms.UserCreationForm, "send_mail"
        ) as mock_send:
            response = self.client.post(
                reverse("signup"), post_data
            )
```

```
        self.assertEqual(response.status_code, 302)
        self.assertTrue(
            models.User.objects.filter(
                email="user@domain.com"
            ).exists()
        )
        self.assertTrue(
            auth.get_user(self.client).is_authenticated
        )
        mock_send.assert_called_once()
```

For the view, we are testing two cases, the first rendering and the successful submission. For a failed submission, Django will not trigger the form_valid() function and will not redirect to the success_url; it will simply be a page reload, which the first test covers a bit already.

A successful submission triggers a few things worth testing. We are using the mock module to test that the send_mail() function was called, instead of checking that an e-mail went out. For the actual sending, we already have a test in the previous file.

Other things we are testing are that

- The response is an HTTP 302 Redirect

- A new User model for that e-mail has been created

- That the new user has been logged in

ModelForm in More Detail

As mentioned earlier, ModelForm is a special type of form. It is created by associating a model to it and, consequently, all the corresponding fields in the form are created and mapped automatically. You also need to specify the fields that you want to include (or exclude).

```python
class Lead(models.Model):
    name = models.CharField(max_length=32)

class LeadForm(forms.ModelForm):
    class Meta:
        model = Lead
        fields = ('name', )

# Creating a form to add a lead.
>>> form = LeadForm()

# Create a form instance with POST data for a new lead
>>> form = LeadForm(request.POST)

# Creating a form to change an existing lead.
>>> lead = Lead.objects.get(pk=1)
>>> form = LeadForm(instance=lead)

# Create a form instance with POST data for an existing lead
>>> form = LeadForm(request.POST, instance=lead)

# Creates the lead entry in the database, or
# triggers an update if an instance was passed in.
>>> new_lead = form.save()
```

The preceding code includes some examples of interaction. By specifying in the Meta class of the class that inherits from forms.ModelForm the model and the fields, a form that manages loading, validation, and saving is generated for you. You can use this ModelForm pattern along with any FormView.

The form that we saw above, UserCreationForm, is just a subclass of ModelForm, with a few extra functionalities.

Messages Framework and Message Levels

As shown previously, the messages framework is used for displaying messages to the user, without persisting them. The next time Django returns an HTTP response, the message will no longer be present. Creating messages is easy:

```
messages.debug(request, '%s SQL statements were executed.' % count)
messages.info(request, 'You signed up successfully.')
messages.success(request, 'Profile details updated.')
messages.warning(request, 'Your account expires in three days.')
messages.error(request, 'Product does not exist.')
```

All we have to do to display these messages is display them somewhere in the templates rendered to the user. In our case, we will do so in the base template main/templates/base.html, just before the content block:

```
...
</nav>

{% for message in messages %}
  <div class="alert alert-{{ message.tags }}">{{ message }}</div>
{% endfor %}

{% block content %}
...
```

This will be enough to always render messages at any page view. The message tags in our case will correspond to debug, info, success, and so on, and these can be used to style that block differently.

When to Use Forms or Views

Whereas the boundaries between models, views, and templates are well marked, the boundaries between views and forms are blurred. Views can do all the things that forms can do, but forms neatly wrap a pattern that is very common: form rendering and validation.

Forms do not interact with the `request object` directly and therefore are limited in what they can do. They normally interact with `request.POST` or, in some specific cases, other attributes of the request.

In some cases you may see the `request object` passed to forms and used in some of the form methods. If we decide to do so, we have to be conscious when creating code that modifies the state of the request from multiple places, because readability of the code may diminish.

Creating a Login Page

The next step after creating a registration page is to create the login page. Our page will ask for an e-mail address and password and try to authenticate the data the user submits. Django offers a view called `LoginView` that we can reuse, but we need to create a custom form for it as we have our own `User` model.

Let's add this to `main/forms.py`:

```python
from django.contrib.auth import authenticate

...

class AuthenticationForm(forms.Form):
    email = forms.EmailField()
    password = forms.CharField(
        strip=False, widget=forms.PasswordInput
    )
```

```python
    def __init__(self, request=None, *args, **kwargs):
        self.request = request
        self.user = None
        super().__init__(*args, **kwargs)

    def clean(self):
        email = self.cleaned_data.get("email")
        password = self.cleaned_data.get("password")

        if email is not None and password:
            self.user = authenticate(
                self.request, email=email, password=password
            )
            if self.user is None:
                raise forms.ValidationError(
                    "Invalid email/password combination."
                )
            logger.info(
                "Authentication successful for email=%s", email
            )

        return self.cleaned_data

    def get_user(self):
        return self.user
```

In this form, differently from the previous one, we need to override the __init__() method to accept the request object. The request object will be used in the validation because the authenticate() function requires it.

Given that there is a view already included in Django for us, we will use that directly in the main/urls.py file, passing some parameters to override the default values:

```
from django.contrib.auth import views as auth_views
from main import forms
...

urlpatterns = [
    path(
        "login/",
        auth_views.LoginView.as_view(
            template_name="login.html",
            form_class=forms.AuthenticationForm,
        ),
        name="login",

    ),
    ...
]
```

We need to create the template previously mentioned. Here is our version, the result of which is shown in Figure 4-2:

```
{% extends "base.html" %}

{% block content %}
<h2>Login</h2>
<p>Please fill the form below.</p>
<form method="POST">
  {% csrf_token %}

  {{ form.non_field_errors }}

  <div class="form-group">
    {{ form.email.label_tag }}
    <input
      type="email"
```

```
        class="form-control {% if form.email.errors %}
        is-invalid{% endif %}"
        id="id_email"
        name="email"
        placeholder="Your email"
        value="{{ form.email.value|default:"" }}">
      {% if form.email.errors %}
        <div class="invalid-feedback">
          {{ form.email.errors }}
        </div>
      {% endif %}
    </div>
    <div class="form-group">
      {{ form.password.label_tag }}
      <input
        type="password"
        class="form-control{% if form.password.errors %}
        is-invalid{% endif %}"
        id="id_password"
        name="password"
        value="{{ form.password.value|default:"" }}">
        {% if form.password.errors %}
        <div class="invalid-feedback">
          {{ form.password.errors }}
        </div>
      {% endif %}
    </div>
    <button type="submit" class="btn btn-primary">Submit</button>
</form>
{% endblock content %}
```

BookTime   ☰

Login

Please fill the form below.

Email:

Your email

Password:

Submit

Figure 4-2. *Login page*

This is similar to the standard form templates that we saw already. Notice form.non_field_errors, which is used when rendering our invalid user/password error. We use that because the error is not field-specific.

To finish this, we will define an extra setting called LOGIN_REDIRECT_ URL in our Django settings. We will set this to a defined URL, such as /. If we did not define this, the default URL would be /accounts/profile/, which does not exist.

Managing Users' Addresses

Now that we have users in the system, we need to start managing some of the users' information, starting with addresses. We are going to use this information later when we build the checkout system. This is the model we are going to work on:

```
class Address(models.Model):
    SUPPORTED_COUNTRIES = (
        ("uk", "United Kingdom"),
        ("us", "United States of America"),
    )
```

```python
    user = models.ForeignKey(User, on_delete=models.CASCADE)
    name = models.CharField(max_length=60)
    address1 = models.CharField("Address line 1", max_length=60)
    address2 = models.CharField(
        "Address line 2", max_length=60, blank=True
    )
    zip_code = models.CharField(
        "ZIP / Postal code", max_length=12
    )
    city = models.CharField(max_length=60)
    country = models.CharField(
        max_length=3, choices=SUPPORTED_COUNTRIES
    )
    def __str__(self):
        return ", ".join(
            [
                self.name,
                self.address1,
                self.address2,
                self.zip_code,
                self.city,
                self.country,
            ]
        )
```

Our Address model contains the most common fields that describe an address. The only thing worth noting here is the choices attribute on the country field: it is used to restrict the content of the field to a given set of entries.

This modifier takes a list (or a tuple) of pairs. The pairs are structured with the first entry being the value stored, and the second being the value displayed. In this way, we limit the amount of storage we need to three characters, while keeping the ability to display longer strings.

At this point, run ./manage.py makemigrations, followed by ./manage.py migrate if the generated migration is correct for the preceding model.

The next step is to offer users a way to add, change, and remove their addresses. Luckily for us, Django makes this high-level operation easy to do with these class-based views: ListView, CreateView, UpdateView, and DeleteView.

```python
from django.urls import reverse_lazy
from django.contrib.auth.mixins import LoginRequiredMixin
from django.views.generic.edit import FormView, CreateView,
UpdateView, DeleteView
from django.views.generic.edit import (
    FormView,
    CreateView,
    UpdateView,
    DeleteView,
)

...

class AddressListView(LoginRequiredMixin, ListView):
    model = models.Address

    def get_queryset(self):
        return self.model.objects.filter(user=self.request.user)

class AddressCreateView(LoginRequiredMixin, CreateView):
    model = models.Address
    fields = [
        "name",
        "address1",
        "address2",
        "zip_code",
```

```python
            "city",
            "country",
        ]
        success_url = reverse_lazy("address_list")

        def form_valid(self, form):
            obj = form.save(commit=False)
            obj.user = self.request.user
            obj.save()
            return super().form_valid(form)

class AddressUpdateView(LoginRequiredMixin, UpdateView):
    model = models.Address
    fields = [
        "name",
        "address1",
        "address2",
        "zip_code",
        "city",
        "country",
    ]
    success_url = reverse_lazy("address_list")

    def get_queryset(self):
        return self.model.objects.filter(user=self.request.user)

class AddressDeleteView(LoginRequiredMixin, DeleteView):
    model = models.Address
    success_url = reverse_lazy("address_list")

    def get_queryset(self):
        return self.model.objects.filter(user=self.request.user)
```

With these views added to our `main/views.py` file, we have enough functionality to offer the user the features we planned. There is a lot to describe here. All the views listed take a `model` parameter, and this specifies the model these views are creating, updating, listing, or deleting. For the creating and updating operations, the list of fields of the model that the view uses needs to be explicit.

Each user must be able to operate only on their own addresses, however, and that is why the `get_queryset()` methods in the previous code are prefiltering them based on user ownership. The address creation view does not need prefiltering, but needs the user to be set internally to the right value, which is why we make use of `self.request.user` in the `form_valid()` method.

All these views are only accessible when logged in, because they require a user, and that is the function of the mixin `LoginRequiredMixin`.

The last three views in the previous code are changing the database, and they are operations that have two steps:

- Creation flow has a data entry step and a data submission step.

- Update flow has a data editing step and a data submission step.

- Deletion flow has a confirmation step and a deletion step.

At the end of the second step, all these views redirect to the URL specified in `success_url`. The `reverse_lazy()` function used there is similar to the `url` template tag: it looks up the named URL specified and returns its URL.

We are going to proceed by assigning the following URLs and names to what we have written so far in `main/urls.py`:

```python
urlpatterns = [
    path(
        "address/",
        views.AddressListView.as_view(),
        name="address_list",
    ),
    path(
        "address/create/",
        views.AddressCreateView.as_view(),
        name="address_create",
    ),
    path(
        "address/<int:pk>/",
        views.AddressUpdateView.as_view(),
        name="address_update",
    ),
    path(
        "address/<int:pk>/delete/",
        views.AddressDeleteView.as_view(),
        name="address_delete",
    ),
    ...
```

As the update and delete operations always operate on an existing model, these views accept a pk parameter passed through the URL. In case you would like to use a slug for the model, the support for this is already built into the `SingleObjectMixin` that this class is using.

These views now require templates. If the template names are not specified, as in our case, the names are automatically generated by using the model name and the view type. They follow the pattern <app_name>/ <model_name>_<operation_name>.html.

For ListView, the template is main/templates/main/address_list.html:

```
{% extends "base.html" %}

{% block content %}
  <h1>List of your addresses:</h1>
  {% for address in object_list %}
    <p>
      {{ address.name }}<br>
      {{ address.address1 }}<br>
      {{ address.address2 }}<br>
      {{ address.city }}<br>
      {{ address.get_country_display }}<br>
    </p>
    <p>
      <a href="{% url "address_update" address.id %}">Update
      address</a>
    </p>
    <p>
      <a href="{% url "address_delete" address.id %}">Delete
      address</a>
    </p>
    {% if not forloop.last %}
      <hr>
    {% endif %}
  {% endfor %}
  <p>
    <a href="{% url "address_create" %}">Add new address</a>
  </p>
{% endblock content %}
```

This very basic layout is enough for us to visualize all users' addresses.

Next one is creation. For the CreateView, the template goes in main/templates/main/address_form.html:

```
{% extends "base.html" %}

{% block content %}
<h2>Add a new address</h2>
<form method="POST">
  {% csrf_token %}
  {{ form.as_p }}
  <button type="submit" class="btn btn-primary">Submit</button>
</form>
{% endblock content %}
```

Unlike in the form templates we've seen so far, we are using a shortcut here. We are using the as_p method of the form to automatically render all the fields, using <p> as a separator. This is not going to be very helpful for production sites, but it will suffice for now.

Our next operation is update. The UpdateView will load main/templates/main/address_update.html. The template is almost exactly the same as the previous one:

```
{% extends "base.html" %}

{% block content %}
  <h2>Add a new address</h2>
  <form method="POST">
    {% csrf_token %}
    {{ form.as_p }}
    <button type="submit" class="btn btn-primary">Submit</button>
  </form>
{% endblock content %}
```

The last template is for the deletion action. There will be no form here, only a page that asks for confirmation.

The template for the DeleteView is main/templates/main/address_confirm_delete.html:

```
{% extends "base.html" %}
{% block content %}
  <h2>Delete address</h2>
  <form method="POST">
    {% csrf_token %}
    <p>Are you sure you want to delete it?</p>
    <button type="submit" class="btn btn-primary">Submit
    </button>
  </form>
{% endblock content %}
```

This concludes all the views we need to use this functionality from the Web. For this to be complete, it is worth writing tests for the overrides that we have done to the CBVs. We are going to test that the user is able to see only their own addresses and that the address creation associates to the current user. We add those tests to the existing test_views.py file:

```
...

    def test_address_list_page_returns_only_owned(self):
        user1 = models.User.objects.create_user(
            "user1", "pw432joij"
        )
        user2 = models.User.objects.create_user(
            "user2", "pw432joij"
        )
        models.Address.objects.create(
            user=user1,
            name="john kimball",
            address1="flat 2",
```

143

```python
            address2="12 Stralz avenue",
            city="London",
            country="uk",
        )
        models.Address.objects.create(
            user=user2,
            name="marc kimball",
            address1="123 Deacon road",
            city="London",
            country="uk",
        )

        self.client.force_login(user2)
        response = self.client.get(reverse("address_list"))
        self.assertEqual(response.status_code, 200)

        address_list = models.Address.objects.filter(user=user2)
        self.assertEqual(
            list(response.context["object_list"]),
            list(address_list),
        )
    def test_address_create_stores_user(self):
        user1 = models.User.objects.create_user(
            "user1", "pw432joij"
        )
        post_data = {
            "name": "john kercher",
            "address1": "1 av st",
            "address2": "",
            "zip_code": "MA12GS",
            "city": "Manchester",
            "country": "uk",
        }
```

```
self.client.force_login(user1)
self.client.post(
    reverse("address_create"), post_data
)

self.assertTrue(
    models.Address.objects.filter(user=user1).exists()
)
```

Creating the Basket Functionality

The concept of Basket, or Shopping Cart, is the cornerstone of any e-commerce site. Without this functionality, the user would not be able to purchase products, and the site would not be able to make money online. To build this basket, we are going to start by adding the following to our main/models.py file:

```
from django.core.validators import MinValueValidator

...

class Basket(models.Model):
    OPEN = 10
    SUBMITTED = 20
    STATUSES = ((OPEN, "Open"), (SUBMITTED, "Submitted"))

    user = models.ForeignKey(
        User, on_delete=models.CASCADE, blank=True, null=True
    )
    status = models.IntegerField(choices=STATUSES, default=OPEN)

    def is_empty(self):
        return self.basketline_set.all().count() == 0
```

```
    def count(self):
        return sum(i.quantity for i in self.basketline_set.all())

class BasketLine(models.Model):
    basket = models.ForeignKey(Basket, on_delete=models.CASCADE)
    product = models.ForeignKey(
        Product, on_delete=models.CASCADE
    )
    quantity = models.PositiveIntegerField(
        default=1, validators=[MinValueValidator(1)]
    )
```

We are going to start with this very simple basket. Please generate the migrations and apply them to your database.

We have one model for the basket itself, and many BasketLine models that link back to it. Each BasketLine model will then connect to a specific product and have an extra field called quantity to store how many of this product are in the basket.

I already explained the choices parameter in a previous section, but here we use it with an integer field. This parameter can be applied to any type of field, but integers are the most space efficient, and therefore I have picked those.

In the second model, for the quantity field, we are passing an extra parameter called validators. Validators add extra checks on data to prevent saving. In this case we want to make sure that the value of the quantity field is never below one. The only way to set it to zero is to delete the model.

Now that we have the models, we are going to introduce a feature of Django we have not seen yet, middlewares. In Django, a middleware is a function (more precisely, a callable) that wraps and offer additional functionalities to views. They are able to modify requests as they come in to the views and responses as they come out of the views.

We are going to use this to automatically connect baskets to HTTP requests. We are doing it in a middleware because we are going to use baskets in several views and templates, and this helps us avoid repeating identical calls to a particular piece of code.

Write this in main/middlewares.py:

```python
from . import models

def basket_middleware(get_response):
    def middleware(request):
        if 'basket_id' in request.session:
            basket_id = request.session['basket_id']
            basket = models.Basket.objects.get(id=basket_id)
            request.basket = basket
        else:
            request.basket=None

        response = get_response(request)
        return response
    return middleware
```

We can clearly see here that there is some code proceeding every view activation, which happens when the get_response() method is called. Before that, the code checks whether the session, which is coming from another middleware that Django provides, contains a basket_id. If so, it will load the basket and assign it to request.basket.

Middlewares can depend on other middlewares, and this is what is happening here: we have a dependency on the SessionMiddleware. To use basket_middleware, we need to add it to the constant MIDDLEWARES in the Django settings.py file, after the session middleware:

```python
MIDDLEWARE = [
    'django.contrib.sessions.middleware.SessionMiddleware',
    ...
    'main.middlewares.basket_middleware',
]
```

Having added this middleware, we can now render the basket in every template. To demonstrate this, we will add this snippet to the base template main/templates/base.html, just before the {% block content %}:

```
...
    {% if request.basket %}
      <div>
        {{ request.basket.count }}
        items in basket
      </div>
    {% endif %}
...
```

Add to Basket View

Now we are ready to start working on the views. The first view that we will create is to add products to the basket. We are going to use a function-based view instead of a class-based view, so it is different from the syntax you have seen so far:

```
from django.http import HttpResponseRedirect
from django.urls import reverse

...

def add_to_basket(request):
    product = get_object_or_404(
        models.Product, pk=request.GET.get("product_id")
    )
    basket = request.basket
    if not request.basket:
        if request.user.is_authenticated:
            user = request.user
```

```
    else:
        user = None
    basket = models.Basket.objects.create(user=user)
    request.session["basket_id"] = basket.id

basketline, created = models.BasketLine.objects.get_or_create(
    basket=basket, product=product
)
if not created:
    basketline.quantity += 1
    basketline.save()
return HttpResponseRedirect(
    reverse("product", args=(product.slug,))
)
```

In this view we can rely on the middleware to position the existing basket inside the `request.basket` attribute. This will only work if the basket exists, and its id is in the session already. This view will also take care of creating a basket if it does not exist yet, and do the necessary steps for the middleware to work for any following request.

Implementing this as a class-based view is possible, but there would not be much we can reuse in terms of built-in CBVs. Doing this as a class will end up being more code for no more functionality, and that is why I wrote this as a function.

To make this usable from templates, it needs a URL:

```
urlpatterns = [
    ...
    path(
        "add_to_basket/",
        views.add_to_basket,
```

```
        name="add_to_basket",
    ),
    ...
]
```

It is now possible to refer to this view from the product detail template.
Add the following lines after `</table>`:

```
...
<a
  href="{% url "add_to_basket" %}?product_id={{ object.id }}">
  Add to basket
</a>
```

To finalize and test this, we can use this test:

```
...

class TestPage(TestCase):
    ...

    def test_add_to_basket_loggedin_works(self):
        user1 = models.User.objects.create_user(
            "user1@a.com", "pw432joij"
        )
        cb = models.Product.objects.create(
            name="The cathedral and the bazaar",
            slug="cathedral-bazaar",
            price=Decimal("10.00"),
        )
        w = models.Product.objects.create(
            name="Microsoft Windows guide",
            slug="microsoft-windows-guide",
            price=Decimal("12.00"),
        )
```

```python
self.client.force_login(user1)
response = self.client.get(
    reverse("add_to_basket"), {"product_id": cb.id}
)
response = self.client.get(
    reverse("add_to_basket"), {"product_id": cb.id}
)

self.assertTrue(
    models.Basket.objects.filter(user=user1).exists()
)
self.assertEquals(
    models.BasketLine.objects.filter(
        basket__user=user1
    ).count(),
    1,
)

response = self.client.get(
    reverse("add_to_basket"), {"product_id": w.id}
)
self.assertEquals(
    models.BasketLine.objects.filter(
        basket user=user1
    ).count(),
    2,
)
```

This test covers all the code in the previous view: basket creation, reuse, and BasketLine operations.

Manage Basket View

The second view that our site needs is a page to change quantities and delete lines from the basket. We are going to use another functionality of Django that we have not used yet: formsets.

Formsets are a way to work with multiple forms of the same type. It is very handy when modifying many entries of a form on the same page. To create formsets there are a few "factory" functions:

- formset_factory(): The simplest way, works best with normal forms

- modelformset_factory(): The equivalent of modelforms but applied to formsets

- inlineformset_factory(): Like the above but more specific for related objects (via foreign key) to a base object

In our project we want to build a page to modify the content of the basket. We want a form for every basket line connected to a basket. In our case we can use inlineformset_factory(). We are going to add this to our main/forms.py file:

```
from django.forms import import inlineformset_factory

...
BasketLineFormSet = inlineformset_factory(
    models.Basket,
    models.BasketLine,
    fields=("quantity",),
    extra=0,
)
```

This formset will automatically build forms for all basket lines connected to the basket specified; the only editable fields will be quantity and there will be no extra form to add new entries, as we do that through the add_to_basket view.

Django does not include any class-based views coupled with formsets. We will have to do so ourselves by writing the whole function-based view for it.

This is the view that needs to go in main/views.py:

```python
from django.shortcuts import get_object_or_404, render
...

def manage_basket(request):
    if not request.basket:
        return render(request, "basket.html", {"formset": None})

    if request.method == "POST":
        formset = forms.BasketLineFormSet(
            request.POST, instance=request.basket
        )
        if formset.is_valid():
            formset.save()
    else:
        formset = forms.BasketLineFormSet(
            instance=request.basket
        )

    if request.basket.is_empty():
        return render(request, "basket.html", {"formset": None})

    return render(request, "basket.html", {"formset": formset})
```

The preceding view will render no formset if the user does not have a basket yet or has one but it is empty. If the basket is not empty, the formset will be rendered for GET requests, and the submission will be handled when the form is submitted back through a POST request.

The template that goes with the above view goes in main/templates/basket.html:

```
{% extends "base.html" %}

{% block content %}
  <h2>Basket</h2>
  {% if formset %}
    <p>You can adjust the quantities below.</p>
    <form method="POST">
      {% csrf_token %}
      {{ formset.management_form }}
      {% for form in formset %}
        <p>
          {{ form.instance.product.name }}
          {{ form }}
        </p>
      {% endfor %}
      <button type="submit" class="btn btn-default">Update
      basket</button>
    </form>
  {% else %}
    <p>You have no items in the basket.</p>
  {% endif %}
{% endblock content %}
```

This template renders the product name, which is excluded by the form, by accessing the model directly through instance. A requisite for formsets to work is to render the management_form attribute in the template. This is used for the extra functionalities formsets provide on top of forms.

To end this functionality, let's add the URL:

```
urlpatterns = [
    path('basket/', views.manage_basket, name="basket"),
    ...
]
```

Figure 4-3. *Manage basket view*

Given that the view is reasonably simple and the bulk of the functionality is managed by formsets, there will be no test for this.

Merging Baskets at Login Time

Our core basket functionality is almost complete, but there are still some edge cases that could be handled better. One of these is handling the case of a user putting books in the basket and then logging in only to discover that the chosen books are no longer in the basket. This apparently odd behavior occurs because the logged-in user is attached to a different Django session.

To fix that we need to implement some code that merges baskets. We will do so as soon as the user logs in, and to do so we can leverage another built-in signal called user_logged_in. Here is some code that shows you how (main/signals.py):

```python
from django.contrib.auth.signals import user_logged_in
from .models import Basket

...

@receiver(user_logged_in)
def merge_baskets_if_found(sender, user, request,**kwargs):
    anonymous_basket = getattr(request,"basket",None)
    if anonymous_basket:
        try:
            loggedin_basket = Basket.objects.get(
                user=user, status=Basket.OPEN
            )
            for line in anonymous_basket.basketline_set.all():
                line.basket = loggedin_basket
                line.save()
            anonymous_basket.delete()
            request.basket = loggedin_basket
            logger.info(
                "Merged basket to id %d", loggedin_basket.id
            )
        except Basket.DoesNotExist:
            anonymous_basket.user = user
            anonymous_basket.save()
            logger.info(
                "Assigned user to basket id %d",
                anonymous_basket.id,
            )
```

This code implements the behavior that is described. To conclude, a test is advisable.

We will test this flow with a test, in main/tests/test_views.py:

```
from django.contrib import auth
from django.urls import reverse
...

    def test_add_to_basket_login_merge_works(self):
        user1 = models.User.objects.create_user(
            "user1@a.com", "pw432joij"
        )
        cb = models.Product.objects.create(
            name="The cathedral and the bazaar",
            slug="cathedral-bazaar",
            price=Decimal("10.00"),
        )
        w = models.Product.objects.create(
            name="Microsoft Windows guide",
            slug="microsoft-windows-guide",
            price=Decimal("12.00"),
        )
        basket = models.Basket.objects.create(user=user1)
        models.BasketLine.objects.create(
            basket=basket, product=cb, quantity=2
        )
        response = self.client.get(
            reverse("add_to_basket"), {"product_id": w.id}
        )
        response = self.client.post(
            reverse("login"),
            {"email": "user1@a.com", "password": "pw432joij"},
        )
```

```python
        self.assertTrue(
            auth.get_user(self.client).is_authenticated
        )
        self.assertTrue(
            models.Basket.objects.filter(user=user1).exists()
        )
        basket = models.Basket.objects.get(user=user1)
        self.assertEquals(basket.count(),3)
```

A Better Widget for Basket Quantities

One last touch we will apply to our basket is a better widget to manage changes to product quantities. We want to present separate bigger buttons with plus and minus signs to make it easy for the user to change the numbers.

In order to do so, we need to change the way the quantity field is rendered in forms. Because the field is inheriting from IntegerField, Django by default will use the built-in NumberInput widget.

Let's start by creating main/widgets.py and including the code for our first widget:

```python
from django.forms.widgets import Widget

class PlusMinusNumberInput(Widget):
    template_name = 'widgets/plusminusnumber.html'

    class Media:
        css = {
            'all': ('css/plusminusnumber.css',)
        }
        js = ('js/plusminusnumber.js',)
```

The widget is referring to an external template for its HTML. Here we also define a Media subclass with some extra CSS and JavaScript to include in the output. While template_name is a specific widget functionality, defining a Media subclass is a functionality that can be applied to both widgets and forms as well.

We will use this HTML for the widget (main/templates/widgets/ plusminusnumber.html):

```
<input
  type="number"
  name="{{ widget.name }}"
  class="form-control quantity-number"
  value="{{ widget.value }}"
  min="1"
  max="10"
  {% include "django/forms/widgets/attrs.html" %} />
<button
  type="button"
  class="btn btn-default btn-number btn-minus"
  data-type="minus"
  data-field="{{ widget.name }}">
  -
</button>
<button
  type="button"
  class="btn btn-default btn-number btn-plus"
  data-type="plus"
  data-field="{{ widget.name }}">
  +
</button>
```

We will also customize the input box with some CSS and add some interactivity with JavaScript. These changes are very basic, but it is a good starting point for you to take these lessons and apply them to more complex scenarios.

Here is the CSS we will need, which goes in main/static/css/plusminusnumber.css:

```css
.quantity-number {
  -moz-appearance:textfield;
}
.quantity-number:: -webkit-inner-spin-button,
.quantity-number:: -webkit-outer-spin-button {
  -webkit-appearance: none;
  -moz-appearance: none;
  appearance: none;
  margin: 0;
}
```

And some JavaScript to add the interactions (main/static/js/plusminusnumber.js):

```javascript
$(function () {
  $('.btn-number').click(function (e) {
    e.preventDefault();
    fieldName = $(this).attr('data-field');
    type = $(this).attr('data-type');
    var input = $("input[name='" + fieldName + "']");
    var currentVal = parseInt(input.val());
    if (type == 'minus') {
      if (currentVal > input.attr('min')) {
        input
          .val(currentVal - 1)
          .change();
      }
```

```
    if (parseInt(input.val()) == input.attr('min')) {
      $(this).attr('disabled', true);
    }
  } else if (type == 'plus') {
    if (currentVal < input.attr('max')) {
      input
        .val(currentVal + 1)
        .change();
    }
    if (parseInt(input.val()) == input.attr('max')) {
      $(this).attr('disabled', true);
    }
  }
 });
});
```

Particularly for the JavaScript, we need to make sure that the loading of this happens after the loading of any dependencies. In our case, given that we included jQuery in our base template, we need to make sure this appears before. To do so, we will add an empty block in the base template main/templates/base.html. This block will be overridden in the templates that need to inject additional JavaScript.

```
{% load static %}
<!doctype html>
<html lang="en">

    ...

    <script src="{% static "js/jquery.min.js" %}"></script>
    <script src="{% static "js/popper.min.js" %}"></script>
    <script src="{% static "js/bootstrap.min.js" %}"></script>
```

```
    {% block js %}
    {% endblock js %}
  </body>
</html>
```

To conclude, we will instruct the formset factory to use this widget, in main/forms.py:

```
from . import widgets

...

BasketLineFormSet = inlineformset_factory(
    models.Basket,
    models.BasketLine,
    fields=("quantity",),
    extra=0,
    widgets={"quantity": widgets.PlusMinusNumberInput()},
)
```

And we will override the content of this block from our basket.html template:

```
{% extends "base.html" %}

{% block content %}
...
{% endblock content %}

{% block js %}
  {% if formset %}
    {{ formset.media }}
  {% endif %}
{% endblock js %}
```

Orders and Checkout

A critical step for any e-commerce site is to go from a full basket to having an order in the system. The flow that the user needs to traverse is called "checkout."

We will create a simple flow with the structure highlighted in Figure 4-4.

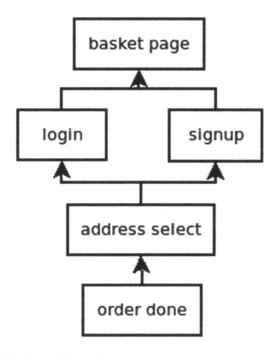

Figure 4-4. *Checkout funnel*

Base Models

To start with these features, we will lay the foundations first with a series of models. Like we did for the Basket and BasketLine models, we will add an Order model and an OrderLine model. While the underlying principle of having this pair is similar (linking the order/basket to many products), our OrderLine model will have an important difference.

While BasketLine can contain a number of products, OrderLine will have exactly one entry per product ordered. The reason for this is that we want a status field to have the granularity of a single ordered item.

```python
class Order(models.Model):
    NEW = 10
    PAID = 20
    DONE = 30
    STATUSES = ((NEW, "New"), (PAID, "Paid"), (DONE, "Done"))

    user = models.ForeignKey(User, on_delete=models.CASCADE)
    status = models.IntegerField(choices=STATUSES, default=NEW)

    billing_name = models.CharField(max_length=60)
    billing_address1 = models.CharField(max_length=60)
    billing_address2 = models.CharField(
        max_length=60,  blank=True
    )
    billing_zip_code = models.CharField(max_length=12)
    billing_city = models.CharField(max_length=60)
    billing_country = models.CharField(max_length=3)

    shipping_name = models.CharField(max_length=60)
    shipping_address1 = models.CharField(max_length=60)
    shipping_address2 = models.CharField(
        max_length=60, blank=True
    )
    shipping_zip_code = models.CharField(max_length=12)
    shipping_city = models.CharField(max_length=60)
    shipping_country = models.CharField(max_length=3)

    date_updated = models.DateTimeField(auto_now=True)
    date_added = models.DateTimeField(auto_now_add=True)
```

```python
class OrderLine(models.Model):
    NEW = 10
    PROCESSING = 20
    SENT = 30
    CANCELLED = 40
    STATUSES = (
        (NEW, "New"),
        (PROCESSING, "Processing"),
        (SENT, "Sent"),
        (CANCELLED, "Cancelled"),
    )

    order = models.ForeignKey(
        Order, on_delete=models.CASCADE, related_name="lines"
    )
    product = models.ForeignKey(
    Product, on_delete=models.PROTECT
    )
    status = models.IntegerField(choices=STATUSES, default=NEW)
```

As for any main/models.py file change, please generate and apply the migrations.

Like what we have done for the Basket model, we will use status fields to manage the workflows in our e-commerce store. For sake of simplicity, we will not build an online payment system. Customer service will mark orders as PAID, and dispatch managers will mark lines with the relevant status.

Every order will have associated a user and a billing/shipping address. Here we are not using any foreign keys; instead, we copy the content of the Address model. This will make orders snapshots in time and any subsequent change to a user's addresses will not affect existing orders.

The order has also a couple of timestamps associated with it: note the auto_now and auto_now_add attributes. These are managed by Django and are automatically updated on update and creation of the model.

The line model also has a couple of new things worth explaining. The parameter related_name is used to specify a better name when accessing the order lines from the Order instance. By specifying this, we can access all the lines of an order with order.lines.all() instead of the more verbose default order.orderline_set.all().

The ForeignKey field for products in the line model has the specifier models.PROTECT. This is a change from our usual models.CASCADE. The behavior we are enforcing at the database level is impeding deletion of any products that are in an order.

To generate orders, we will write a creation method to attach to the Basket model:

```python
import logging

logger = logging.getLogger(__name__)

...

    def create_order(self, billing_address, shipping_address):
        if not self.user:
            raise exceptions.BasketException(
                "Cannot create order without user"
            )

        logger.info(
            "Creating order for basket_id=%d"
            ", shipping_address_id=%d, billing_address_id=%d",
            self.id,
            shipping_address.id,
            billing_address.id,
        )
```

```python
order_data = {
    "user":self.user,
    "billing_name": billing_address.name,
    "billing_address1": billing_address.address1,
    "billing_address2": billing_address.address2,
    "billing_zip_code": billing_address.zip_code,
    "billing_city": billing_address.city,
    "billing_country": billing_address.country,
    "shipping_name": shipping_address.name,
    "shipping_address1": shipping_address.address1,
    "shipping_address2": shipping_address.address2,
    "shipping_zip_code": shipping_address.zip_code,
    "shipping_city": shipping_address.city,
    "shipping_country": shipping_address.country,
}
order = Order.objects.create(**order_data)
c=0
for line in self.basketline_set.all():
    for item in range(line.quantity):
        order_line_data = {
            "order": order,
            "product": line.product,
        }
        order_line = OrderLine.objects.create(
            **order_line_data
        )
        c += 1
logger.info(
    "Created order with id=%d and lines_count=%d",
    order.id,
    c,
)
```

```
        self.status = Basket.SUBMITTED
        self.save()
        return order
```

Given how important this code is, we will add a test to test_models.py:

...

```python
    def test_create_order_works(self):
        p1 = models.Product.objects.create(
            name="The cathedral and the bazaar",
            price=Decimal("10.00"),
        )
        p2 = models.Product.objects.create(
            name="Pride and Prejudice", price=Decimal("2.00")
        )

        user1 = models.User.objects.create_user(
            "user1", "pw432joij"
        )
        billing = models.Address.objects.create(
            user=user1,
            name="John Kimball",
            address1="127 Strudel road",
            city="London",
            country="uk",
        )
        shipping = models.Address.objects.create(
            user=user1,
            name="John Kimball",
            address1="123 Deacon road",
            city="London",
            country="uk",
        )
```

```python
basket = models.Basket.objects.create(user=user1)
models.BasketLine.objects.create(
    basket=basket, product=p1
)
models.BasketLine.objects.create(
    basket=basket, product=p2
)

with self.assertLogs("main.models", level="INFO") as cm:
    order = basket.create_order(billing, shipping)

self.assertGreaterEqual(len(cm.output), 1)

order.refresh_from_db()

self.assertEquals(order.user, user1)
self.assertEquals(
    order.billing_address1, "127 Strudel road"
)
self.assertEquals(
    order.shipping_address1, "123 Deacon road"
)

# add more checks here

self.assertEquals(order.lines.all().count(), 2)
lines = order.lines.all()
self.assertEquals(lines[0].product, p1)
self.assertEquals(lines[1].product, p2)
```

You will notice how much data we need to set up. In the following chapters I will present a way to alleviate this, but this will do for now. Calling the create_order() method would return an order, but to make sure we are working on a clean copy, the refresh_from_db() method is called.

Checkout Flow

To implement the checkout flow described at the beginning of this section, we will need a few changes of existing code and a few new things. We will start by building the pages first, before connecting them. The new page is the address selection page, which will need a form:

```python
class AddressSelectionForm(forms.Form):
    billing_address = forms.ModelChoiceField(
            queryset=None)
    shipping_address = forms.ModelChoiceField(
            queryset=None)

    def __init__(self, user, *args, **kwargs):
        super().__init__(*args, **kwargs)
        queryset = models.Address.objects.filter(user=user)
        self.fields['billing_address'].queryset = queryset
        self.fields['shipping_address'].queryset = queryset
```

This form, unlike the ones seen so far, dynamically specifies the parameters in the declared fields. In this case we are restricting addresses to the ones that are connected to the current user. The reason for this is easy: we would not want the user to be able to select any available address in the system.

To manage this form, we can create a corresponding view that inherits from FormView and fills the class with the customizations we want:

```python
class AddressSelectionView(LoginRequiredMixin, FormView):
    template_name = "address_select.html"
    form_class = forms.AddressSelectionForm
    success_url = reverse_lazy('checkout_done')
```

```python
    def get_form_kwargs(self):
        kwargs = super().get_form_kwargs()
        kwargs['user'] = self.request.user
        return kwargs

    def form_valid(self, form):
        del self.request.session['basket_id']
        basket = self.request.basket
        basket.create_order(
            form.cleaned_data['billing_address'],
            form.cleaned_data['shipping_address']
        )
        return super().form_valid(form)
```

The methods specified here do most of the work: get_form_kwargs()
extracts the user from the request and returns it in a dictionary. This
dictionary is then passed to the form by the superclass. The FormView
superclass calls this function automatically, as it is a very common pattern
used to pass extra variables to forms.

In the form_valid() method, we delete the basket from the session
and we call the create_order() method on it, with the submitted
addresses data.

We need to fill the missing pieces now, starting with the
main/templates/address_select.html template:

```html
{% extends "base.html" %}

{% block content %}
  <h2>Select the billing/shipping addresses</h2>
  <form method="POST">
    {% csrf_token %}
    {{ form.as_p }}
```

```
<button type="submit" class="btn btn-primary">Submit</button>
<a class="btn btn-primary" href="{% url "address_create"
%}">Add a new one</a>
</form>
{% endblock content %}
```

This is a very standard form template. The only addition is a link to the address creation page that we created at the beginning of this chapter. This page needs to be linked from the basket template. This is the revised version of main/templates/basket.html:

```
{% extends "base.html" %}

{% block content %}
<h2>Basket</h2>
{% if formset %}
  <p>You can adjust the quantities below.</p>
  <form method="POST">
    {% csrf_token %}
    {{ formset.management_form }}
    {% for form in formset %}
      <p>
        {{ form.instance.product.name }}
        {{ form }}
      </p>
    {% endfor %}
    <button type="submit" class="btn btn-default">Update
    basket</button>
    {% if user.is_authenticated %}
      <a href="{% url "address_select" %}" class="btn
      btn-primary">Place order</a>
```

```
        {% else %}
          <a
            href="{% url "signup" %}?next={% url"address_select" %}"
            class="btn btn-primary">Signup</a>
          <a
            href="{% url "login" %}?next={% url "address_select" %}"
            class="btn btn-primary">Login</a>
        {% endif %}
      </form>
  {% else %}
    <p>You have no items in the basket.</p>
  {% endif %}
{% endblock content %}

{% block js %}
  {% if formset %}
    {{ formset.media }}
  {% endif %}
{% endblock js %}
```

Note the extra link to go to the next step. The next step in this funnel is either signup or login, in the case where the user is not authenticated, or address selection in the case where the user is already logged in (as shown in Figure 4-5).

Figure 4-5. *Address selection page*

Earlier in this chapter, we created both signup and login pages in a way that, if a GET parameter called next is specified, the value of that parameter will be the URL the user is redirected to, if the form submission was successful. We are going to use this feature to compose the funnel.

Before we define the URLs (and have a functioning funnel), we are going to define the last page of the funnel, which is the URL that earlier in this section is named checkout_done. We are going to add a very simple template for it, inside main/templates/order_done.html:

```
{% extends "base.html" %}
{% block content %}
    <p>Thanks for your order.</p>
{% endblock content %}
```

The final step is adding the URLs for both views we previously created:

```
...

urlpatterns = [
    path(
        "order/done/",
```

```
        TemplateView.as_view(template_name="order_done.html"),
        name="checkout_done",
    ),
    path(
        "order/address_select/",
        views.AddressSelectionView.as_view(),
        name="address_select",
    ),
...
```

Our checkout flow is now done. What this funnel needs now is a touch of styling. We said in Chapter 2 that we were using Bootstrap, and there are a few CSS classes in the HTML that are part of that, but the rest is up to you.

Finally in this chapter, we are going to talk about Django Admin and how to visualize in it the checkout data.

Displaying Checkout Data in the Django admin

Both the Basket model and the Order model have a corresponding "lines" model linked to it. When displaying a basket or an order, it would be helpful if the Django admin could display all these linked models along with the original model. Django supports this by using "inlines".

To start with, add these to your main/admin.py file:

```
class BasketLineInline(admin.TabularInline):
    model = models.BasketLine
    raw_id_fields = ("product",)

@admin.register(models.Basket)
class BasketAdmin(admin.ModelAdmin):
    list_display = ("id", "user", "status", "count")
    list_editable = ("status",)
```

```python
    list_filter = ("status",)
    inlines = (BasketLineInline,)

class OrderLineInline(admin.TabularInline):
    model = models.OrderLine
    raw_id_fields = ("product",)

@admin.register(models.Order)
class OrderAdmin(admin.ModelAdmin):
    list_display = ("id", "user", "status")
    list_editable = ("status",)
    list_filter = ("status", "shipping_country", "date_added")
    inlines = (OrderLineInline,)
    fieldsets = (
        (None, {"fields": ("user", "status")}),
        (
            "Billing info",
            {
                "fields": (
                    "billing_name",
                    "billing_address1",
                    "billing_address2",
                    "billing_zip_code",
                    "billing_city",
                    "billing_country",
                )
            },
        ),
        (
            "Shipping info",
            {
```

```
        "fields": (
            "shipping_name",
            "shipping_address1",
            "shipping_address2",
            "shipping_zip_code",
            "shipping_city",
            "shipping_country",
        )
    },
),
)
```

Above we declared instances of `ModelAdmin` that are nested inside other instances (via the `inlines` attribute). For models like `Basket` and `Order`, which have foreign keys pointing from their relevant `line` model, we need to use an Inline to show the related data.

The property `raw_id_fields` is used to change the way foreign keys are rendered. By default, foreign key widgets are rendered with a select box, and all possible relationships are rendered in the select options. If, like in our case, there are many possible relationship, the list becomes very long, which can have a performance impact or even trigger a timeout, given enough records.

Most of the other properties have been introduced already, either in this chapter or the previous one. If you do not remember, I encourage you to go back and find what they are used for. Obviously, all this information is also available in the official Django documentation.

We registered these new classes using the `@admin.register()` decorator instead of a direct call to `admin.register()`. Both ways work.

Summary

In this chapter we started by redefining the User model to remove usernames and make e-mails mandatory. We then created the models that our checkout needs, including baskets and orders.

We also added to the site login and registration pages for users, along with views to add and manage items that are in the user's basket.

Middlewares were used to manage basket rendering in templates and use in related views. Django widgets functionality was also introduced on the basket management page.

We used ModelForms and Django messages in some parts of the chapter as a way to generate forms automatically and manage the ephemeral messages that illustrate to the user what happened in the view that was executed.

This chapter, the longest in the book, introduced a lot of functionality. In the next chapter we are going to step back from the depths of databases and talk about static assets.

CHAPTER 5

Adding CSS/JavaScript to Our Django Project

Every site nowadays uses CSS and JavaScript, some more heavily than others. This chapter provides an overview of these technologies and how they can be integrated with Django.

Our survey of these technologies will not be extensive—most tools in the frontend ecosystem evolve too quickly for a book to stay updated. Rather, we'll take a minimalistic approach by using only a few, reasonably stable libraries. However, keep in mind that you may still have to adapt what you read here to the future versions of the tools presented.

Managing Static Files

A *static file* is anything that is served straight to the browser as a result of an HTTP request. These are some examples of static files:

- CSS files
- JavaScript files
- Images
- Videos
- Fonts
- Data files for the frontend

© Federico Marani 2019
F. Marani, *Practical Django 2 and Channels 2*,
https://doi.org/10.1007/978-1-4842-4099-1_5

All these resources are managed in the same way by Django. Static resources can be specific to a Django app or stored at the project level. When using its development server, Django will serve the content of every static folder of every app under STATIC_URL, as mentioned in Chapter 1, regardless of what type it is.

We have seen an example of this in Chapter 4 when we introduced a widget to update basket quantities. We have placed the supporting CSS and JavaScript inside main/static/css and main/static/js, respectively, and if our project setup was correct, it will serve these files along with the widget.

For simple JavaScript and CSS, this is all you may need. As long as these files are ready to be interpreted by the client, there is not more to do. In the past few years, though, tools to preprocess CSS and JavaScript have become more common, allowing you to use more advanced features such as the latest versions of JavaScript.

These preprocessors can be integrated with Django. We are going to look at some of these in the following sections.

CSS Preprocessors

CSS preprocessors bring to the CSS world a bit more sophistication. Historically, CSS has been an extremely simple language, with selectors and properties but not much more. For the sake of maintainability, this may not be enough.

The intent of this chapter is not to force you to choose a CSS preprocessor, or any preprocessor, but to show you how powerful preprocessors can be and how they can be used alongside Django. If your project does not require any of this, you can safely skip to the next chapter.

Sass (https://sass-lang.com) is one of the most commonly used preprocessors. Originally written in Ruby, now there is a C version that is easier to integrate with existing Django projects. On top of CSS, it adds support for variables, mixins, inline imports, inheritance, and so on.

Less (`http://lesscss.org`) is another famous preprocessor. The syntax has stayed closer to CSS from the beginning. Unlike SASS, it is written in JavaScript, and it can run in Node and in the browser.

Stylus (`http://stylus-lang.com`) is yet another preprocessor, although it is less commonly used than Sass and Less. It is the more sophisticated one, with plenty of features. It is also written in JavaScript and requires Node to run.

Using JavaScript Frameworks...or Not

There is no arguing that JavaScript holds an important spot in frontend development. In recent years the language has gone through some major evolutions, and interpreters in browsers have become very sophisticated.

Unlike Python, JavaScript does not come with "batteries included." When you install Python, you install a fairly big standard library with it. JavaScript does not come with a standard library. In a normal frontend development workflow, you will likely need to pull in external libraries.

JavaScript is the only language available in web browsers, which in turn are available for almost any type of computer, so the language itself is ubiquitous. Its use transforms dummy HTML and CSS into something that adds logic and interaction to websites.

Do you need logic and dynamic interactions on your site? If so, by all means, learn from this chapter and do your own research, and use it extensively. Please note that not all websites need this level of sophistication: sometimes bare HTML is the best option. On the other hand, users expect modern-era websites to show a certain level of speed and intelligence. Using JavaScript may be the only way to meet users' expectations.

JavaScript usage on our websites can be as heavy or as light as we want it to be. We can use JavaScript to add dynamism to sections of specific pages, and we can use it to completely override functionalities that normally would reside in the backend: URL routing, templating, form validation, and more. The extent of its use is up to us to decide.

The extent and sophistication of the JavaScript that we want to integrate should drive our decision of whether or not to use frameworks. The concept of frameworks applies as much to Python as to JavaScript. It is about time efficiency, and it is about not reinventing the wheel. However, it must also be about sticking to the framework's conventions.

The following is a (nonexhaustive) list of currently common JavaScript projects that can be used to manage our website UI:

- *React* (`https://reactjs.org`): A library created by Facebook for building user interfaces. Smaller in scope than any of the following libraries, it offers a good ecosystem of projects to expand its core functionalities. It is a common choice.

- *Vue.js* (`https://vuejs.org`): A very flexible JavaScript framework that offers more than React out of the box. It is a younger project but with many users already.

- *Angular* (`https://angular.io`): One of the older and more complete JavaScript frameworks. It is especially suited to be used for single-page applications (SPAs) and for very complex user interfaces. In my experience, it is more enterprise-focused.

- *jQuery* (`https://jquery.com`): Possibly the first very successful JavaScript library. It was not born to manage UI but to wrap parts of the language (and Document Object Model) that were not standardized at the time, when browsers were not as advanced as today. Despite its age, it is still widely used. The ecosystem built around this library is the biggest compared to the other libraries in this list.

SPAs and Consequences for Django

A *single-page application (SPA)* is a web application (or website) that, instead of relying on the standard browser page reloading, uses JavaScript to dynamically rewrite the active page content. In doing so, an SPA usually creates a smoother experience for the end user.

When deciding whether or not to use this approach on our site, we need to take into account its consequences. We are going to move all the UI concerns to the client, which is going to contain a lot more logic than what HTML-only websites do.

These architectures are going to be a lot thinner on the server. Most SPAs are structured to work directly with REST APIs (or more recently, GraphQL) and compose the views on this data directly in the browser. Moving all the templating and URL routing to the client side makes the backend more likely to contain mostly views that return JSON or XML data, rather than HTML.

SPAs also come with some drawbacks. Using SPAs makes websites difficult to optimize for search engines. Google has recently started to crawl and execute JavaScript that is found on pages, but with many limitations; therefore, it may be unwise to rely solely on this.

Google is not the only search engine. Other search engines may also act similarly, but again, execution of JavaScript at this scale is not an easy matter and so we should not assume that search engines will properly crawl an SPA.

In practical terms, it is entirely possible to have SPAs in Django. Besides the SPA's bundle of JS and CSS files, you will need a bootstrap HTML page, which loads an empty page with a root container, normally a `<div>` tag.

In addition to this, SPAs handle routing client-side. We need to make sure that routing to specific sections does not happen server-side. The solution to this is to serve the same bootstrap page for all the links that are managed on the client side.

This is an example set of URLs that is typical in this scenario:

```
from django.views.generic import TemplateView

urlpatterns = [
    path('api/', include(api_patterns)),
    ...
    path(' ', TemplateView.as_view(template_name="spa.html")),
    # Catchall URL
    re_path(r'^.*/$', TemplateView.as_view(template_name=
    "spa.html")),
```

And the bootstrap page, spa.html, would contain something along these lines:

```
{% load staticfiles }
<!DOCTYPEhtml>

<html>
    <head>
        <title>SPA</title>
    </head>
    <body>
        <div id="main-app">
            Loading...
        </div>
        <script src="{% static 'js/spa.bundle.js' %}"></script>
    </body>
</html>
```

How JavaScript Testing Fits In

In a simple Django project, you will find most of the complexity in the backend, and that is where most of the automated testing will happen. However, if the complexity in the frontend increases, it is important that automated testing also happens there.

Complexity in the frontend is normally in the UI interactions, something that the backend does not cover. In more advanced use cases, the frontend also requires storing state in the browser. While stateless interactions are easier to test, as the frontend gets more stateful, testing techniques need to be changed accordingly.

Finally, Django comes also equipped for functional/system testing. At this level, we need to tread lightly. Having said that, system testing the most important user flows may be the thing that saves us from having to explain why online sales suddenly stopped working.

Unit, Integration, and End-to-End Testing

Tests normally fall within three categories, based on the amount of code involved in the test:

- *Unit testing*: A test of a single component, which could be a Python function, or a Django view activation. The intention here is to be as specific as possible about what code to test. If your test involves some external resource, such as a database or network, it is not a unit test.

- *Integration testing*: Testing of the interaction of multiple components. Most of the testing that we wrote in the previous chapters was related to setting up data in the database. Given that this process involves multiple systems, Postgres and Django in our case, it is safe to say those tests are integration tests.

185

- *End-to-end (E2E) testing*: Sometimes called functional testing, involves testing the whole system in its entirety. That includes everything in between our project database and what the user does in the browser. This type of test is difficult to write and slow to run; therefore, a project should limit the number of E2E tests.

Note that browsers involved in end-to-end testing can be real or headless. A *headless browser* is a browser that does not show any window on the developer's monitor but does still go through the actions required to process and render a page. Headless browsers are faster than real browsers because they do not present the rendered site to a screen, but they are not what the end user has.

In general, unless you have some performance requirements, use a real browser. When tests are running, you will be able to see a lot more than what your code considers a failure, even though your code is not testing for it. You will see the errors on your screen.

Adding an Image Switcher on Product Page

We are going from theory to practice now by applying some of the knowledge that we have acquired. In our project we have the possibility of uploading many images per product, but we have not yet built an intelligent way to display the images. We are going to build a very simple image switcher that will display the original image when the related thumbnail is clicked.

We are going to use React to do the JavaScript, but any framework works. Please do not focus on my choice of framework, but rather on the final solution. For now, we will also keep things as simple as possible regarding Django integration.

Let's add the React component on the product page. We will do so by modifying main/templates/main/product_detail.html:

```
{% extends"base.html" %}

{% block content %}
  <h1>products</h1>
  <table class="table">
    <tr>
      <th>Name</th>
      <td>{{ object.name }}</td>
    </tr>
    <tr>
      <th>Cover images</th>
      <td>
        <div id="imagebox">
          Loading...
        </div>
      </td>
    </tr>
    ...
</table>
{% endblock content %}

{% block js %}
<script
  src="https://unpkg.com/react@16/umd/react.production.min.js">
</script>
<script
  src="https://unpkg.com/react-dom@16/umd/react-dom.production.
  min.js">
</script>
```

```
<style type="text/css" media="screen">
.image{
    margin: 10px;
    display: inline-block;
}
</style>

<script>
const e=React.createElement;

class ImageBox extends React.Component{
  constructor(props){
    super(props);
    this.state = {
        currentImage: this.props.imageStart
    }
  }

  click(image){
    this.setState({
        currentImage: image
    });
  }

  render(){
    const images = this.props.images.map((i)=>
        e('div', {className: "image", key: i.id},
        e('img', {onClick: this.click.bind(this, i),
                width: "100",
                src: i.thumbnail}),
        ),
    );
```

```
    return e('div', {className: "gallery"},
        e('div', {className: "current-image"},
          e('img',{src: this.state.currentImage.image})
          ),
        images)
  }
}

document.addEventListener("DOMContentLoaded",
  function(event) {
    var images = [
    {% for image in object.productimage_set.all %}
        {"image": "{{ image.image.url|safe }}",
        "thumbnail": "{{ image.thumbnail.url|safe }}"},
    {% endfor %}
    ]
    ReactDOM.render(
        e(ImageBox, {images: images, imageStart: images[0]}),
        document.getElementById('imagebox')
    );
  });
</script>
{% endblock %}
```

This is enough to add the switching functionality. If you click any of the small images on the page, a full version of it will be displayed in the bigger box above. There is also some basic CSS for a bare minimum of styling. The resulting page is shown in Figure 5-1.

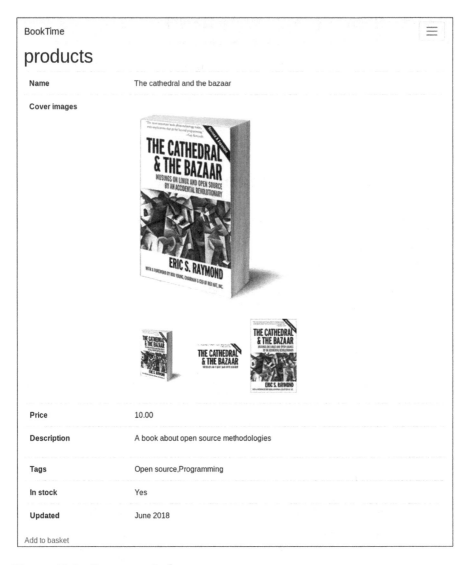

Figure 5-1. *Image switcher*

E2E Testing with Selenium

We are ready to start building the first end-to-end test. To do so we have to install some packages first. From the main project folder, where the Pipfile is, type the following:

```
$ pipenv install selenium
```

This will install the Selenium driver. Selenium is a testing framework for web applications. It is used to automate all operations that a user could do on a website, such as keyboard and mouse events. Selenium will spin up a copy of a browser (e.g., Firefox) and pilot it without our intervention.

We are going to use Firefox for this test. Please make sure you have Firefox installed. You also need to install Geckodriver, which is software that acts as a bridge between Firefox and Selenium. You can find this on the Mozilla GitHub page at https://github.com/mozilla/geckodriver/releases.

Make sure that the Geckodriver binary you download from GitHub is installed in a path that is in your executable paths. On Linux, a good place would be /usr/local/bin.

On a Mac, the entire installation can be done with the command brew install geckodriver.

Once we have done all this setup, which we have to do only once, we can start with our first end-to-end test. Put the following in main/tests/test_e2e.py:

```
from decimal import Decimal
from django.urls import reverse
from django.core.files.images import ImageFile
from django.contrib.staticfiles.testing import (
    StaticLiveServerTestCase
)
from selenium.webdriver.firefox.webdriver import WebDriver
from main import models
```

```python
class FrontendTests(StaticLiveServerTestCase):
    @classmethod
    def setUpClass(cls):
        super().setUpClass()
        cls.selenium = WebDriver()
        cls.selenium.implicitly_wait(10)

    @classmethod
    def tearDownClass(cls):
        cls.selenium.quit()
        super().tearDownClass()

    def test_product_page_switches_images_correctly(self):
        product = models.Product.objects.create(
            name="The cathedral and the bazaar",
            slug="cathedral-bazaar",
            price=Decimal("10.00"),
        )
        for fname in ["cb1.jpg", "cb2.jpg", "cb3.jpg"]:
            with open("main/fixtures/cb/ s" %fname, "rb") as f:
                image = models.ProductImage(
                    product=product,
                    image=ImageFile(f, name=fname),
                )
                image.save()

        self.selenium.get(
            "%s%s"
            % (
                self.live_server_url,
                reverse(
                    "product",
```

```python
            kwargs={"slug":"cathedral-bazaar"},
        ),
    )
)
current_image = self.selenium.find_element_by_css_selector(
    ".current-image > img:nth-child(1)"
).get_attribute(
    "src"
)
self.selenium.find_element_by_css_selector(
    "div.image:nth-child(3) > img:nth-child(1)"
).click()
new_image = self.selenium.find_element_by_css_selector(
    ".current-image > img:nth-child(1)"
).get_attribute("src")
self.assertNotEqual(current_image, new_image)
```

This test will start Firefox, create a product with three images, load the product page, and click one of the thumbnails at the bottom of the image switcher. The final assertion tests that the full image has changed to the one the test clicked.

Before running the preceding test, make sure you have three sample images inside main/fixtures/cb/, named accordingly.

Unlike the tests we have seen so far, this test inherits from StaticLiveServerTestCase. While the standard TestCase uses a very simple HTTP client, this instead will provide enough functionality to have real browsers connect and use it. This test server will run in its own independent database—it will not reuse the existing database.

There are areas for improvement here, starting from JavaScript integration. We are going to be looking now at integrating a JavaScript build tool.

CSS/JavaScript Build Tools

In the modern development workflow, there is normally a CSS/JS build tool that applies transformations to the original JavaScript. There are many types of transformations, the most common being compilation and minification. Another common step done by these tools is to preprocess CSS files.

Many build tools are available, but recently, a build tool that seems to be getting a lot of attention is Webpack (https://webpack.js.org). Webpack takes JavaScript modules with dependencies and generates bundles that contain all the dependencies the code needs to run. It is also able to minify and take out unused code.

Webpack is written in Node.js. In order to use this tool, you need to make sure that both Node and Npm are installed. Once this is done, we will integrate this in our project. From the top folder (where manage.py is), launch these commands:

```
$ # create a package.json file
$ npm init -y

$ # install webpack as dev dependencies
$ npm install webpack webpack-cli --save-dev

$ # install webpack-bundle-tracker as dev dependencies
$ npm install webpack-bundle-tracker --save-dev

$ # install react dependencies
$ npm install react react-dom --save

$ # install Django package connected to webpack-bundle-tracker
$ pipenv install django-webpack-loader
```

After having issued these commands, we will change a few sections of package.json as shown next. We will also create a Webpack config that declares multiple entries and adds our bundle tracker plug-in.

Our package.json file is as follows:

```json
{
  "name": "booktime",
  "version": "1.0.0",
  "description": "",
  "private": true,
  "scripts": {
    "test": "echo \"Error: no test specified\" && exit 1",
    "build": "webpack"
  },
  "keywords": [],
  "author": "",
  "license": "ISC",
  "devDependencies": {
    "webpack": "^4.12.0",
    "webpack-bundle-tracker": "^0.3.0",
    "webpack-cli": "^3.0.8"
  },

  "dependencies": {
    "react": "^16.4.1",
    "react-dom": "^16.4.1"
  }
}
```

This is the content for `webpack.config.js`:

```
const path = require('path');
const BundleTracker = require('webpack-bundle-tracker')

module.exports = {
  mode: 'development',
  entry: {
      imageswitcher: './frontend/imageswitcher.js'
  },
  plugins:[
    new BundleTracker({filename: './webpack-stats.json'}),
  ],
  output:{
    filename: '[name].bundle.js',
    path: path.resolve(dirname, 'main/static/bundles')
  }
};
```

On the Django side, we will integrate the Webpack loader library in `settings.py`:

```
...

WEBPACK_LOADER = {
    'DEFAULT': {
        'BUNDLE_DIR_NAME': 'bundles/',
        'STATS_FILE': os.path.join(BASE_DIR, 'webpack-stats.
        json'),
    }
}
```

```
INSTALLED_APPS = [
    ...
    'webpack_loader',
    ...
]
```

It is time now to move all the JavaScript code that was in the product detail template into its separate file. We will call this imageswitcher.js and place it in a new top-level folder called frontend/, as previously shown in the Webpack config file.

```
const React = require("react");
const ReactDOM = require("react-dom");
const e = React.createElement;

var imageStyle = {
    margin: "10px",
    display: "inline-block"
}

class ImageBox extends React.Component{
  constructor(props) {
    super(props);
    this.state = {
        currentImage: this.props.imageStart
    }
  }

  click(image){
    this.setState({
        currentImage: image
    });
  }
```

```
render(){
    const images = this.props.images.map((i) =>
        e('div', {style: imageStyle, className: "image", key:i.
        image},
          e('img', {onClick: this.click.bind(this,i),
          width: "100", src: i.thumbnail})
          )
    );
    return e('div', {className: "gallery"},
        e('div', {className: "current-image"},
         e('img', {src: this.state.currentImage.image})
         ),
        images)
  }
}
window.React = React
window.ReactDOM = ReactDOM
window.ImageBox = ImageBox

module.exports = ImageBox
```

The preceding code is similar to what we had before, with some important differences. The import statements were not in the previous version, along with inline styles and the final assignments to window and module.exports. The assignments to the window object are required for this code to be used from other locations in the page.

At this point, you should be able to run webpack by typing

```
$ npm run build

> booktime@1.0.0 build /..../booktime
> webpack
```

```
(node:23880) DeprecationWarning: Tapable.plugin is deprecated.
Use new API on `.hooks` instead
Hash: 828b5178a3e3974adde0
Version: webpack 4.12.0
Time: 488ms
Built at: 07/30/2018 8:54:08 AM
                    Asset    Size  Chunks          Chunk Names
imageswitcher.bundle.js 713 KiB  imageswitcher [emitted]
                                                    imageswitcher
[./frontend/imageswitcher.js] 931 bytes {imageswitcher} [built]
    + 21 hidden modules
```

Now you have a Webpack bundle generated, and some new entries in the webpack-stats.json file. django-webpack-loader will use this last file to insert bundle references in templates.

All the window assignments previously mentioned will be available in the product_detail.html template after having included the bundle:

```
{% extends "base.html" %}
{% load render_bundle from webpack_loader %}

{% block content %}
...
{% endblock content %}

{% block js %}
  {% render_bundle 'imageswitcher" js' %}
  <script>
    document.addEventListener("DOMContentLoaded", function
    (event){
      var images = [
        {% for image in object.productimage_set.all %}
```

```
        {
          "image":"{{ image.image.url }}",
          "thumbnail": "{{ image.thumbnail.url }}"
        },
      {% endfor %}
    ]
    ReactDOM.render(React.createElement(ImageBox,{
      images: images,
      imageStart: images[0]
    }),document.getElementById( 'imagebox'));
  });
</script>
{% endblock %}
```

This is one of the possible ways to integrate Webpack with Django. The React components are fairly separate, and data is loaded through component instantiation, directly on the page, without the help of an API. The rendering location is also specified directly in the page template, so this can easily be changed if the component is loaded from a different page.

To verify that we have not broken this functionality, we can run the end-to-end test that we wrote in the previous section. If it works, you followed all the steps correctly.

JavaScript Unit Tests

We are now relying on a full browser to test the image switcher that we have created, although there is a better, faster way. Given how self-contained this component is, we can test it in isolation, in an environment that is a lot simpler than a full-fledged browser.

To do so we will use a JavaScript tool called Jest (https://jestjs.io). Jest is a test runner that is becoming common nowadays. Again, the specific choice of tool is not important here. There are other test runners such as QUnit (https://qunitjs.com), Jasmine (https://jasmine.github.io), and Mocha (https://mochajs.org). They all use Node.js as their runtime, and therefore they are all executed in a similar way.

Type these commands from the top folder:

```
$ npm install jest enzyme enzyme-adapter-react-16 --save-dev
```

Now we can integrate our first test in our project. Given that we started with the convention of having all JavaScript assets in the frontend/ directory, we will place our test there with the name of imageswitcher.test.js:

```
const React = require("react");
const ImageBox = require('./imageswitcher');
const renderer = require('react-test-renderer');
const Enzyme = require('enzyme');
const Adapter = require('enzyme-adapter-react-16');

Enzyme.configure({ adapter: new Adapter() });

test('ImageBox switches images correctly', ()=>{
  var images = [
    {"image": "1.jpg",
    "thumbnail": "1.thumb.jpg"},
    {"image": "2.jpg",
    "thumbnail": "2.thumb.jpg"},
    {"image": "3.jpg",
    "thumbnail": "3.thumb.jpg"}
  ]
  const wrapper = Enzyme.shallow(
    React.createElement(ImageBox, {images: images, imageStart:
    images[0]})
  );
```

```
const currentImage = wrapper.find('.current-image > img').
first().prop('src');
wrapper.find('div.image').at(2).find('img').simulate('click');
const newImage = wrapper.find('.current-image > img').
first().prop('src');

expect(currentImage).not.toEqual(newImage);
});
```

This test loads the component from frontend/imageswitcher.js and renders it, then it simulates a using clicking the third image. The assertion at the end tests that the click changed the current image.

Jest requires a bit of configuration to do test discovery, which we will add to package.json:

```
...
"scripts": {
  "test": "jest",
  "build": "webpack"
},
...
"jest": {
  "moduleDirectories": [
    "node_modules",
    "frontend"
  ],
  "testURL": "http://localhost/"
},
...
```

With this configuration, we can run the tests with the command npm test:

```
$ npm test

> jest
```

```
PASS frontend/imageswitcher.test.js
 v ImageBox switches images correctly (24ms)

Test Suites: 1 passed, 1 total
Tests:       1 passed, 1 total
Snapshots:   0 total
Time:        1.65s, estimated 2s
Ran all test suites.
```

This is enough of a start for us. This test runner is different from the Django test runner and it would need to be run separately from the backend tests. If we had a Continuous Integration system, this would need to be integrated in the pipeline, along with Django tests.

Summary

In modern websites, there is a lot happening on the frontend. Many websites use asset preprocessors for both CSS and JavaScript, and in this chapter we saw a possible way to integrate those.

We also looked at how to use tools such as Webpack, React, and Selenium to add interactivity to the site, without leaving the testing part neglected. However, Selenium tests are slow, and therefore it is best to limit those to the most critical parts of the web application. Jest, on the other hand, tests React on its own, and it is much faster.

The libraries that I picked for this chapter are by no means the only ones present in this space. There are many tools available and you should decide which ones suit your needs and desires. The choice of tools here was mainly made based on the usage in the Django community.

In the next chapter we will talk about some external Django libraries that are commonly used to add to Django even more power.

CHAPTER 6

Using External Libraries in Our Project

This chapter presents how easy it is to include external Django libraries in our project, and how we can use some of these libraries to speed up development or add features that otherwise would not be available in vanilla Django.

Using Django Extensions

Django Extensions[1] library offers some useful additional commands that our project could use. To see what they are, we need to install the library first:

```
$ pipenv install django-extensions
$ pipenv install pydotplus    # for graph_models
$ pipenv install ipython      # for shell_plus
$ pipenv install werkzeug     # for runserver_plus
```

We also need to add the library to INSTALLED_APPS:

```
INSTALLED_APPS = [
    "django.contrib.admin",
    "django.contrib.auth",
```

---

[1]https://github.com/django-extensions/django-extensions

© Federico Marani 2019
F. Marani, *Practical Django 2 and Channels 2*,
https://doi.org/10.1007/978-1-4842-4099-1_6

```
    "django.contrib.contenttypes",
    "django.contrib.sessions",
    "django.contrib.messages",
    "django.contrib.staticfiles",
    'webpack_loader',
    'django_extensions',
    "main.apps.MainConfig",
]
```

Once we have done that, we should be able to see, among the standard commands, the new commands as well:

```
$ ./manage.py

Type 'manage.py help <subcommand>' for help on a specific
subcommand.

Available subcommands:

[auth]
    changepassword
    createsuperuser

[contenttypes]
    remove_stale_contenttypes

[django]
    check
    compilemessages
    createcachetable
    dbshell

    ...

    test
    testserver
```

```
[django_extensions]
    admin_generator
    clean_pyc
    clear_cache
    compile_pyc

    ...

    sync_s3
    syncdata
    unreferenced_files
    update_permissions
    validate_templates

[main]
    import_data

[sessions]
    clearsessions

[staticfiles]
    collectstatic
    findstatic
    runserver
```

There are a lot of commands that this library offers. I will not describe them all in this chapter, but just the ones that are more commonly used. You can find a full list of these management commands in the online Django documentation.[2]

This first command generates a graph with all the models and the connections between them, through foreign keys:

```
$ ./manage.py graph_models -a -o booktime_models.png
```

---

[2]https://docs.djangoproject.com/en/2.0/ref/django-admin/

You can see the graph for our project in Figure 6-1.

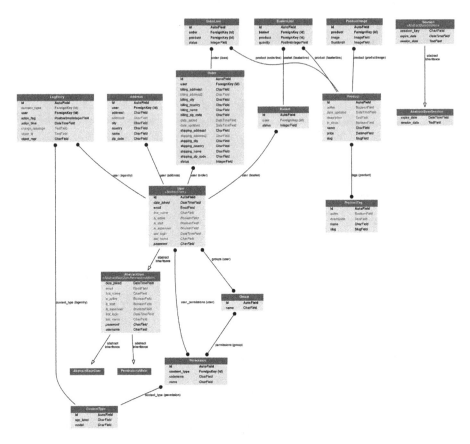

Figure 6-1. *graph_models command output*

Another useful command is shell_plus, which starts a shell (using the library IPython installed at the beginning of this section) that offers history, autocomplete, automatic imports for our models, and so on:

```
$ ./manage.py shell_plus
# Shell Plus Model Imports
from django.contrib.admin.models import LogEntry
from django.contrib.auth.models import Group, Permission
from django.contrib.contenttypes.models import ContentType
```

```
from django.contrib.sessions.models import Session
from main.models import Address, Basket, BasketLine, ...
# Shell Plus Django Imports
from django.core.cache import cache
from django.conf import settings
from django.contrib.auth import get_user_model
from django.db import transaction
from django.db.models import Avg, Case, Count, F, ...
from django.utils import timezone
from django.urls import reverse
Python 3.6.3 (default, Oct 3 2017, 21:45:48)
Type 'copyright', 'credits' or 'license' for more information
IPython 6.4.0 -- An enhanced Interactive Python. Type '?' for help.

In [1]:
```

Along with the library, there is also an enhanced version of the
runserver command we use to start the development server. This
command is runserver_plus:

```
$ ./manage.py runserver_plus
Performing system checks...

System check identified no issues (0 silenced).

Django version 2.0.7, using settings 'booktime.settings'
Development server is running at http://[127.0.0.1]:8000/
Using the Werkzeug debugger (http://werkzeug.pocoo.org/)
Quit the server with CONTROL-C.
 * Debugger is active!
 * Debugger PIN: 130-358-807
```

When using this to browse the site, the Django error page will be
substituted with Werkzeug (http://werkzeug.pocoo.org), which offers an
interactive debugger, very useful to debug problems quickly, as shown in
Figure 6-2.

builtins.NameError

```
NameError: name 'error' is not defined
```

Traceback (most recent call last)

```
File "/home/flagz/.local/share/virtualenvs/booktime-8-1qP2a4/lib/python3.6/site-packages/django/contrib/staticfiles/handlers.py",
line 66, in __call__
  return self.application(environ, start_response)
```

```
File "/home/flagz/.local/share/virtualenvs/booktime-8-1qP2a4/lib/python3.6/site-packages/django/core/handlers/wsgi.py", line 146,
in __call__

    def __call__(self, environ, start_response):
        set_script_prefix(get_script_name(environ))
        signals.request_started.send(sender=self.__class__, environ=environ)
        request = self.request_class(environ)
        response = self.get_response(request)


        response._handler_class = self.__class__


        status = '%d %s' % (response.status_code, response.reason_phrase)
        response_headers = list(response.items())
[console ready]
>>>
```

```
File "/home/flagz/.local/share/virtualenvs/booktime-8-1qP2a4/lib/python3.6/site-packages/django/core/handlers/base.py", line 81,
in get_response
  response = self._middleware_chain(request)
```

```
File "/home/flagz/.local/share/virtualenvs/booktime-8-1qP2a4/lib/python3.6/site-packages/django/core/handlers/exception.py", line
37, in inner
  response = response_for_exception(request, exc)
```

```
File "/home/flagz/.local/share/virtualenvs/booktime-8-1qP2a4/lib/python3.6/site-packages/django/core/handlers/exception.py", line
87, in response_for_exception
  response = handle_uncaught_exception(request, get_resolver(get_urlconf()), sys.exc_info())
```

```
File "/home/flagz/.local/share/virtualenvs/booktime-8-1qP2a4/lib/python3.6/site-packages/django/core/handlers/exception.py", line
122, in handle_uncaught_exception
```

Figure 6-2. *Werkzeug debugger with runserver_plus example*

Better Tests with factory_boy

The factory_boy library[3] simplifies the generation of data for tests.
Historically in Django, data for tests was either loaded from files, called
fixtures, or directly embedded in the code. For cases that require a lot of
setup data, having data hard-coded can create maintenance problems,
especially for fixtures.

---

[3]https://factoryboy.readthedocs.io/en/latest/

To solve this, the factory_boy library gives us a way to generate data for tests automatically, based on constraints that we can specify in the test. This library generates fake data for names, addresses, and so on, at every run. It also generates data on all fields, unless you specify otherwise.

We can install this library with

```
$ pipenv install factory_boy
```

To demonstrate the power of this library, we will modify one test file that in our project is particularly heavy in terms of data setup: `main/tests/test_models.py`. Before doing so, we will create some factories in `main/factories.py`:

```python
import factory
import factory.fuzzy
from . import models

class UserFactory(factory.django.DjangoModelFactory):
    email="user@site.com"

    class Meta:
        model = models.User
        django_get_or_create = ('email',)

class ProductFactory(factory.django.DjangoModelFactory):
    price = factory.fuzzy.FuzzyDecimal(1.0, 1000.0, 2)

    class Meta:
        model = models.Product

class AddressFactory(factory.django.DjangoModelFactory):
    class Meta:
        model = models.Address
```

Factories are classes used to generate data for specific models. These are called by the tests. This is our updated version of main/tests/test_models.py:

```python
from decimal import Decimal
from django.test import TestCase
from main import models
from main import factories

class TestModel(TestCase):
    def test_active_manager_works(self):
        factories.ProductFactory.create_batch(2, active=True)
        factories.ProductFactory(active=False)
        self.assertEqual(len(models.Product.objects.active()), 2)

    def test_create_order_works(self):
        p1 = factories.ProductFactory()
        p2 = factories.ProductFactory()
        user1 = factories.UserFactory()
        billing = factories.AddressFactory(user=user1)
        shipping = factories.AddressFactory(user=user1)

        basket = models.Basket.objects.create(user=user1)
        models.BasketLine.objects.create(
            basket=basket, product=p1
        )
        models.BasketLine.objects.create(
            basket=basket, product=p2
        )

        with self.assertLogs("main.models", level="INFO") as cm:
            order = basket.create_order(billing, shipping)
```

```
self.assertGreaterEqual(len(cm.output), 1)

order.refresh_from_db()

self.assertEquals(order.user, user1)
self.assertEquals(
    order.billing_address1, billing.address1
)
self.assertEquals(
    order.shipping_address1, shipping.address1
)

self.assertEquals(order.lines.all().count(), 2)
lines = order.lines.all()
self.assertEquals(lines[0].product, p1)
self.assertEquals(lines[1].product, p2)
```

As you can see, we are taking out a lot of extra information, such as product names, shipping lines, and so forth, from the setup of these two tests. If, in the future, we decide to add another field to any of the models called (e.g., Address), the test would still pass, without needing an update.

Django Debug Toolbar

Django Debug Toolbar[4] is a well-known library that displays a lot of useful information about the loaded web page. It includes information about the HTTP request/response, Django internal settings, SQL queries triggered, templates used, cache calls, and other details.

This library is also extensible with plug-ins in case what is included does not cover the information you want to be displayed. There are several plug-ins available online.

---

[4]https://github.com/jazzband/django-debug-toolbar

To install Django Debug Toolbar, you can use the following command:

```
$ pipenv install django-debug-toolbar
```

In addition to installing it, some additional settings are required, starting from some changes to booktime/settings.py:

```
...

INSTALLED_APPS = [
    ....
    'debug_toolbar',
    "main.apps.MainConfig",
]

MIDDLEWARE = [
    "debug_toolbar.middleware.DebugToolbarMiddleware",
    ...
]

INTERNAL_IPS = ['127.0.0.1']

...
```

Make the following addition to the end of booktime/urls.py as well:

```
...

if settings.DEBUG:
    import debug_toolbar
    urlpatterns = [
        path('__debug__/', include(debug_toolbar.urls)),
    ] + urlpatterns
```

This is enough to start using the tool. A black bar will appear on the right side of the screen, with clickable sections that can be opened to see a particular category of information. Figure 6-3 shows the SQL queries that are generated when displaying the product page.

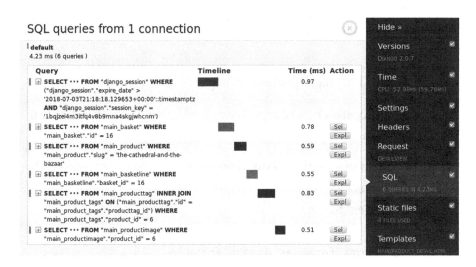

Figure 6-3. *SQL queries on the product page*

The other panels are Settings, to see the current Django configuration, Request, to see information about the current view, Templates, to see which templates have been used to compose the response and with what variables passed in, and Cache, to see all the cache calls done by the view.

For the case of BookTime, our book e-commerce system, this library works well, because all pages are templates returned by Django. If in your project you had an SPA architecture with backend APIs, this approach would not work as well, because Django Debug Toolbar relies on the backend returning HTML to the browser. In that case, you might want to take a look at Django Silk.

Visualizing Orders with django-tables2 and django-filter

The django-tables2[5] and django-filter[6] libraries, which are independent but often used in conjunction, can help us speed up the process of creating very simple dashboards. Here we are going to develop a filterable order list for internal users:

```
$ pipenv install django-tables2 django-filter
```

Using these libraries is very easy. We will add an authenticated view to our list of views in main/views.py:

```
from django.contrib.auth.mixins import (
    LoginRequiredMixin,
    UserPassesTestMixin
)
from django import forms as django_forms
from django.db import models as django_models
import django_filters
from django_filters.views import FilterView

...


...


class DateInput(django_forms.DateInput):
    input_type = 'date'

class OrderFilter(django_filters.FilterSet):
    class Meta:
        model = models.Order
```

---

[5]https://django-tables2.readthedocs.io/en/latest/
[6]https://django-filter.readthedocs.io/en/master/

```
    fields = {
            'user__email': ['icontains'],
            'status': ['exact'],
            'date_updated': ['gt', 'lt'],
            'date_added': ['gt', 'lt'],
            }
    filter_overrides = {
            django_models.DateTimeField: {
                'filter_class': django_filters.DateFilter,
                'extra': lambda f:{
                    'widget': DateInput}}}

class OrderView(UserPassesTestMixin, FilterView):
    filterset_class = OrderFilter
    login_url = reverse_lazy("login")

    def test_func(self):
        return self.request.user.is_staff is True
```

OrderView is a view that is only available to users that have access to
the admin interface as well, as the test_func function checks for that. This
view inherits from FilterView, with a filterset_class that specifies what
filters are available in the page.

The FilterSet class format is similar to Django's own ModelForm,
where you can define the filters directly or use the Meta class to generate
the filters automatically. In the previous example, we define the fields to
filter on and the lookup expressions active on them. We also want to make
sure that we use an HTML5 date input field for dates.

Along with this view, we will add a template (in the default location for the view, main/templates/main/order_filter.html):

```
{% extends "base.html" %}
{% load render_table from django_tables2 %}

{% block content %}
  <h2>Order dashboard</h2>
  <form method="get">
    {{ filter.form.as_p }}
    <input type="submit"/>
  </form>
  <p>
    {% render_table filter.qs %}
  </p>
{% endblock content %}
```

This template makes use of django-tables2 to render the table, along with sorting controls. It simplifies the job of printing headers and cycling through results with only one template tag. This tag, however, needs to be installed. We will do so in settings.py:

```
INSTALLED_APPS = [
    ...
    'django_tables2',
    "main.apps.MainConfig",
]

...

DJANGO_TABLES2_TEMPLATE = 'django_tables2/bootstrap.html'
```

This library also allows us to specify what templates to use when rendering tables. In our instance, we need the CSS styles of the Bootstrap framework.

When any Django library is added to the INSTALLED_APPS list, Django will add its static and templates folders to the search paths for static files and template files. This is how this library, by specifying an initial template, will then be able to bring in all its dependencies.

The next (and last) operation is to make this available in main/urls.py:

```
urlpatterns = [
    ...
    path(
        "order-dashboard/",
        views.OrderView.as_view(),
        name="order_dashboard",
    ),
]
```

This newly created dashboard will now be available at the URL indicated above. After you enter some orders in your project, you will be able to see some results in the dashboard and use the filters that we set up, as shown in Figure 6-4.

BookTime

0 items in basket

Order dashboard

User email address contains: [ ]

Status: [--------- ▾]

Date updated is greater than: [dd / mm / yyyy]

Date updated is less than: [dd / mm / yyyy]

Date added is greater than: [dd / mm / yyyy]

Date added is less than: [dd / mm / yyyy]

[Submit Query]

ID	User	Status	Billing Name	Billing address1	Billing address2	Billing Zip Code	Billing City	Billing Country
6	admin@admin.com	New	Federico Marani	1 Home road	—	-	London	uk
7	test@client.com	Paid	John Kimball	-	—	-	-	-
8	test@aa.com	Done	Matt Smith	1 Avenue road	—	RS99AC	Roechester	uk

Figure 6-4. *Simple order dashboard*

As you can see, with a small amount of code we have built a very functional dashboard.

django-widget-tweaks

This library[7] is helpful when dealing with complex form templates that require a certain structure. The Bootstrap CSS framework, for example, requires every input to be marked with the `form-control` CSS class. In standard Django, this would be achievable by either specifying the complete HTML tag or injecting the class in Python. If you find yourself doing either of these things, especially modifying the `form` classes to output the right CSS styles, you are handling design concerns in code, which is not a very good separation between these two domains.

With the help of this library, we can rewrite and simplify some of the templates in the BookTime project. First, let's install it:

```
$ pipenv install django-widget-tweaks
```

It also needs to be included in the settings:

```
INSTALLED_APPS = [
    ...
    'widget_tweaks',
    "main.apps.MainConfig",
]
```

As soon as we have that, all the template tags from this library are available to be used from templates. We can build on the built-in Django widget rendering, adding the CSS classes and HTML structure that we need.

---

[7]https://github.com/jazzband/django-widget-tweaks

Django templates, besides extending others, can also use the `include` template tag, which we will start using. Let's extract all the field rendering HTML in its own template, called `main/templates/includes/field.html`:

```
{% load widget_tweaks %}

<div class="form-group">
  {{ field.label_tag }}
  {{ field|add_class:"form-control"|add_error_class:"is-invalid" }}
  {% if field.errors %}
    <div class="invalid-feedback">
      {{ field.errors }}
    </div>
  {% endif %}
</div>
```

The `field` variable is a widget, and it has a few tags applied to it that modify the output. We are adding some CSS classes, one always and another in case of error.

This snippet now can be included by other templates. This is how the `main/templates/login.html` template would use it:

```
{% extends "base.html" %}

{% block content %}
  <h2>Login</h2>
  <p>Please fill the form below.</p>
  <form method="POST">
    {% csrf_token %}
    {{ form.non_field_errors }}
    {% include "includes/field.html" with field=form.email %}
    {% include "includes/field.html" with field=form.password %}
```

```
<button type="submit" class="btn btn-primary">Submit</button>
</form>
{% endblock content %}
```

A similar restructuring could be done on `signup.html` and `contact_form.html` (inside `main/templates/`). The rest of our templates use the `{{ form }}` shortcut. To use this there, that template variable would need to be broken down by iterating through its `fields`.

Building an API Using Django Rest Framework for Order Fulfillment

For e-commerce organizations, order dispatch commonly is managed by a third-party dispatch service. This external entity may be using its own delivery management system, in which case a data integration is required.

We will cover these use cases with the API:

- The dispatch service needs to be able to see orders and their order lines coming through the system, but only after they have been paid.

- The dispatch service needs to be able to filter the preceding list by status or order.

- The dispatch service will mark order lines as "processing" to acknowledge them.

- The dispatch service will mark order lines as "sent" or "canceled" to inform the central office about their status.

- The dispatch service can change the shipping address of orders if it needs to.

Curl Demo Flow

We will use the curl command to show the APIs. Curl is a very simple command-line tool available on many platforms (https://curl.haxx.se). You can consider it the equivalent of browsers but for APIs. If you do not have this tool installed already, you can use a package manager to install it.

This is the API flow that we are about to implement.

To get the list of order lines that are ready to be shipped (status 10), we will use the following command:

```
$ curl -H 'Accept: application/json; indent=4' \
    -u dispatch@booktime.domain:abcabcabc \
    http://127.0.0.1:8000/api/orderlines/

{
    "count": 2,
    "next": null,
    "previous": null,
    "results": [
        {
            "id": 10,
            "order": "http://127.0.0.1:8000/api/orders/9/",
            "product": "Siddhartha",
            "status": 10
        },
        {
            "id": 11,
            "order": "http://127.0.0.1:8000/api/orders/9/",
            "product": "Backgammon for dummies",
            "status": 10
        }
    ]
}
```

To get the shipping address of order number 9:

```
$ curl -H 'Accept: application/json; indent=4' \
    -u dispatch@bookime.domain:abcabcabc \
    http://127.0.0.1:8000/api/orders/9/

{

    "shipping_name": "John Smith",
    "shipping_address1": "1 the road",
    "shipping_address2": "",
    "shipping_zip_code": "LC11RA",
    "shipping_city": "Smithland",
    "shipping_country": "uk",
    "date_updated": "2018-07-07T11:46:09.367227Z",
    "date_added": "2018-07-05T22:22:01.067294Z"
}
```

Once the dispatch system has order lines and orders lists, it will be able to start progressively marking these lines as "processing" (status 20) or "sent" (status 30):

```
$ curl -H 'Accept: application/json; indent=4' \
    -u dispatch@booktime.domain:abcabcabc -XPUT \
    -H 'Content-Type: application/json' \
    -d '{"status": 20}' http://127.0.0.1:8000/api/
        orderlines/10/

{

    "id": 10,
    "order": "http://127.0.0.1:8000/api/orders/9/",
    "product": "Siddhartha",
    "status": 20
}
```

```
$ curl -H 'Accept: application/json; indent=4' \
    -u dispatch@bookime.domain:abcabcabc -XPUT \
    -H 'Content-Type: application/json' \
    -d '{"status": 30}' http://127.0.0.1:8000/api/
        orderlines/11/

{

    "id": 11,
    "order": "http://127.0.0.1:8000/api/orders/9/",
    "product": "Backgammon for dummies",
    "status": 30
}
$ curl -H 'Accept: application/json; indent=4' \
    -u dispatch@bookime.domain:abcabcabc -XPUT \
    -H 'Content-Type: application/json' \
    -d '{"status": 30}' http://127.0.0.1:8000/api/
        orderlines/10/

{

    "id": 10,
    "order": "http://127.0.0.1:8000/api/orders/9/",
    "product": "Siddhartha",
    "status": 30
}
```

We use numeric status codes because that is how we defined them in the status choices list of the OrderLine model.

Having numeric statuses give us some advantages, like space efficiency and orderability, but it is not always clear what these numbers mean. It is important to document this in the API docs.

Once all lines are marked as "sent" or "cancelled", these lines will not be available in the order lines list anymore:

```
$ curl -H 'Accept: application/json; indent=4' \
    -u dispatch@bookime.domain:abcabcabc \
    http://127.0.0.1:8000/api/orderlines/

{
    "count": 0,
    "next": null,
    "previous": null,
    "results": []
}
```

Framework Installation and Configuration

Django Rest Framework[8] is integrated with django-filter, and we will
use that for filtering. Make sure you have it installed. To install Django Rest
Framework, type the following command:

```
$ pipenv install djangorestframework
```

After it is installed, configure it in settings.py:

```
INSTALLED_APPS = [
    ...
    'rest_framework',
    "main.apps.MainConfig",
]

...

REST_FRAMEWORK = {
    'DEFAULT_AUTHENTICATION_CLASSES':
    ('rest_framework.authentication.SessionAuthentication',
     'rest_framework.authentication.BasicAuthentication'),
```

---

[8]http://www.django-rest-framework.org/

```
    'DEFAULT_PERMISSION_CLASSES':
    ('rest_framework.permissions.DjangoModelPermissions',),
    'DEFAULT_FILTER_BACKENDS':
    ('django_filters.rest_framework.DjangoFilterBackend',),
    'DEFAULT_PAGINATION_CLASS':
    'rest_framework.pagination.PageNumberPagination',
    'PAGE_SIZE': 100
}
```

This configuration is flexible enough for our use case, and more. The authentication classes are used to verify whether user/password combinations correspond to what is stored in the database. The permission classes are used to understand what a user can or cannot do on the system.

In our case, we are leveraging the built-in permissions that are generated by default when models are created.

In addition to these, we are setting django-filter to be our filtering backend, and setting a default pagination of 100 items per page.

Finally, we need add some additional URLs, which we will do in booktime/urls.py:

```
urlpatterns = [
    ...
    path('api-auth/', include('rest_framework.urls')),
    path("", include("main.urls")),
] + ...
```

Users and Permissions

We will create a user in the system to use when calling the APIs. This user will need at least two permissions:

- Can change order
- Can change order line

As you can see in Figure 6-5, this is the user that we are using in the previous examples. Feel free to use whatever user/password you want, but remember to update the `curl` commands appropriately.

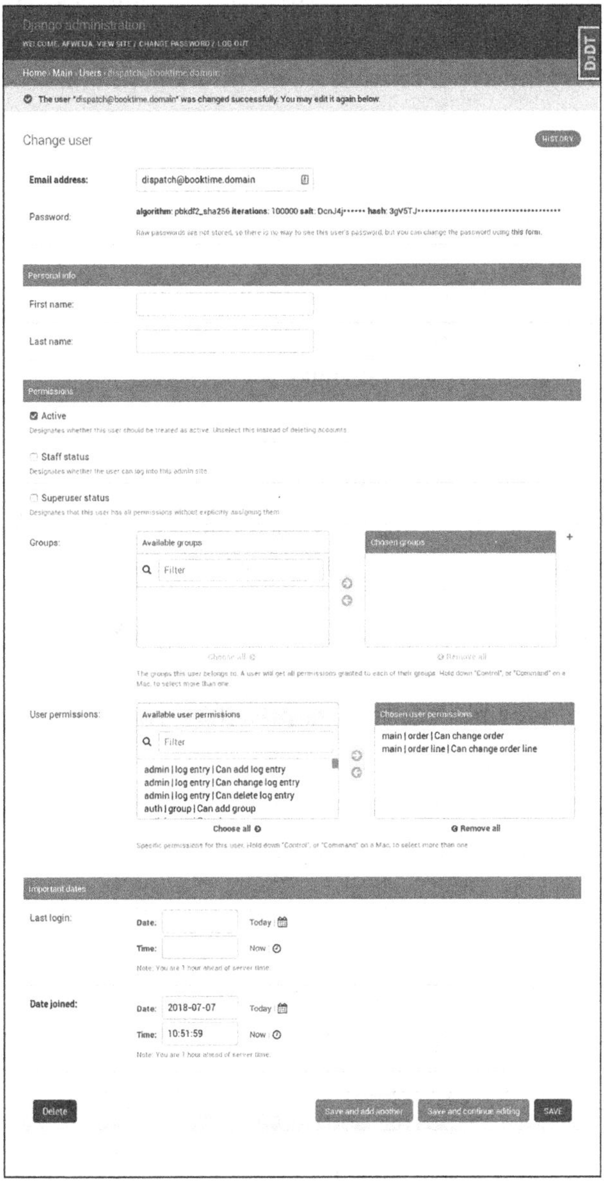

Figure 6-5.   *REST user*

API Endpoints

Django Rest Framework is a very flexible library, with a lot of functionalities. There is enough material to write many pages about it, but this is not the focus of this book. The following is some code that uses this library and covers the use cases that we mentioned; put this code in main/endpoints.py:

```python
from rest_framework import serializers, viewsets
from . import models

class OrderLineSerializer(serializers.
HyperlinkedModelSerializer):
    product = serializers.StringRelatedField()

    class Meta:
        model = models.OrderLine
        fields = ('id', 'order', 'product', 'status')
        read_only_fields = ('id', 'order', 'product')

class PaidOrderLineViewSet(viewsets.ModelViewSet):
    queryset = models.OrderLine.objects.filter(
        order__status=models.Order.PAID).order_by("-order__
        date_added")
    serializer_class = OrderLineSerializer
    filter_fields = ('order', 'status')

class OrderSerializer(serializers.HyperlinkedModelSerializer):
    class Meta:
        model = models.Order
        fields = ('shipping_name',
                  'shipping_address1',
                  'shipping_address2',
                  'shipping_zip_code',
```

```
                    'shipping_city',
                    'shipping_country',
                    'date_updated',
                    'date_added')

class PaidOrderViewSet(viewsets.ModelViewSet):
    queryset = models.Order.objects.filter(
        status=models.Order.PAID).order_by("-date_added")
    serializer_class = OrderSerializer
```

We need to assign URLs to the preceding views. We will do so in main/
urls.py:

```
...

from django.urls import path, include
from rest_framework import routers
from main import endpoints

router = routers.DefaultRouter()
router.register(r'orderlines', endpoints.PaidOrderLineViewSet)
router.register(r'orders', endpoints.PaidOrderViewSet)

urlpatterns = [
    ...
    path('api/', include(router.urls)),
]
```

Order Completion Using Signals

Now that we have enough for the dispatcher to mark orders as sent, we
need to make sure that the marked orders do not appear in the list api
anymore. We will do this in a way that is not dependent on how they are
marked, either through the REST API or through Django admin.

To do so we will again use Django signals. This new signal will be inserted in main/signals.py:

```
...

from django.db.models.signals import pre_save, post_save
from .models import ProductImage, Basket, OrderLine, Order

...

@receiver(post_save, sender=OrderLine)
def orderline_to_order_status(sender, instance, **kwargs):
    if not instance.order.lines.filter(status__lt=OrderLine.
    SENT).exists():
        logger.info(
            "All lines for order %d have been processed.
            Marking as done.", instance.order.id,
        )
        instance.order.status = Order.DONE
        instance.order.save()
```

This signal will be executed after saving instances of the OrderLine model. The first thing it does is check whether any order lines connected to the order have statuses below "sent." If there is any, the execution is terminated. If there is no line below the "sent" status, the whole order is marked as "done."

To try this flow, you would need to use the curl commands we have listed above. You would need two terminals open, one with the Django runserver command running, and other one for typing the curl commands.

Using the DRF Web Client

Besides using `curl` to test the API, it is possible to use the Django Rest
Framework (DRF) web client, which is available when browsing the API
URLs directly through a browser.

Figure 6-6 is a screenshot of the web client. It is useful to showcase the
API and test quickly when preferable over the command line.

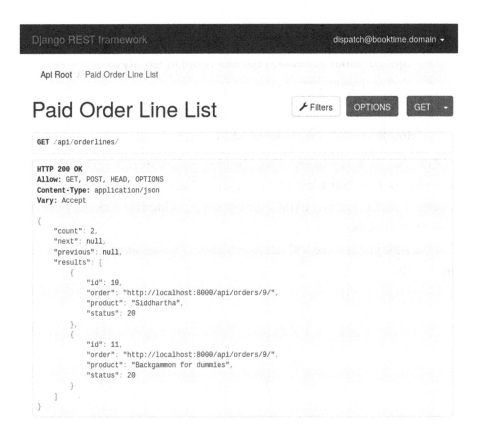

Figure 6-6. *DRF web client*

Summary

In this chapter we have seen these libraries:

- django-extensions: Includes some very useful commands not included in Django

- factory-boy: Generates data dynamically for tests

- django-debug-toolbar: Tool that gives us a lot of information when debugging

- django-widget-tweaks: Provides more flexibility to define frontend attributes

- django-rest-framework: A framework within a framework that is all about REST

Of course, there are many other libraries available online. This chapter was meant to show you some of the ways in which Django could be extended. I encourage you to do your research online and pick the ones that suit your needs.

In the next chapter we will talk again about Django admin, this time more deeply.

CHAPTER 7

Making an Internal Dashboard for the Company

In this chapter we will build a dashboard for Booktime company employees on top of the Django admin interface. We will discuss why and how to do this, along with different types of users in the company.

We will cover these topics:

- Configuring the admin interface

- Adding admin views

- Configuring users and permissions

- Creating internal reports

- Generating PDFs

Reasons to Use Django admin

In this chapter we are using the Django admin interface to demonstrate how customizable this app is. With only some basic customizations we are already able to manage our products and order data, as we have seen in the previous chapters. We are also already able to filter and search for products and orders in our system.

© Federico Marani 2019
F. Marani, *Practical Django 2 and Channels 2*,
https://doi.org/10.1007/978-1-4842-4099-1_7

The Django admin interface comes with a built-in authentication and permission system. You can easily configure multiple users to be able to see and change only parts of your data. This interface also has a built-in log to track who changed what models in the database.

This app allows us to get an adequate state without much effort. In this chapter we will continue building upon the customizations that we already did by creating new views integrated in the admin interface, modifying the permissions of the users, integrating reporting functions, and customizing its look.

All of this is possible by mostly overriding the base classes, although this approach has limits. Given that, when customizing the admin interface, we are always overriding built-in behavior with additional code, it is advisable to not overcustomize it because your code will quickly become hard to read.

Another limitation of this approach is that you cannot fundamentally alter the user flow of the app. Just like the choice between class-based views and function-based views, if you spend more time overriding built-in behavior than codifying your own, customizing the admin interface is not the right approach.

In this chapter we will try to stretch this interface to its limits to achieve support for all the standard operations an e-commerce company should be able to do, or at least for the ones that our fictitious book-selling company requires.

Views in the admin interface

To list all exposed views in the admin, we can use the `show_urls` command from the `django-extensions` library. Here is a small snippet of its output:

...

```
/admin/
    django.contrib.admin.sites.index
    admin:index
/admin/<app_label>/
    django.contrib.admin.sites.app_index
    admin:app_list
/admin/auth/user/
    django.contrib.admin.options.changelist_view
    admin:auth_user_changelist
/admin/auth/user/<id>/password/
    django.contrib.auth.admin.user_change_password
    admin:auth_user_password_change
/admin/auth/user/<path:object_id>/
    django.views.generic.base.RedirectView
/admin/auth/user/<path:object_id>/change/
    django.contrib.admin.options.change_view
    admin:auth_user_change
/admin/auth/user/<path:object_id>/delete/
    django.contrib.admin.options.delete_view
    admin:auth_user_delete
/admin/auth/user/<path:object_id>/history/
    django.contrib.admin.options.history_view
    admin:auth_user_history
/admin/login/
    django.contrib.admin.sites.login
    admin:login
/admin/logout/
    django.contrib.admin.sites.logout
    admin:logout
```

...

As you can see, for an instance of Django admin, there are many pages (not all of which are shown in the preceding snippet):

- *Index view*: The initial page, which lists all the Django apps and their models

- *App list view*: The list of models of a single Django app

- *Change list view*: The list of all entries for a Django model

- *Change view*: A view to change a single entity of a Django model

- *Add view*: A view to add a new entity of a Django model

- *Delete view*: A confirmation view to delete a single entity of a Django model

- *History view*: A list of all changes done through Django admin interface of a single entity

- *Support views*: Login, logout, and change password views

Each of these views is customizable through overriding specific methods in the right admin class (we will explore an example of this). Each of these views also uses a template that can be customized:

- *Index view*: `admin/index.html`

- *App list view*: `admin/app_index.html`

- *Change list view*: `admin/change_list.html`

- *Change item view*: `admin/change_form.html`

- *Add item view*: `admin/change_form.html`

- *Delete item view on one item*: `admin/delete_confirmation.html`

- *Delete item view on multiple items*: admin/delete_ selected_confirmation.html

- *History view*: admin/object_history.html

There are many more templates that represent specific sections of the screen of some of these views. I encourage you to explore these templates to understand their structure. You can find them in your Python virtualenv or online on GitHub[1].

Django admin interface comes with a built-in set of views, but you can add new views. You can define views both at the top level and at the model level. The new views will inherit all the security checks and URL namespacing of the correspondent admin instance. This makes it possible to add, for instance, all the reporting views to our admin instance, with the proper authorization checks in place.

In addition to all the preceding features, it is possible to have multiple Django admin interfaces running on one site, each with its own customizations. Up to this point we have used django.contrib.admin. site, which is an instance of django.contrib.admin.AdminSite, but nothing stops us from having many instances of it.

Configuring User Types and Permissions for the Company

Before writing any code, it is important to clarify the different types of users that you have in the system and the way each type is allowed to interact with the system. We have three types of users in the BookTime company:

- Owners
  - Can see and operate on all useful models

---

[1]https://github.com/django/django/tree/master/django/contrib/admin/ templates/admin

- Central office employees

    - Can flag orders as paid

    - Can change order data

    - Can see reports about the site's performance

    - Can manage products and related information

- Dispatch office

    - Can flag order lines as shipped (or canceled)

    - Can flag products as out of stock

In Django, we will store the membership information in this way:

- *Owners*: Any user for whom the is_superuser field is set
  to True

- *Central office employees*: Any user belonging to the
  "Employees" group

- *Dispatch office*: Any user belonging to the "Dispatchers"
  group

To create these user types in the system we will use a data fixture,
which is the same principle as a test fixture. Put this content in main/data/
user_groups.json:

```
[
  {
    "model": "auth.group",
    "fields": {
      "name": "Employees",
      "permissions": [
        [ "add_address", "main", "address" ],
        [ "change_address", "main", "address" ],
        [ "delete_address", "main", "address" ],
```

```json
      [ "change_order", "main", "order" ],
      [ "add_orderline", "main", "orderline" ],
      [ "change_orderline", "main", "orderline" ],
      [ "delete_orderline", "main", "orderline" ],
      [ "add_product", "main", "product" ],
      [ "change_product", "main", "product" ],
      [ "delete_product", "main", "product" ],
      [ "add_productimage", "main", "productimage" ],
      [ "change_productimage", "main", "productimage" ],
      [ "delete_productimage", "main", "productimage" ],
      [ "change_producttag", "main", "producttag" ]
    ]
  }
},
{
  "model": "auth.group",
  "fields": {
    "name": "Dispatchers",
    "permissions": [
      [ "change_orderline", "main", "orderline" ],
      [ "change_product", "main", "product" ]
    ]
  }
}
]
```

To load the preceding code, type the following:

```
$ ./manage.py loaddata main/data/user_groups.json
Installed 2 object(s) from 1 fixture(s)
```

We are also going to add a few helper functions to our User model, to help us identify what type of user it is:

```python
class User(AbstractUser):
    ...

    @property
    def is_employee(self):
        return self.is_active and (
            self.is_superuser
            or self.is_staff
            and self.groups.filter(name="Employees").exists()
        )

    @property
    def is_dispatcher(self):
        return self.is_active and (
            self.is_superuser
            or self.is_staff
            and self.groups.filter(name="Dispatchers").exists()
        )
```

Implementing Multiple admin interfaces for Users

We are going to start with a bunch of code that I will explain inline with code comments. Starting from main/admin.py, we are going to replace all we have with a more advanced version of it, supporting all the use cases that we listed.

```python
from datetime import datetime, timedelta
import logging
from django.contrib import admin
```

```python
from django.contrib.auth.admin import (
    UserAdmin as DjangoUserAdmin
)
from django.utils.html import format_html
from django.db.models.functions import TruncDay
from django.db.models import Avg, Count, Min, Sum
from django.urls import path
from django.template.response import TemplateResponse

from . import models

logger = logging.getLogger(__name__)

class ProductAdmin(admin.ModelAdmin):
    list_display = ("name", "slug", "in_stock", "price")
    list_filter = ("active", "in_stock", "date_updated")
    list_editable = ("in_stock",)
    search_fields = ("name",)
    prepopulated_fields = {"slug": ("name",)}
    autocomplete_fields = ("tags",)

    # slug is an important field for our site, it is used in
    # all the product URLs. We want to limit the ability to
    # change this only to the owners of the company.
    def get_readonly_fields(self, request, obj=None):
        if request.user.is_superuser:
            return self.readonly_fields
        return list(self.readonly_fields) + ["slug", "name"]

    # This is required for get_readonly_fields to work
    def get_prepopulated_fields(self, request, obj=None):
        if request.user.is_superuser:
            return self.prepopulated_fields
        else:
            return {}
```

```python
class DispatchersProductAdmin(ProductAdmin):
    readonly_fields = ("description", "price", "tags", "active")
    prepopulated_fields = {}
    autocomplete_fields = ()

class ProductTagAdmin(admin.ModelAdmin):
    list_display = ("name", "slug")
    list_filter = ("active",)
    search_fields = ("name",)
    prepopulated_fields = {"slug": ("name",)}

    # tag slugs also appear in urls, therefore it is a
    # property only owners can change
    def get_readonly_fields(self, request, obj=None):
        if request.user.is_superuser:
            return self.readonly_fields
        return list(self.readonly_fields) + ["slug", "name"]

    def get_prepopulated_fields(self, request, obj=None):
        if request.user.is_superuser:
            return self.prepopulated_fields
        else:
            return {}

class ProductImageAdmin(admin.ModelAdmin):
    list_display = ("thumbnail_tag", "product_name")
    readonly_fields = ("thumbnail",)
    search_fields = ("product__name",)

    # this function returns HTML for the first column defined
    # in the list_display property above
    def thumbnail_tag(self, obj):
        if obj.thumbnail:
            return format_html(
```

```python
            '<img src="%s"/>' % obj.thumbnail.url
        )
    return "-"

    # this defines the column name for the list_display
    thumbnail_tag.short_description = "Thumbnail"

    def product_name(self, obj):
        return obj.product.name

class UserAdmin(DjangoUserAdmin):
    # User model has a lot of fields, which is why we are
    # reorganizing them for readability
    fieldsets = (
        (None, {"fields": ("email", "password")}),
        (
            "Personal info",
            {"fields": ("first_name", "last_name")},
        ),
        (
            "Permissions",
            {
                "fields": (
                    "is_active",
                    "is_staff",
                    "is_superuser",
                    "groups",
                    "user_permissions",
                )
            },
        ),
        (
            "Important dates",
```

```python
                {"fields": ("last_login", "date_joined")},
        ),
    )
    add_fieldsets = (
        (
            None,
            {
                "classes": ("wide",),
                "fields": ("email", "password1", "password2"),
            },
        ),
    )
    list_display = (
        "email",
        "first_name",
        "last_name",
        "is_staff",
    )
    search_fields = ("email", "first_name", "last_name")
    ordering = ("email",)

class AddressAdmin(admin.ModelAdmin):
    list_display = (
        "user",
        "name",
        "address1",
        "address2",
        "city",
        "country",
    )
    readonly_fields = ("user",)
```

```python
class BasketLineInline(admin.TabularInline):
    model = models.BasketLine
    raw_id_fields = ("product",)

class BasketAdmin(admin.ModelAdmin):
    list_display = ("id", "user", "status", "count")
    list_editable = ("status",)
    list_filter = ("status",)
    inlines = (BasketLineInline,)

class OrderLineInline(admin.TabularInline):
    model = models.OrderLine
    raw_id_fields = ("product",)

class OrderAdmin(admin.ModelAdmin):
    list_display = ("id", "user", "status")
    list_editable = ("status",)
    list_filter = ("status", "shipping_country", "date_added")
    inlines = (OrderLineInline,)
    fieldsets = (
        (None, {"fields": ("user", "status")}),
        (
            "Billing info",
            {
                "fields": (
                    "billing_name",
                    "billing_address1",
                    "billing_address2",
                    "billing_zip_code",
                    "billing_city",
                    "billing_country",
                )
            },
        ),
```

```python
        (
            "Shipping info",
            {
                "fields": (
                    "shipping_name",
                    "shipping_address1",
                    "shipping_address2",
                    "shipping_zip_code",
                    "shipping_city",
                    "shipping_country",
                )
            },
        ),
    )

# Employees need a custom version of the order views because
# they are not allowed to change products already purchased
# without adding and removing lines

class CentralOfficeOrderLineInline(admin.TabularInline):
    model = models.OrderLine
    readonly_fields = ("product",)

class CentralOfficeOrderAdmin(admin.ModelAdmin):
    list_display = ("id", "user", "status")
    list_editable = ("status",)
    readonly_fields = ("user",)
    list_filter = ("status", "shipping_country", "date_added")
    inlines = (CentralOfficeOrderLineInline,)
    fieldsets = (
        (None, {"fields": ("user", "status")}),
        (
            "Billing info",
```

```
    {
        "fields": (
            "billing_name",
            "billing_address1",
            "billing_address2",
            "billing_zip_code",
            "billing_city",
            "billing_country",
        )
    },
),
(
    "Shipping info",
    {
        "fields": (
            "shipping_name",
            "shipping_address1",
            "shipping_address2",
            "shipping_zip_code",
            "shipping_city",
            "shipping_country",
        )
    },
),
)
```

```python
# Dispatchers do not need to see the billing address in the fields

class DispatchersOrderAdmin(admin.ModelAdmin):
    list_display = (
        "id",
        "shipping_name",
        "date_added",
        "status",
    )
    list_filter = ("status", "shipping_country", "date_added")
    inlines = (CentralOfficeOrderLineInline,)
    fieldsets = (
        (
            "Shipping info",
            {
                "fields": (
                    "shipping_name",
                    "shipping_address1",
                    "shipping_address2",
                    "shipping_zip_code",
                    "shipping_city",
                    "shipping_country",
                )
            },
        ),
    )

    # Dispatchers are only allowed to see orders that
    # are ready to be shipped
    def get_queryset(self, request):
        qs = super().get_queryset(request)
        return qs.filter(status=models.Order.PAID)
```

```python
# The class below will pass to the Django Admin templates a couple
# of extra values that represent colors of headings

class ColoredAdminSite(admin.sites.AdminSite):
    def each_context(self, request):
        context = super().each_context(request)
        context["site_header_color"] = getattr(
            self, "site_header_color", None
        )
        context["module_caption_color"] = getattr(
            self, "module_caption_color", None
        )
        return context

# The following will add reporting views to the list of
# available urls and will list them from the index page

class ReportingColoredAdminSite(ColoredAdminSite):
    def get_urls(self):
        urls = super().get_urls()
        my_urls = [
            path(
                "orders_per_day/",
                self.admin_view(self.orders_per_day),
            )
        ]
        return my_urls + urls

    def orders_per_day(self, request):
        starting_day = datetime.now() - timedelta(days=180)
        order_data = (
            models.Order.objects.filter(
                date_added__gt=starting_day
            )
```

```
        .annotate(
            day=TruncDay("date_added")
        )
        .values("day")
        .annotate(c=Count("id"))
    )
    labels = [
        x["day"].strftime("%Y-%m-%d") for x in order_data
    ]
    values = [x["c"] for x in order_data]

    context = dict(
        self.each_context(request),
        title="Orders per day",
        labels=labels,
        values=values,
    )
    return TemplateResponse(
        request, "orders_per_day.html", context
    )

def index(self, request, extra_context=None):
    reporting_pages = [
        {
            "name": "Orders per day",
            "link": "orders_per_day/",
        }
    ]
    if not extra_context:
        extra_context = {}
    extra_context = {"reporting_pages": reporting_pages}
    return super().index(request, extra_context)
```

```python
# Finally we define 3 instances of AdminSite, each with their own
# set of required permissions and colors

class OwnersAdminSite(ReportingColoredAdminSite):
    site_header = "BookTime owners administration"
    site_header_color = "black"
    module_caption_color = "grey"

    def has_permission(self, request):
        return (
            request.user.is_active and request.user.is_superuser
        )

class CentralOfficeAdminSite(ReportingColoredAdminSite):
    site_header = "BookTime central office administration"
    site_header_color = "purple"
    module_caption_color = "pink"

    def has_permission(self, request):
        return (
            request.user.is_active and request.user.is_employee
        )

class DispatchersAdminSite(ColoredAdminSite):
    site_header = "BookTime central dispatch administration"
    site_header_color = "green"
    module_caption_color = "lightgreen"

    def has_permission(self, request):
        return (
            request.user.is_active and request.user.is_dispatcher
        )

main_admin = OwnersAdminSite()
main_admin.register(models.Product, ProductAdmin)
```

```
main_admin.register(models.ProductTag, ProductTagAdmin)
main_admin.register(models.ProductImage, ProductImageAdmin)
main_admin.register(models.User, UserAdmin)
main_admin.register(models.Address, AddressAdmin)
main_admin.register(models.Basket, BasketAdmin)
main_admin.register(models.Order, OrderAdmin)

central_office_admin = CentralOfficeAdminSite(
    "central-office-admin"
)
central_office_admin.register(models.Product, ProductAdmin)
central_office_admin.register(models.ProductTag,
ProductTagAdmin)
central_office_admin.register(
    models.ProductImage, ProductImageAdmin
)
central_office_admin.register(models.Address, AddressAdmin)
central_office_admin.register(
    models.Order, CentralOfficeOrderAdmin
)

dispatchers_admin = DispatchersAdminSite("dispatchers-admin")
dispatchers_admin.register(
    models.Product, DispatchersProductAdmin
)
dispatchers_admin.register(models.ProductTag, ProductTagAdmin)
dispatchers_admin.register(models.Order, DispatchersOrderAdmin)
```

That's a lot of code! First of all, there are three instances of Django admin, one for each type of user we declared in the previous section. Each instance has a different set of models registered, depending on what is relevant for that type of user.

The Django admin sites will be color-coded. Colors are injected through some custom CSS. The owners' and central office's admin interfaces have also some extra views for reporting. The extra views are inserted in three steps: the actual view (orders_per_day), the URL mapping (in get_urls()), and the inclusion in the index template (index()).

Specifically to DispatchersAdminSite, we have special a version of ModelAdmin for Product and Order. DispatchersOrderAdmin overrides the get_queryset() method because the dispatch office only needs to see the orders that have been marked as paid already. On those, they only need to see the shipping address.

For anyone else other than owners, we are also limiting the ability to change the slugs because they are part of the URLs. If they were changed, Google or any other entity that links to our site would have broken links.

The new instances of Django admin interfaces now need an entry in urlpatterns in main/urls.py, as follows. Do not forget to remove the old entry for admin/ in booktime/urls.py. If you forget to remove it, you will have some problems with clashing path names.

```
...

from main import admin

urlpatterns = [
    ...
    path("admin/", admin.main_admin.urls),
    path("office-admin/", admin.central_office_admin.urls),
    path("dispatch-admin/", admin.dispatchers_admin.urls),
]
```

To finish this setup, we need to override a couple of admin templates. First, we are going to add a directory named templates to the top folder, for overridden templates. This implies a change in booktime/settings.py:

```
TEMPLATES = [
    ...
    {
        "DIRS": [os.path.join(BASE_DIR, 'templates')],
    ...
```

Then we override the templates. This is our new admin base template, which will take care of setting the colors in the CSS. Place the following in templates/admin/base_site.html:

```
{% extends "admin/base.html" %}

{% block title %}
  {{ title }} | {{ site_title|default:_('Django site admin') }}
{% endblock %}

{% block extrastyle %}
  <style type="text/css" media="screen">
    #header {
      background: {{site_header_color}};
    }
    .module caption {
      background: {{module_caption_color}};
    }
  </style>
{% endblock extrastyle %}

{% block branding %}
  <h1 id="site-name">
    <a href="{% url 'admin:index' %}">
      {{ site_header|default:_('Django administration') }}
    </a>
  </h1>
{% endblock %}

{% block nav-global %}{% endblock %}
```

In the code we have seen above the index view had some extra template variables. To display those, a new template is required. We will place this file in `templates/admin/index.html`, and it will be a customization of a built-in admin template.

Let's take a copy of this admin template for our project. From our top-level folder, run the following command.

```
cp $VIRTUAL_ENV/lib/python3.6/site-packages/django/contrib/
admin/templates/admin/index
```

The new template will need to be changed, at the beginning of the content block. Here is the modified template content:

```
{% extends "admin/base_site.html" %}
...

{% block content %}
<div id="content-main">

  {% if reporting_pages %}
    <div class="module">
      <table>
        <caption>
          <a href="#" class="section">Reports</a>
        </caption>
        {% for page in reporting_pages %}
          <tr>
            <th scope="row">
                <a href="{{ page.link }}">
                    {{ page.name }}
                </a>
            </th>
            <td> </td>
            <td> </td>
          </tr>
```

```
        {% endfor %}
      </table>
    </div>
  {% else %}
    <p>No reports</p>
  {% endif %}

  ...

{% endblock %}
```

...

We now have the three dashboards that we want to give to our internal team. Please go ahead and open the URLs in your browser, after having logged in as a superuser. Bear in mind that the reporting section is not finished yet.

In the next section we will talk more about reporting with the Django ORM. The code was included above (`orders_per_day()`), but given how important it is, it deserves to be explained in its own section.

Reporting on Orders

When it comes to reporting, SQL queries tend to become a bit more complicated, using aggregate functions, `GROUP BY` clauses, etc. The purpose of the Django ORM is to map database rows to `Model` objects. It can be used to do reports, but that is not its primary function. This can lead to some difficult-to-understand ORM expressions, so be warned.

In Django, there are two classes of aggregation: one that acts on all entries in a `QuerySet` and another that acts on each entry of it. The first uses the `aggregate()` method, and the second `annotate()`. Another way to explain it is that `aggregate()` returns a Python dictionary, while `annotate()` returns a `QuerySet` where each entry is annotated with additional information.

There is an exception to this rule, and that is when the annotate() function is used with values(). In that case, annotations are not generated for each item of the QuerySet, but rather on each unique combination of the fields specified in the values() method.

When in doubt, you can see the SQL that the ORM is generating by checking the property query on any QuerySet.

The next few sections present some reports, and break down the ORM queries.

Numbers of Orders Per Day

In the code above there is a view called orders_per_day that runs this aggregation query:

```
order_data = (
    models.Order.objects.filter(
        date_added__gt=starting_day
    )
    .annotate(
        day=TruncDay("date_added")
    )
    .values("day")
    .annotate(c=Count("id"))
)
```

The query that comes out in Postgres is as follows:

```
SELECT DATE_TRUNC('day', "main_order"."date_added" AT TIME ZONE
'UTC') AS "day",
    COUNT("main_order"."id") AS "c" FROM "main_order"
    WHERE "main_order"."date_added" > 2018-01-16
    19:20:01.262472+00:00
    GROUP BY DATE_TRUNC('day', "main_order"."date_added" AT
    TIME ZONE 'UTC')
```

The preceding ORM code does a few things:

- Creates a temporary/annotated day field, populating it with data based on the date_added field

- Uses the new day field as a unit for aggregation

- Counts orders for specific days

The preceding query includes two annotate() calls. The first acts on all rows in the order table. The second, instead of acting on all rows, acts on the result of the GROUP BY clause, which is generated by the values() call.

To finish the reporting functionality presented in the previous section, we need to create a template in main/templates/orders_per_day.html:

```
{% extends "admin/base_site.html" %}
{% block extrahead %}
  <script
    src="https://cdnjs.cloudflare.com/ajax/libs/Chart.js/2.7.2/
    Chart.bundle.min.js"
    integrity="sha256-XF29CBwU1MWLaGEnsELogU6Y6rcc5nCkhhx
    89nFMIDQ="
    crossorigin="anonymous"></script>
{% endblock extrahead %}
{% block content %}
  <canvas id="myChart" width="900" height="400"></canvas>
  <script>
    var ctx = document.getElementById("myChart");
    var myChart = new Chart(ctx, {
      type: 'bar',
      data: {
        labels: {{ labels|safe }},
        datasets: [
          {
            label: 'No of orders',
```

```
        backgroundColor: 'blue',
        data: {{ values|safe }}
      }
    ]
  },
  options: {
    responsive: false,
    scales: {
      yAxes: [
        {
          ticks: {
            beginAtZero: true
          }
        }
      ]
    }
  }
});
</script>
{% endblock %}
```

In the template we are using an open source library called Chart.js. Using a charting library for reporting views is a common theme, and you should familiarize yourself with a few charting libraries and the format they require the data to be in.

Viewing the Most Bought Products

We are going to add another view that shows what are the most bought products. Differently from orders_per_day(), we are going to do this with a bit more customization, and with integration tests, to show that you can apply the same concepts of normal views to admin views.

These are the bits of main/admin.py that we will add for this view:

```python
from django import forms

...

class PeriodSelectForm(forms.Form):
    PERIODS = ((30, "30 days"), (60, "60 days"), (90, "90 days"))
    period = forms.TypedChoiceField(
        choices=PERIODS, coerce=int, required=True
    )

class ReportingColoredAdminSite(ColoredAdminSite):
    def get_urls(self):
        urls = super().get_urls()
        my_urls = [
            ...
            path(
                "most_bought_products/",
                self.admin_view(self.most_bought_products),
                name="most_bought_products",
            ),
        ]
        return my_urls + urls

    ...

    def most_bought_products(self, request):
        if request.method == "POST":
            form = PeriodSelectForm(request.POST)
            if form.is_valid():
                days = form.cleaned_data["period"]
                starting_day = datetime.now() - timedelta(
                    days=days
                )
```

```python
            data = (
                models.OrderLine.objects.filter(
                    order__date_added__gt=starting_day
                )
                .values("product__name")
                .annotate(c=Count("id"))
            )
            logger.info(
                "most_bought_products query: %s", data.query
            )
            labels = [x["product__name"] for x in data]
            values = [x["c"] for x in data]
    else:
        form = PeriodSelectForm()
        labels = None
        values = None

    context = dict(
        self.each_context(request),
        title="Most bought products",
        form=form,
        labels=labels,
        values=values,
    )
    return TemplateResponse(
        request, "most_bought_products.html", context
    )

def index(self, request, extra_context=None):
    reporting_pages = [
            ...
            {
```

```
            "name": "Most bought products",
            "link": "most_bought_products/",
        },
    ]
    ...
```

As you can see, we can use forms inside this view. We created a simple form to select how far back we want the report for.

Additionally, we are going to create main/templates/most_bought_ products.html:

```
{% extends "admin/base_site.html" %}
{% block extrahead %}
  <script
    src="https://cdnjs.cloudflare.com/ajax/libs/Chart.js/2.7.2/
    Chart.bundle.min.js"
    integrity="sha256-XF29CBwU1MWLaGEnsELogU6Y6rcc5nCkhhx
    89nFMIDQ="
    crossorigin="anonymous"></script>
{% endblock extrahead %}
{% block content %}
  <p>
    <form method="POST">
      {% csrf_token %}
      {{ form }}
      <input type="submit" value="Set period" />
    </form>
  </p>
  {% if labels and values %}
    <canvas id="myChart" width="900" height="400"></canvas>
    <script>
```

```
      var ctx = document.getElementById("myChart");
      var myChart = new Chart(ctx, {
        type: 'bar',
        data: {
          labels: {{ labels|safe }},
          datasets: [
            {
              label: 'No of purchases',
              backgroundColor: 'blue',
              data: {{ values|safe }}
            }
          ]
        },
        options: {
          responsive: false,
          scales: {
            yAxes: [
              {
                ticks: {
                  beginAtZero: true
                }
              }
            ]
          }
        }
      });
    </script>
  {% endif %}
{% endblock %}
```

The preceding template is very similar to the previous one, the only difference being that we are rendering the graph only when the form has been submitted. The selected period is needed for the query. The resulting page is shown in the Figure 7-1.

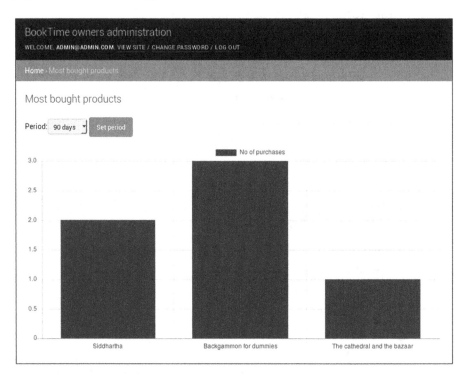

Figure 7-1. *Most bought products view*

To conclude this functionality, we are going to add our first admin views tests. We will create a new file called main/tests/test_admin.py:

```
from django.test import TestCase
from django.urls import reverse
from main import factories
from main import models

class TestAdminViews(TestCase):
    def test_most_bought_products(self):
```

```
products = [
    factories.ProductFactory(name="A", active=True),
    factories.ProductFactory(name="B", active=True),
    factories.ProductFactory(name="C", active=True),
]
orders = factories.OrderFactory.create_batch(3)
factories.OrderLineFactory.create_batch(
    2, order=orders[0], product=products[0]
)
factories.OrderLineFactory.create_batch(
    2, order=orders[0], product=products[1]
)
factories.OrderLineFactory.create_batch(
    2, order=orders[1], product=products[0]
)
factories.OrderLineFactory.create_batch(
    2, order=orders[1], product=products[2]
)
factories.OrderLineFactory.create_batch(
    2, order=orders[2], product=products[0]
)
factories.OrderLineFactory.create_batch(
    1, order=orders[2], product=products[1]
)

user = models.User.objects.create_superuser(
    "user2", "pw432joij"
)
self.client.force_login(user)

response = self.client.post(
    reverse("admin:most_bought_products"),
    {"period": "90"},
```

```
    )
    self.assertEqual(response.status_code, 200)
    data = dict(
        zip(
            response.context["labels"],
            response.context["values"],
        )
    )
    self.assertEqual(data,  {"B": 3, "C": 2, "A": 6})
```

This test makes heavy use of factories to create enough data for the report to contain some useful information. Here are the new factories we added in main/factories.py:

```
...

class OrderLineFactory(factory.django.DjangoModelFactory):
    class Meta:
        model = models.OrderLine

class OrderFactory(factory.django.DjangoModelFactory):
    user = factory.SubFactory(UserFactory)

    class Meta:
        model = models.Order
```

Bulk Updates to Products

In the Django admin interface it is possible to apply actions in bulk. An example of this is deletion: from the change list view we can select multiple items and then select the delete action from the drop-down menu at the top of the table.

These are called "actions," and it is possible to add custom actions to specific instances of ModelAdmin. We are going to add a couple to mark products as active or inactive.

To do so, let's change `main/admin.py`:

```
...
def make_active(self, request, queryset):
    queryset.update(active=True)

make_active.short_description = "Mark selected items as active"

def make_inactive(self, request, queryset):
    queryset.update(active=False)

make_inactive.short_description = (
    "Mark selected items as inactive"
)

class ProductAdmin(admin.ModelAdmin):
    ...

    actions = [make_active, make_inactive]
```

As you can see, it is a very simple change. The result of this can be seen in the product list page by clicking the drop-down button on the left before the column names, as shown in Figure 3-5.

Printing Order Invoices (As PDFs)

The last thing we are going to tackle is a common occurrence for e-commerce shops: printing invoices. In Django there is no facility to generate PDFs, so we will need to install a third-party library.

There are multiple Python PDF libraries available online; in our case we will choose WeasyPrint. This library allows us to create PDFs out of HTML pages, and that is how we will start here. If you want more flexibility, perhaps you should rely on a different library.

WeasyPrint requires a couple of system libraries installed in the system: Cairo and Pango. They are both used for rendering the document. You can install those with your package manager. You also require the fonts required to render the CSS properly.

Let's install WeasyPrint:

```
$ pipenv install WeasyPrint
```

We will create an admin view for this that we can add to the relevant AdminSite classes:

```
...

from django.shortcuts import get_object_or_404, render
from django.http import HttpResponse
from django.template.loader import render_to_string
from weasyprint import HTML
import tempfile

...

class InvoiceMixin:
    def get_urls(self):
        urls = super().get_urls()
        my_urls = [
            path(
                "invoice/<int:order_id>/",
                self.admin_view(self.invoice_for_order),
                name="invoice",
            )
        ]
        return my_urls + urls

    def invoice_for_order(self, request, order_id):
        order = get_object_or_404(models.Order, pk=order_id)
```

```python
if request.GET.get("format") == "pdf":
    html_string = render_to_string(
        "invoice.html", {"order": order}
    )
    html = HTML(
        string=html_string,
        base_url=request.build_absolute_uri(),
    )

    result = html.write_pdf()

    response = HttpResponse(
        content_type="application/pdf"
    )
    response[
        "Content-Disposition"
    ] = "inline; filename=invoice.pdf"
    response["Content-Transfer-Encoding"] = "binary"
    with tempfile.NamedTemporaryFile(
        delete=True
    ) as output:
        output.write(result)
        output.flush()
        output = open(output.name, "rb")
        binary_pdf = output.read()
        response.write(binary_pdf)

    return response

return render(request, "invoice.html", {"order": order})
# This mixin will be used for the invoice functionality, which is
# only available to owners and employees, but not dispatchers
```

```python
class OwnersAdminSite(InvoiceMixin, ReportingColoredAdminSite):
    ...

class CentralOfficeAdminSite(
    InvoiceMixin, ReportingColoredAdminSite
):
    ...
```

This Django view has two rendering modes, HTML and PDF. Both modes use the same invoice.html template, but in the case of PDF, WeasyPrint is used to post-process the output of the templating engine.

When generating PDFs, instead of using the normal render() call, we use the render_to_string() method and store the result in memory. The PDF library will then use this to generate the PDF body, which we will store in a temporary file. In our case, the temporary file will be deleted, but we could persist this in a FileField if we wanted to.

The template used in our case is main/templates/invoice.html:

```html
{% load static %}
<!doctype html>
<html lang="en">
  <head>
    <link
      rel="stylesheet"
      href="{% static "css/bootstrap.min.css" %}">
    <title>Invoice</title>
  </head>
  <body>
    <div class="container-fluid">
      <div class="row">
        <div class="col">
          <h1>BookTime</h1>
          <h2>Invoice</h2>
```

```
    </div>
  </div>
  <div class="row">
    <div class="col-8">
      Invoice number BT{{ order.id }}
      <br/>
      Date:
      {{ order.date_added|date }}
    </div>
    <div class="col-4">
      {{ order.billing_name }}<br/>
      {{ order.billing_address1  }}<br/>
      {{ order.billing_address2  }}<br/>
      {{ order.billing_zip_code }}<br/>
      {{ order.billing_city }}<br/>
      {{ order.billing_country }}<br/>
    </div>
  </div>
  <div class="row">
    <div class="col">
      <table
        class="table"
        style="width: 95%; margin: 50px 0px 50px 0px">
        <tr>
          <th>Product name</th>
          <th>Price</th>
        </tr>
        {% for line in order.lines.all %}
          <tr>
            <td>{{ line.product.name }}</td>
            <td>{{ line.product.price }}</td>
          </tr>
```

```
            {% endfor %}
          </table>
        </div>
      </div>
      <div class="row">
        <div class="col">
          <p>
            Please pay within 30 days
          </p>
          <p>
            BookTime inc.
          </p>
        </div>
      </div>
    </div>
  </body>
</html>
```

This is enough to have the functionality working, but it is not visible in the admin interface yet. To make it visible, we will add buttons to the change order view, as shown in Figure 7-2.

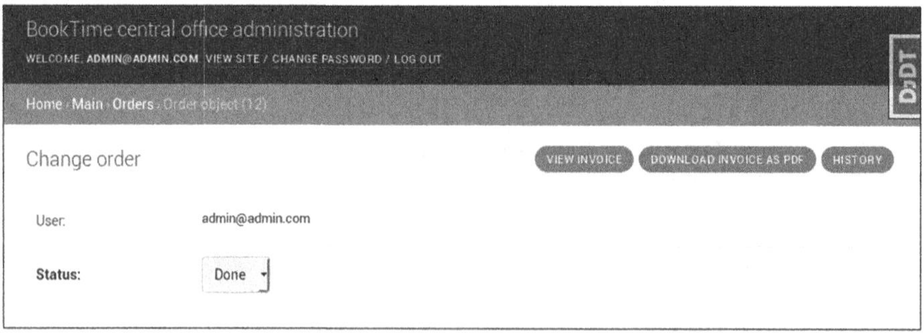

Figure 7-2. *Invoice buttons*

Django admin allows us to override templates that are specific to a model view. We have already overridden some admin templates by creating new ones in the `templates/` folder, and we will follow a similar approach. We are going to create `templates/admin/main/order/change_form.html`:

```
{% extends "admin/change_form.html" %}

{% block object-tools-items %}
  {% url 'admin:invoice' original.pk as invoice_url %}
  {% if invoice_url %}
    <li>
      <a href="{{ invoice_url }}">View Invoice</a>
    </li>
    <li>
      <a href="{{ invoice_url }}?format=pdf">
        Download Invoice as PDF
      </a>
    </li>
  {% endif %}
  {{ block.super }}
{% endblock %}
```

At this point, please go ahead and try to retrieve and view the PDF. If it does not generate correctly, you may have to go on the WeasyPrint forums and work out why. You will find most times that the issue is a missing dependency in your system.

Testing Invoice Generation

The last thing this functionality needs is a test. We want to make sure that, given an order with some specific data, the results for both HTML and PDF versions are exactly what we expect.

This test relies on two fixtures, the HTML invoice and the PDF version. Before running this test, create an order with the test data as shown next and download both the invoices to the right folders.

```python
from datetime import datetime
from decimal import Decimal
from unittest.mock import patch
...

class TestAdminViews(TestCase):
    ...

    def test_invoice_renders_exactly_as_expected(self):
        products = [
            factories.ProductFactory(
                name="A", active=True, price=Decimal("10.00")
            ),
            factories.ProductFactory(
                name="B", active=True, price=Decimal("12.00")
            ),
        ]
        with patch("django.utils.timezone.now") as mock_now:
            mock_now.return_value = datetime(
                2018, 7, 25, 12, 00, 00
            )
            order = factories.OrderFactory(
                id=12,
                billing_name="John Smith",
                billing_address1="add1",
                billing_address2="add2",
                billing_zip_code="zip",
                billing_city="London",
                billing_country="UK",
            )
```

```python
factories.OrderLineFactory.create_batch(
    2, order=order, product=products[0]
)
factories.OrderLineFactory.create_batch(
    2, order=order, product=products[1]
)
user = models.User.objects.create_superuser(
    "user2", "pw432joij"
)
self.client.force_login(user)
response = self.client.get(
    reverse(
        "admin:invoice", kwargs={"order_id": order.id}
    )
)
self.assertEqual(response.status_code, 200)
content = response.content.decode("utf8")
with open(
    "main/fixtures/invoice_test_order.html", "r"
) as fixture:
    expected_content = fixture.read()
self.assertEqual(content, expected_content)
response = self.client.get(
    reverse(
        "admin:invoice", kwargs={"order_id": order.id}
    ),
    {"format": "pdf"}
)
self.assertEqual(response.status_code, 200)
content = response.content
```

```
with open(
    "main/fixtures/invoice_test_order.pdf", "rb"
) as fixture:
    expected_content = fixture.read()
self.assertEqual(content, expected_content)
```

Summary

This chapter was a deep dive into the Django admin interface. We saw how customizable this app can be. We also talked about the dangers of pushing this app too far: if the user flow we want to offer is different from the simple create/edit/delete approach, customizing the admin may not be worth it, and instead adding custom views outside of the admin may be better.

We also talked about reporting and how to structure ORM queries for this. Django documentation goes a lot deeper on this, and I encourage you to research it for more advanced queries.

We also covered PDF generation. In our case, this is done only for people in the back office. Some sites offer invoice generation directly available to website users. In that case, it would be easy to adapt the code in this chapter to offer it in a normal (non-admin) view.

In the next chapter we will talk about an extension of Django called Channels, and how we can use this to build a chat page to interact with our customers.

CHAPTER 8

Backend for a Mobile Customer-Service App

In this chapter we will move away from HTML and normal HTTP. We will create the necessary infrastructure to support a mobile app, including asynchronous communication using WebSocket and HTTP server-side events.

This chapter is centered on Django Channels, including these topics:

- How to integrate it

- How to build WebSocket consumers

- How to integrate it with Redis

- How to use it to serve content asynchronously

Django Channels

Django Channels is a recent addition to the Django ecosystem. It is officially supported by Django, and all development happens on GitHub alongside Django itself. It is not, however, included when installing Django.

Channels allows us to write asynchronous code to deal with incoming requests, which is helpful in case we have a naturally asynchronous interaction between client and server—for example, a chat session.

© Federico Marani 2019
F. Marani, *Practical Django 2 and Channels 2*,
https://doi.org/10.1007/978-1-4842-4099-1_8

While it is technically possible to build a chat server with normal Django views if the real-time component is not critical, synchronous systems will not be able to scale up as well as asynchronous systems when the number of clients increases.

That said, development is much easier on synchronous systems. Do not consider asynchronous programming to be always a better paradigm, because, as anything in computing, it comes with trade-offs.

Asynchronous Code vs. Synchronous Code

Synchronous programming is a very well-understood execution model. Your code is executed from beginning to end, before returning control to Django. On the other end, in asynchronous programming, this is not always the case. Your asynchronous code operates in coordination with an `asyncio` event loop. There is a lot of documentation online that I encourage you to look, like[1].

Fortunately, you do not need to understand everything about asynchronous programming before using Django Channels. Some of the underlying details are hidden by this library, which simplifies your job. One of the most important things to understand is that you cannot mix synchronous and asynchronous code freely. Every time you do so, you need to cross a boundary[2].

I encourage you to spend some time reading about asynchronous programming online. It will help you to follow the code and concepts presented in this chapter.

Installation and Configuration

To install Channels on our system, we will set it up along with Redis, an open source in-memory data structure server (`https://redis.io`). This is for the same reasons that we used PostgreSQL at the start: to always

---

[1] `https://asyncio.readthedocs.io/en/latest/`

[2] `https://www.aeracode.org/2018/02/19/python-async-simplified/`

work on environments that are the same that production deployments will use.

Go ahead and download and install Redis on your operating system. After you have done so, proceed with installing Channels:

```
pipenv install channels
pipenv install channels_redis
```

Our project will need a new file, routing.py, to be placed in the same folder of settings.py. This file, for now, will not declare any route besides the built-in ones.

The contents of booktime/routing.py are this:

```
from channels.routing import ProtocolTypeRouter

application = ProtocolTypeRouter({})
```

We will connect this file with a configuration for Channels using Redis. The application channels needs to be the first because it overrides the runserver command of standard Django:

```
INSTALLED_APPS = [
    'channels',
    ...
]
ASGI_APPLICATION = "booktime.routing.application"

CHANNEL_LAYERS = {
    'default': {
        'BACKEND': 'channels_redis.core.RedisChannelLayer',
        'CONFIG': {
            "hosts": [('127.0.0.1', 6379)],
        },
    },
}
```

You are ready now to use this library. This is the output of the new runserver command:

```
$ ./manage.py runserver
Performing system checks...

System check identified no issues (0 silenced).
August 15, 2018 - 18:56:30
Django version 2.1, using settings 'booktime.settings'
Starting ASGI/Channels version 2.1.2 development server at...
Quit the server with CONTROL-C.
2018-08-15 18:56:30,270 - INFO - server - HTTP/2 support not enabled
2018-08-15 18:56:30,271 - INFO - server - Configuring endpoint...
2018-08-15 18:56:30,272 - INFO - server - Listening on 127.0.0.1:8000
```

Use of Redis

As previously mentioned, Redis is an in-memory data structure server. It can be used as a very simple database, a cache, or a message broker. It has a very different set of operations from normal databases, and its use case is very different.

In our setup, Channels will be using Redis to pass messages between different instances of the running Django application. Redis will also enable us to do message passing between instances running on different machines as well as running on a single server.

Besides requiring Redis to support the communication between processes, the code in this chapter will use Redis directly to create a simple presence mechanism. By default, Channels does not offer a way to ascertain whether or not certain users are connected to our endpoints.

Consumers

We can consider *consumers* in Channels as the equivalent of class-based views, with the difference that consumers are not as high level and numerous as CBVs. There are two base consumer classes, `SyncConsumer` and `AsyncConsumer`. Their interfaces are the same except that asynchronous code relies on the Python `async`/`await` syntax.

The structure of consumers is based on a combination of message handlers using class methods and the `send()` built-in method. Consumers can have multiple message handlers, and the routing of messages is based on the `type` value of the message.

Every consumer, when the class is initialized, will receive a `scope` object, stored in `self.scope`. It contains information about the initial request such as:

- `scope["path"]`: The path of the request

- `scope["user"]`: The current user (only when authentication is enabled)

- `scope["url_route"]`: Contains the matched route (if using a URL router)

There are several subclasses of the original consumer:

- `WebsocketConsumer` and `AsyncWebsocketConsumer`

- `JsonWebsocketConsumer` and `AsyncJsonWebsocketConsumer`

- `AsyncHttpConsumer`

Each one of those subclasses adds a few helper methods, for example, to manage JSON encoding/decoding or WebSockets.

Channels, Channel Layers, and Groups

One of the core concepts of this library is channels. A channel is essentially a mailbox, and each consumer gets one automatically when it is instantiated as part of request handling, and it is removed when the consumer terminates. This is how messages are dispatched from the outside to a given consumer.

A channel layer is the equivalent of a mailman. They are needed to transport messages between various instances of Django. This layer can deliver messages either to a single consumer (by knowing its channel name) or to a set of consumers (by knowing their group channel name).

Sending messages to a single consumer is not a common use case. It is more common to send messages to all consumers associated with a particular user (useful in case he or she opened the site on multiple tabs), or to all consumers of a particular set of users (like in our chat case).

To this end, Channels offers an abstraction called *groups*. Groups are entities you can send messages to, which then will be forwarded to all the consumers' channels connected to it. The connection of channels to groups is made through the methods group_add() and group_discard() on the channel layer.

To send messages to a group, you can use group_send(). When a message is sent through this method, the channel layers will forward the message to all the consumers' channels connected. Then, the consumers will automatically handle the message by calling the message handler for that specific message type.

It is then the responsibility of the handler to either forward back to the HTTP client the message (by using send()) or do the required computation.

Routing and Middleware

Channels includes various routers, which are used to route requests to specific consumers. Routing can be based on a protocol (HTTP or WebSocket), URLs, or channel names.

In our project we will initially use `ProtocolTypeRouter` because we need to separate WebSocket-handling code from normal Django views. We will use routers together with special middleware provided by Channels.

Middleware here is not the same as middleware in standard Django. This middleware is fully asynchronous. It offers something that in principle is similar to Django middleware: filtering, blocking, and adding additional information to scopes.

In our application we shall be using `AuthMiddlewareStack`, which is a combination of authentication, session, and cookie middleware components. This middleware stack will take care of loading the user session, establishing whether the connection is authenticated, and, if so, loading the user object in the consumer scope.

Chat for Our Customer-Service Operators

Let's start building something concrete with Channels: the internal chat page for customer-service operators. We will start by downloading a must-have, `reconnecting-websocket`, which will deal with unstable connections for us:

```
$ curl -o main/static/js/reconnecting-websocket.min.js \
    https://raw.githubusercontent.com/joewalnes/reconnecting-
    websocket/
    \master/reconnecting-websocket.min.js
```

We will offer to our customer-service representatives a very simple chat page, which you are free to style as you wish. This is the content of main/templates/chat_room.html:

```
{% load static %}
<!DOCTYPE html>

<html>
  <head>
    <meta charset="utf-8"/>
    <title>Chat Room</title>
    <script
      src="{% static "js/reconnecting-websocket.min.js" %}"
      charset="utf-8"></script>
  </head>
  <body>
    <textarea id="chat-log" cols="100" rows="20"></textarea><br/>
    <input id="chat-message-input" type="text" size="100"/><br/>
    <input id="chat-message-submit" type="button" value="Send"/>
  </body>
  <script>
    var roomName = {{ room_name_json }};
    var chatSocket = new ReconnectingWebSocket(
      'ws://' + window.location.host + '/ws/customer-service/' +
      roomName + '/'
    );
    chatSocket.onmessage = function (e) {
      var data = JSON.parse(e.data);
      var username = data['username'];
      if (data['type'] == "chat_join") {
        message = (username + ' joined\n ');
      } else if (data['type'] == "chat_leave") {
        message = (username + ' left\n ');
```

```
  } else {
    message = (username + ': ' + data['message'] + '\n');
  }
  document
    .querySelector('#chat-log')
    .value += message;
};
chatSocket.onclose = function (e) {
  console.error('Chat socket closed unexpectedly');
};
document
  .querySelector('#chat-message-input')
  .focus();
document
  .querySelector('#chat-message-input')
  .onkeyup = function (e) {
    if (e.keyCode === 13) { // enter, return
      document
        .querySelector('#chat-message-submit')
        .click();
    }
  };
document
  .querySelector('#chat-message-submit')
  .onclick = function (e) {
    var messageInputDom = document.querySelector(
      '#chat-message-input'
    );
    var message = messageInputDom.value;
    chatSocket.send(
      JSON.stringify({'type': 'message', 'message': message})
    );
```

```
        messageInputDom.value = ";
      };
    setInterval(function () {
      chatSocket.send(JSON.stringify({'type': 'heartbeat'}));
    }, 10000);
  </script>
</html>
```

This is our customized version of an example included in the Channels repository. It is a simple message visualizer/sender that sends and receives JSON messages over a WebSocket connection.

WebSocket Protocol Format

We are going to define a very simple format for WebSocket messages, server to client:

```
{
    type: "TYPE",
    username: "who is the originator of the event",
    message: "This is the displayed message" (optional)
}
```

Here, TYPE can have the following values:

- chat_join: The username joined the chat.

- chat_leave: The username left the chat.

- chat_message: The username sent a message.

This is enough to define server to client. Now for the client to server:

```
{
    type: "TYPE",
    message: "This is the displayed message" (optional)
}
```

TYPE in this case can have the following values:

- `message`: The username sent a message.

- `heartbeat`: A ping to let the server know that the user is active.

This describes our entire WebSocket protocol. We are going to use this to build both the customer-service part and the mobile interface for our company's customer.

Heartbeat Mechanism in Redis

Our chat is going to need a presence system that is user-centric rather than connection-centric. Any user, whether a customer-service representative or an end user, will become unavailable once all WebSocket connections initiated by them are closed or become inactive for more than 10 seconds. This will ensure a more robust way to handle network problems or browser crashes.

We are going to rely on the expiration feature of Redis. Redis has a very efficient way to set values for specific keys, only temporarily. When setting values along with an expiration time, Redis will automatically remove these in due time. It is the perfect mechanism for us, as it takes care of recycling keys automatically.

The heartbeat signals coming from clients will issue a Redis `SETEX` command on a key named `customer-service_ORDERID_USEREMAIL` setting a dummy value of 1 with an expiration of 10 seconds.

This is enough to support a page to display a dynamic list of who is connected to what customer-service chat. This page will issue a Redis `KEYS` command with the prefix `customer-service_`, and generate the information from the returned result.

To use Redis directly, we need to add a new dependency to our system:

```
$ pipenv install aioredis
```

Given that we are using asynchronous consumers, we will need asynchronous network libraries with it. The `aioredis` library is the asynchronous version of the Redis Python client.

Bootstrap Page

We are going to add a URL to `main/urls.py` and a view to `main/views.py` to serve the `chat_room.html` template presented earlier. Let's start with the view:

```
...

def room(request, order_id):
    return render(
        request,
        "chat_room.html",
        {"room_name_json": str(order_id)},
    )
...

urlpatterns = [
    ...

    path(
        "customer-service/<int:order_id>/",
        views.room,
        name="cs_chat",
    ),
]
```

The chat bootstrap page is now complete, but its JavaScript will not work because the WebSocket endpoint does not exist yet.

WebSocket Consumer

In the consumer is where most of the work happens. We will put the consumer in main/consumers.py:

```python
import aioredis
import logging
from django.shortcuts import get_object_or_404
from channels.db import database_sync_to_async
from channels.generic.websocket import
AsyncJsonWebsocketConsumer
from . import models

logger = logging.getLogger(__name__)

class ChatConsumer(AsyncJsonWebsocketConsumer):
    EMPLOYEE = 2
    CLIENT = 1

    def get_user_type(self, user, order_id):
        order = get_object_or_404(models.Order, pk=order_id)

        if user.is_employee:
            order.last_spoken_to = user
            order.save()
            return ChatConsumer.EMPLOYEE
        elif order.user == user:
            return ChatConsumer.CLIENT
        else:
            return None

    async def connect(self):
        self.order_id = self.scope["url_route"]["kwargs"][
            "order_id"
        ]
```

```python
self.room_group_name = (
    "customer-service_%s" % self.order_id
)
authorized = False
if self.scope["user"].is_anonymous:
    await self.close()

user_type = await database_sync_to_async(
    self.get_user_type
)(self.scope["user"], self.order_id)

if user_type == ChatConsumer.EMPLOYEE:
    logger.info(
        "Opening chat stream for employee %s",
        self.scope["user"],
    )
    authorized = True
elif user_type == ChatConsumer.CLIENT:
    logger.info(
        "Opening chat stream for client %s",
        self.scope["user"],
    )
    authorized = True
else:
    logger.info(
        "Unauthorized connection from %s",
        self.scope["user"],
    )
    await self.close()

if authorized:
    self.r_conn = await aioredis.create_redis(
        "redis://localhost"
    )
```

```python
        await self.channel_layer.group_add(
            self.room_group_name, self.channel_name
        )
        await self.accept()
        await self.channel_layer.group_send(
            self.room_group_name,
            {
                "type": "chat_join",
                "username": self.scope[
                    "user"
                ].get_full_name(),
            },
        )
    async def disconnect(self, close_code):
        if not self.scope["user"].is_anonymous:
            await self.channel_layer.group_send(
                self.room_group_name,
                {
                    "type": "chat_leave",
                    "username": self.scope[
                        "user"
                    ].get_full_name(),
                },
            )
            logger.info(
                "Closing chat stream for user %s",
                self.scope["user"],
            )
            await self.channel_layer.group_discard(
                self.room_group_name, self.channel_name
            )
```

```python
    async def receive_json(self, content):
        typ = content.get("type")
        if typ == "message":
            await self.channel_layer.group_send(
                self.room_group_name,
                {
                    "type": "chat_message",
                    "username": self.scope[
                        "user"
                    ].get_full_name(),
                    "message": content["message"],
                },
            )
        elif typ == "heartbeat":
            await self.r_conn.setex(
                "%s_%s"
                % (
                    self.room_group_name,
                    self.scope["user"].email,
                ),
                10,  # expiration (in 10 seconds)
                "1",  # dummy value
            )

    async def chat_message(self, event):
        await self.send_json(event)

    async def chat_join(self, event):
        await self.send_json(event)

    async def chat_leave(self, event):
        await self.send_json(event)
```

We derived our consumer from AsyncJsonWebsocketConsumer, which takes care of the WebSocket low-level aspects and JSON encoding. We need to implement receive_json(), connect(), and disconnect() for this class to work.

The first thing connect() does is generate a room name, which will be used as a channel name for the group_*() calls. After this, we need to make sure the user has the permission to be here, and this requires accessing the database.

Accessing the database from an asynchronous consumer requires wrapping the code in a synchronous function, and then using the database_sync_to_async() method. This is because Django itself, especially the ORM, is written in a synchronous manner.

The get_user_type() method in the preceding code, besides checking the user type, stores the name of the last employee the customer has spoken to in the order.

The three main methods, receive_json(), connect(), and disconnect(), are using the channel layer methods group_send(), group_add(), and group_discard() to manage the communication and synchronization between all the different consumer instances of one chat room.

In the method receive_json(), we use the group_send() method to handle the two types of messages we listed in the WebSocket protocol format section. Messages of type "message" are forwarded as is to all connected consumers, and messages of type "heartbeat" are used to update the expiration time of the Redis key (or create the key if it does not exist already).

In the methods connect() and disconnect(), we use the group_send() method to generate the join/leave messages of the various users.

It is important to remember that group_send() is not sending the data back to the browser's WebSocket connection. It is only used to relay information between consumers, using the configured channel layer. Each consumer will receive this data through message handlers.

Finally, in ChatConsumer there are three handlers: `chat_message()`, `chat_join()`, and `chat_leave()`. All of them send the message straight back to the browser WebSocket connection, because all the processing will happen in the frontend.

The name of the message handler that will handle the message is derived from the `type` field. If `group_send()` is called with a `message['type']` of `chat_message`, the receiving consumer will handle this with the `chat_message()` handler.

In light of these last few paragraphs, take your time to re-read the code and cross-reference the things I just mentioned about what the code does. Also consider when reading the code that asynchronous programming is not the default style in Python.

This consumer requires a new field in our database schema. Let's quickly add it to our `main/models.py`:

```
...

class Order(models.Model):
    ...

    last_spoken_to = models.ForeignKey(
        User,
        null=True,
        related_name="cs_chats",
        on_delete=models.SET_NULL,
    )

    ...
```

After this addition, do not forget to run the management commands `makemigrations` and `migrate` to have this applied to the database.

After having defined the consumer and all that it requires, we'll continue with defining the route for this consumer.

Routing

At the moment we have an empty {} routing variable inside booktime/routing.py. We need to change this.

We will manage all routes specific to our site in main/routing.py:

```python
from django.urls import path

from . import consumers

websocket_urlpatterns = [
    path(
        "ws/customer-service/<int:order_id>/",
        consumers.ChatConsumer
    )
]
```

We will manage all the general routes in booktime/routing.py:

```python
from channels.auth import AuthMiddlewareStack
from channels.routing import ProtocolTypeRouter, URLRouter
import main.routing

application = ProtocolTypeRouter({
    # (http->django views is added by default)
    'websocket': AuthMiddlewareStack(
        URLRouter(
            main.routing.websocket_urlpatterns
        )
    ),
})
```

This setup will assign a URL path to our WebSocket consumer and relay WebSocket traffic to this new "websocket" route. If we do not add the "http" protocol type to the main router, Channels will add it automatically to support the standard Django views.

You can now test your page by loading the chat URL in your browser. You should be able to load the chat and type some sentences into the chat. If you load the chat in multiple browsers, you will see that what you type in one window will appear in the other.

Automated Testing

As with anything in this book, I will explain how to test the code that was exposed so far. Channels offers constructs called *communicators*. You can think of communicators as the equivalent to the test clients that are included in the Django TestCase.

Communicators, unlike consumers, do not have a synchronous version and an asynchronous version. They only come with an asynchronous API. To use this with the standard Python Unittest framework, which runs synchronously, we would need to use some low-level asyncio API. That is what we are going to do in the tests.

We will put these tests in main/tests/test_consumers.py:

```
import asyncio
from django.contrib.auth.models import Group
from django.test import TestCase
from channels.db import database_sync_to_async
from channels.testing import WebsocketCommunicator
from main import consumers
from main import factories

class TestConsumers(TestCase):
    def test_chat_between_two_users_works(self):
        def init_db():
            user = factories.UserFactory(
                email="john@bestemails.com",
                first_name="John",
                last_name="Smith",
            )
```

```python
    order = factories.OrderFactory(user=user)
    cs_user = factories.UserFactory(
        email="customerservice@booktime.domain",
        first_name="Adam",
        last_name="Ford",
        is_staff=True,
    )
    employees, _ = Group.objects.get_or_create(
        name="Employees"
    )
    cs_user.groups.add(employees)

    return user, order, cs_user

async def test_body():
    user, order, cs_user = await database_sync_to_async(
        init_db
    )()

    communicator = WebsocketCommunicator(
        consumers.ChatConsumer,
        "/ws/customer-service/%d/" % order.id,
    )
    communicator.scope["user"] = user
    communicator.scope["url_route"] = {
        "kwargs": {"order_id": order.id}
    }
    connected, _ = await communicator.connect()
    self.assertTrue(connected)

    cs_communicator = WebsocketCommunicator(
        consumers.ChatConsumer,
        "/ws/customer-service/%d/" % order.id,
    )
```

```python
        cs_communicator.scope["user"] = cs_user
        cs_communicator.scope["url_route"] = {
            "kwargs": {"order_id": order.id}
        }
        connected, _ = await cs_communicator.connect()
        self.assertTrue(connected)

        await communicator.send_json_to(
            {
                "type": "message",
                "message": "hello customer service",
            }
        )

        await asyncio.sleep(1)

        await cs_communicator.send_json_to(
            {"type": "message", "message": "hello user"}
        )

        self.assertEquals(
            await communicator.receive_json_from(),
            {"type": "chat_join", "username": "John Smith"},
        )
        self.assertEquals(
            await communicator.receive_json_from(),
            {"type": "chat_join", "username": "Adam Ford"},
        )
        self.assertEquals(
            await communicator.receive_json_from(),
            {
                "type": "chat_message",
                "username": "John Smith",
```

```
                    "message": "hello customer service",
                },
            )
            self.assertEquals(
                await communicator.receive_json_from(),
                {
                    "type": "chat_message",
                    "username": "Adam Ford",
                    "message": "hello user",
                },
            )

            await communicator.disconnect()
            await cs_communicator.disconnect()

            order.refresh_from_db()
            self.assertEquals(order.last_spoken_to, cs_user)

        loop = asyncio.get_event_loop()
        loop.run_until_complete(test_body())
```

In this test we are testing that the connection works and the messages are relayed as they should be. To test this we use two communicators, one that represents the customer-service operator and the other the final user.

Note that the preceding test function contains two subfunctions, one for the synchronous database initialization and the other with the main asynchronous body. The main asynchronous body is then run by referencing the asyncio loop directly.

The communicators take as arguments the consumer to connect to and a URL. The URL is not strictly necessary but it is used by the URLRouter to inject the routes in the consumer scope. The URLRouter does not support naming routes, therefore the use of reverse() when referencing URLs is not possible.

Our consumer also needs a test for blocking unauthorized users:

```
...

def test_chat_blocks_unauthorized_users(self):
    def init_db():
        user = factories.UserFactory(
            email="john@bestemails.com",
            first_name="John",
            last_name="Smith",
        )
        order = factories.OrderFactory()

        return user, order

    async def test_body():
        user, order = await database_sync_to_async(init_db)()
        communicator = WebsocketCommunicator(
            consumers.ChatConsumer,
            "/ws/customer-service/%d/" % order.id,
        )
        communicator.scope["user"] = user
        communicator.scope["url_route"] = {
            "kwargs": {"order_id": order.id}
        }
        connected, _ = await communicator.connect()
        self.assertFalse(connected)
```

```
loop = asyncio.get_event_loop()
loop.run_until_complete(test_body())
```

Admittedly, the low-level asyncio functions here are simplistic. If you are going to start writing many asynchronous tests, you may want to look at Pytest, which is what Django Channels uses internally for releases.

Chat Dashboard (with Presence)

Our customer-service representatives need to be able to see if there are customers waiting to be served. We need to build a dashboard that dynamically updates with a list of chat rooms and the various people in it.

We are going to adopt a similar approach to the chat we built before, but instead of WebSockets we will use a simpler unidirectional approach. We will use HTTP server-sent events.

Server-sent events (SSE) is essentially an HTTP connection that stays open and keeps receiving chunks of information, as soon as they happen. Every chunk of information is prefixed with the word "data:" and it terminated with two newline characters.

I invite you to read some documentation online about the protocol format[3]. SSE is not as complex as WebSockets. It is quite easy to implement, and all major browsers support it.

Similarly to what we did before, we will use reconnecting-eventsource, which will deal with unstable connections for us:

```
$ curl -o main/static/js/reconnecting-eventsource.js \
    https://cdn.jsdelivr.net/npm/reconnecting-eventsource@1.0.1/\
    dist/ReconnectingEventSource.js
```

---

[3]https://en.wikipedia.org/wiki/Server-sent_events

In the same spirit of the chat page, this is our very simple dashboard, stored in main/templates/customer_service.html:

```
{% load static %}
<!DOCTYPE html>
<html>
  <head>
    <meta charset="utf-8"/>
    <title>Chat Rooms</title>
    <script
      src="{% static "js/reconnecting-eventsource.js" %}"
      charset="utf-8"></script>
  </head>
  <body>
    <h1>Customer chats</h1>
    <div id="notification-area"></div>
    <script>
      var source = new ReconnectingEventSource('/customer-
      service/notify/');
      source.addEventListener('message', function (e) {
        document
          .getElementById("notification-area")
          .innerHTML = "";
        var data = JSON.parse(e.data);
        var html;
        for (var i = 0; i < data.length; i++) {
          html = '<div><a href="' + data[i]['link'] + '">' +
                  data[i]['text'] + '</a></div>';
          document
            .getElementById("notification-area")
            .innerHTML += html;
        }
```

```
    }, false);
  </script>
 </body>
</html>
```

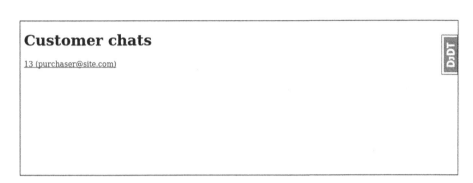

Figure 8-1. *Customer-service dashboard*

We are again going to add a URL to main/urls.py to serve the template above:

```
...

urlpatterns = [
    ...

    path(
        "customer-service/",
        TemplateView.as_view(
            template_name="customer_service.html"
        ),
        name="cs_main",
    ),
]
```

HTTP Server-Sent Events Consumer

The above page will receive dynamic data from a new consumer in main/
consumers.py:

...

```python
import asyncio
import json
from django.urls import reverse
from channels.exceptions import StopConsumer
from channels.generic.http import AsyncHttpConsumer
```

...

```python
class ChatNotifyConsumer(AsyncHttpConsumer):
    def is_employee_func(self, user):
        return not user.is_anonymous and user.is_employee

    async def handle(self, body):
        is_employee = await database_sync_to_async(
            self.is_employee_func
        )(self.scope["user"])

        if is_employee:
            logger.info(

                "Opening notify stream for user %s and params %s",
                self.scope.get("user"),
                self.scope.get("query_string"),
            )
            await self.send_headers(
                headers=[
                    ("Cache-Control", "no-cache"),
                    ("Content-Type", "text/event-stream"),
                    ("Transfer-Encoding", "chunked"),
```

```
            ]
        )
        self.is_streaming = True
        self.no_poll = (
            self.scope.get("query_string") == "nopoll"
        )
        asyncio.get_event_loop().create_task(self.stream())
    else:
        logger.info(
            "Unauthorized notify stream for user %s and
            params %s",
            self.scope.get("user"),
            self.scope.get("query_string"),
        )
        raise StopConsumer("Unauthorized")

async def stream(self):
    r_conn = await aioredis.create_redis("redis://localhost")
    while self.is_streaming:
        active_chats = await r_conn.keys(
            "customer-service_*"
        )

        presences = {}
        for i in active_chats:
            _, order_id, user_email = i.decode("utf8").split(
                "_"
            )
            if order_id in presences:
                presences[order_id].append(user_email)
            else:
                presences[order_id] = [user_email]
        data = []
        for order_id, emails in presences.items():
```

```python
            data.append(
                {
                    "link": reverse(
                        "cs_chat",
                        kwargs={"order_id": order_id}
                    ),
                    "text": "%s (%s)"
                    % (order_id, ", ".join(emails)),
                }
            )

        payload = "data: %s\n\n" % json.dumps(data)
        logger.info(
            "Broadcasting presence info to user %s",
            self.scope["user"],
        )
        if self.no_poll:
            await self.send_body(payload.encode("utf-8"))
            self.is_streaming = False
        else:
            await self.send_body(
                payload.encode("utf-8"),
                more_body=self.is_streaming,
            )
            await asyncio.sleep(5)

async def disconnect(self):
    logger.info(
        "Closing notify stream for user %s",
        self.scope.get("user"),
    )
    self.is_streaming = False
```

This consumer implements the `AsyncHttpConsumer` interface with the `handle()` and `disconnect()` methods. Due to the streaming nature of the endpoint we are trying to build, we need to keep the connection open. We will be calling the `send_headers()` method to start the HTTP response, and we will call `send_body()`, with a `more_body` argument set to `True`, in a separate asynchronous task that stays active.

The `stream()` method activation is added to the event loop, and will stay active until the `disconnect()` method is called (disconnection initiated by the client). When this method is called, it will set an `is_streaming` flag to `False`, which will cause the `stream()` inner loop, running in a different asyncio task, to exit.

The `stream()` method will periodically read from Redis the keys that are not expired, and send them back to the client. If, at connection time, the `nopoll` flag is passed in, it will exit the loop without waiting for a client disconnection.

Streaming only happens for authorized users. For unauthorized users, the `handle()` method will raise a `StopConsumer` exception, which will stop the consumer and close the current connection with the client.

Routing

The SSE consumer is the first HTTP consumer that we have created, and it will require some additional configuration to work. We will define all non-websocket HTTP routes in `main/routing.py`:

```python
from channels.auth import import AuthMiddlewareStack

...

http_urlpatterns = [
    path(
        "customer-service/notify/",
        AuthMiddlewareStack(
```

```
            consumers.ChatNotifyConsumer
        )
    )
]
```

And we will override the default HTTP route in booktime/routing.py with a custom one:

```
from django.urls import re_path
from channels.auth import AuthMiddlewareStack
from channels.routing import ProtocolTypeRouter, URLRouter
from channels.http import AsgiHandler
import main.routing

application = ProtocolTypeRouter(
    {
        "websocket": AuthMiddlewareStack(
            URLRouter(main.routing.websocket_urlpatterns)
        ),
        "http": URLRouter(
            main.routing.http_urlpatterns
            + [re_path(r"", AsgiHandler)]
        ),
    }
)
```

The HTTP route now is associated with a URLRouter that includes our http_urlpatterns defined in main/routing.py and, for all other routes, falls back to AsgiHandler, which in turn forwards to the standard Django handlers.

AsgiHandler is a translator from the Asynchronous Server Gateway Interface (ASGI) protocol to the Web Server Gateway Interface (WSGI) protocol, which is an internal protocol used by core Django.

Automated Testing

Testing for the SSE consumer will use a different type of communicator, HttpCommunicator. We will use that after establishing a WebSocket connection and after the connection timed out, and we will check whether the right events are returned from the SSE request. The timeout is to give time to Redis to remove the entries from memory.

```python
...
import json
from channels.testing import HttpCommunicator

class TestConsumers(TestCase):
    ...

    def test_chat_presence_works(self):
        def init_db():
            user = factories.UserFactory(
                email="user@site.com",
                first_name="John",
                last_name="Smith",
            )
            order = factories.OrderFactory(user=user)
            cs_user = factories.UserFactory(
                email="customerservice@booktime.domain",
                first_name="Adam",
                last_name="Ford",
                is_staff=True,
            )
            employees, _ = Group.objects.get_or_create(
                name="Employees"
            )
```

```
        cs_user.groups.add(employees)

        return user, order, cs_user

    async def test_body():
        user, order, notify_user = await database_sync_to_async(
            init_db
        )()

        communicator = WebsocketCommunicator(
            consumers.ChatConsumer,
            "/ws/customer-service/%d/" % order.id,
        )
        communicator.scope["user"] = user
        communicator.scope["url_route"] = {
            "kwargs": {"order_id": order.id}
        }
        connected, _ = await communicator.connect()
        self.assertTrue(connected)

        await communicator.send_json_to(
            {"type": "heartbeat"}
        )
        await communicator.disconnect()

        communicator = HttpCommunicator(
            consumers.ChatNotifyConsumer,
            "GET",
            "/customer-service/notify/",
        )
        communicator.scope["user"] = notify_user
        communicator.scope["query_string"] = "nopoll"

        response = await communicator.get_response()
        self.assertTrue(
```

```python
            response["body"].startswith(b"data: ")
        )
        payload = response["body"][6:]
        data = json.loads(payload.decode("utf8"))
        self.assertEquals(
            data,
            [
                {
                    "link": "/customer-service/%d/" % order.id,
                    "text": "%d (user@site.com)" % order.id,
                }
            ],
            "expecting someone in the room but no one found",
        )

        await asyncio.sleep(10)

        communicator = HttpCommunicator(
            consumers.ChatNotifyConsumer,
            "GET",
            "/customer-service/notify/",
        )
        communicator.scope["user"] = notify_user
        communicator.scope["query_string"] = "nopoll"
        response = await communicator.get_response()
        self.assertTrue(
            response["body"].startswith(b"data: ")
        )
        payload = response["body"][6:]
        data = json.loads(payload.decode("utf8"))
        self.assertEquals(
            data,
            [],
```

```
                "expecting no one in the room but someone found",
        )

    loop = asyncio.get_event_loop()
    loop.run_until_complete(test_body())
```

Mobile APIs

We will stop using Django Channels for the rest of this chapter. The rest of the APIs that we are planning to use from our mobile app will be built using Django REST Framework (DRF). We will build an authentication endpoint and an API for order retrieval.

Authentication

For our mobile app, we will use a token-based authentication. This is best practice for non-web apps, as it gives us a bit more security in case the client device is compromised. No credentials are stored on the device, besides the token, which can be easily invalidated if needs to be.

To do so, we will need to enable this in Django Rest Framework:

```
INSTALLED_APPS = [
    ...
    "rest_framework",
    "rest_framework.authtoken",
    ...
]

REST_FRAMEWORK = {
    "DEFAULT_AUTHENTICATION_CLASSES": (
        "rest_framework.authentication.SessionAuthentication",
        "rest_framework.authentication.TokenAuthentication",
        "rest_framework.authentication.BasicAuthentication",
```

```
    ),
    ...
}
```

This will add an extra model to our system. The previous step will require running the migrate command. After this, we will automatically generate a token for every new user with a new signal in main/signals.py:

```python
from django.conf import settings
from rest_framework.authtoken.models import Token

...

@receiver(post_save, sender=settings.AUTH_USER_MODEL)
def create_auth_token(
    sender, instance=None, created=False, **kwargs
):
    if created:
        Token.objects.create(user=instance)
```

Every new user, from now on, can access authenticated DRF endpoints with tokens, besides the already-existing methods. Next we need to create the login endpoint, which we can add at the bottom of our main/urls.py:

```python
from rest_framework.authtoken import views as authtoken_views

...

urlpatterns = [
    ...
    path(
        "mobile-api/auth/",
        authtoken_views.obtain_auth_token,
        name="mobile_token",
    ),
]
```

That is it. We have a working mobile authentication endpoint. To complete this, there is the associated test (main/tests/test_endpoints.py):

```
from django.urls import reverse
from rest_framework.test import APITestCase
from main import models

class TestEndpoints(APITestCase):

    def test_mobile_login_works(self):
        user = models.User.objects.create_user(
            "user1", "abcabcabc"
        )
        response = self.client.post(
            reverse("mobile_token"),
            {"username": "user1", "password": "abcabcabc"},
        )
        jsonresp = response.json()
        self.assertIn("token", jsonresp)
```

Retrieving Orders

Our mobile app will need a way to retrieve the orders of the current authenticated user. We will add a new endpoint to our main/endpoints.py:

```
from rest_framework.decorators import (
    api_view,
    permission_classes,
)
from rest_framework.permissions import IsAuthenticated
from rest_framework.response import Response

...
```

```
@api_view()
@permission_classes((IsAuthenticated,))
def my_orders(request):
    user = request.user
    orders = models.Order.objects.filter(user=user).order_by(
        "-date_added"
    )
    data = []
    for order in orders:
        data.append(
            {
                "id": order.id,
                "image": order.mobile_thumb_url,
                "summary": order.summary,
                "price": order.total_price,
            }
        )
    return Response(data)
```

This is a Django Rest Framework API defined as a function. DRF allows us to define, just as Django, endpoints as classes or functions. Because this is a custom read-only endpoint, it is easier to define it as a function rather than as a class.

This view uses some new properties of the Order model:

```
class Order(models.Model):
    ...

    @property
    def mobile_thumb_url(self):
        products = [i.product for i in self.lines.all()]
        if products:
            img = products[0].productimage_set.first()
```

```python
        if img:
            return img.thumbnail.url

    @property
    def summary(self):
        product_counts = self.lines.values(
            "product__name"
        ).annotate(c=Count("product__name"))
        pieces = []
        for pc in product_counts:
            pieces.append(
                "%s x %s" % (pc["c"], pc["product__name"])
            )
        return ", ".join(pieces)

    @property
    def total_price(self):
        res = self.lines.aggregate(
            total_price=Sum("product__price")
        )
        return res["total_price"]
```

Finally, the view needs an URL in main/urls.py:

```python
urlpatterns = [
    ...
    path(
        "mobile-api/my-orders/",
        endpoints.my_orders,
        name="mobile_my_orders",
    ),
]
```

This is enough for this view to work. We are going to add the specific test to main/test/test_endpoints.py, along with the previous one:

```
...

from rest_framework import status
from rest_framework.authtoken.models import Token
from main import factories

class TestEndpoints(APITestCase):
    ...

    def test_mobile_flow(self):
        user = factories.UserFactory(email="mobileuser@site.com")
        token = Token.objects.get(user=user)
        self.client.credentials(
            HTTP_AUTHORIZATION="Token " + token.key
        )

        orders = factories.OrderFactory.create_batch(
            2, user=user
        )
        a = factories.ProductFactory(
            name="The book of A", active=True, price=12.00
        )
        b = factories.ProductFactory(
            name="The B Book", active=True, price=14.00
        )
        factories.OrderLineFactory.create_batch(
            2, order=orders[0], product=a
        )
        factories.OrderLineFactory.create_batch(
            2, order=orders[1], product=b
        )
```

```python
        response = self.client.get(reverse("mobile_my_orders"))
        self.assertEqual(
            response.status_code, status.HTTP_200_OK
        )

        expected = [
            {
                "id": orders[1].id,
                "image": None,
                "price": 28.0,
                "summary": "2 x The B Book",
            },
            {
                "id": orders[0].id,
                "image": None,
                "price": 24.0,
                "summary": "2 x The book of A",
            },
        ]
        self.assertEqual(response.json(), expected)
```

Order Shipment Tracking

BookTime relies on an external company to ship the items bought online.
This company has its own tracking system, and we want to use it to deliver
this extra information back to our mobile app users.

We are going to add a custom endpoint to get the shipment status
of an order. Let's pretend the delivery company has supplied BookTime
with access to an HTTP API that we can use to get real-time information
about the status of the shipment, and that is where this information will
come from.

The API of the delivery company will not be used directly by the mobile app because we may want to add other companies in the future, without having to change the mobile app code.

This is what our system will do:

- Receive mobile app requests for shipment information

- Issue API requests to the third-party company

- Forward shipment information back to the mobile app

To put it succinctly, it will look like a reverse-proxy system.

This is a good use case for Channels given its asynchronous nature. Doing this in an asynchronous manner will make our solution scale to a higher number of simultaneous requests.

If we did this in the standard synchronous way, we would potentially block all threads on waiting for the remote system to return us shipment statuses. If that were to occur, our API would become unresponsive. We need to avoid this.

By using non-blocking, asynchronous code, our APIs will not become unresponsive, even if the third-party system that we are interfacing with goes offline.

To simulate this hypothetical API, we will use Pastebin. Go to `https://pastebin.com`, click the New Paste button, type **In Transit** in the text box, and click Create New Paste. Once you have done so (see Figure 8-2), click the "raw" label to get its raw URL. Copy the URL. We will use this to simulate our API.

Figure 8-2. *Click "raw" to copy the raw Pastebin URL for the API simulation*

Now that we have our, admittedly simple, test API, we can write a client for it. This API will need to be consumed with an asynchronous network library. For the same reasons we used `aioredis` in the previous sections, we will use an HTTP client library called `aiohttp`, which needs to be installed:

```
$ pipenv install aiohttp
```

Having done so, we are ready to write our consumer. We will add this to `main/consumers.py` (replace put_url_here with your Pastebin URL):

```python
import aiohttp
...

...

class OrderTrackerConsumer(AsyncHttpConsumer):
    def verify_user(self, user, order_id):
        order = get_object_or_404(models.Order, pk=order_id)
        return order.user == user
```

```python
async def query_remote_server(self, order_id):
    async with aiohttp.ClientSession() as session:
        async with session.get(
            "http://pastebin.com/put_url_here"
        ) as resp:
            return await resp.read()

async def handle(self, body):
    self.order_id = self.scope["url_route"]["kwargs"][
        "order_id"
    ]
    is_authorized = await database_sync_to_async(
        self.verify_user
    )(self.scope["user"], self.order_id)

    if is_authorized:
        logger.info(
            "Order tracking request for user %s and "
            "order %s",
            self.scope.get("user"),
            self.order_id
        )
        payload = await self.query_remote_server(self.order_id)
        logger.info(
            "Order tracking response %s for user %s and "
            "order %s",
            payload,
            self.scope.get("user"),
            self.order_id
        )
        await self.send_response(200, payload)
    else:
        raise StopConsumer("unauthorized")
```

This consumer is fully asynchronous, with the exception of database queries. It is accepting a request in with an order ID specified in the URL, then forwarding back to the client the result of query_remote_server().

query_remote_server() is using the library that we just installed to issue a GET request to the remote Pastebin we just created. The result of this will simply be passed back to the client.

This consumer will need a URL, which needs to be added to main/routing.py:

```
...

http_urlpatterns = [
    ...
    path(
        "mobile-api/my-orders/<int:order_id>/tracker/",
        AuthMiddlewareStack(consumers.OrderTrackerConsumer),
    )
]
```

You should now be able to test this. Please make sure you have at least one order from your current user in the system. If you navigate to the preceding URL with the correct order ID, you should be seeing the content of your Pastebin in your browser.

The test for this will be inside main/tests/test_consumers.py:

```
from unittest.mock import patch, MagicMock
...

class TestConsumers(TestCase):
    ...

    def test_order_tracker_works(self):
        def init_db():
            user = factories.UserFactory(
                email="mobiletracker@site.com"
            )
```

```python
    order = factories.OrderFactory(user=user)
    return user, order

async def test_body():
    user, order = await database_sync_to_async(
        init_db
    )()

    awaitable_requestor = asyncio.coroutine(
        MagicMock(return_value=b"SHIPPED")
    )

    with patch.object(
        consumers.OrderTrackerConsumer, "query_remote_
        server"
    ) as mock_requestor:
        mock_requestor.side_effect = awaitable_requestor
        communicator = HttpCommunicator(
            consumers.OrderTrackerConsumer,
            "GET",
            "/mobile-api/my-orders/%d/tracker/" % order.id,
        )
        communicator.scope["user"] = user
        communicator.scope["url_route"] = {
            "kwargs": {"order_id": order.id}
        }
        response = await communicator.get_response()
        data = response["body"].decode("utf8")

        mock_requestor.assert_called_once()
        self.assertEquals(
```

```
                    data,
                    "SHIPPED"
            )

        loop = asyncio.get_event_loop()
        loop.run_until_complete(test_body())
```

In the preceding test, we are patching the whole method query_remote_server() with an asynchronous function that returns the string "SHIPPED". In this way, we are excluding the HTTP client from our tests, which makes it faster to run and a good compromise for us, given its simplicity.

Bringing It All Together

There are still a few changes to apply for our mobile integration to go as smoothly as possible. First of all, our token-based authentication, which works only on DRF views at the moment, needs to include WebSocket and async HTTP routes.

We need a custom AuthMiddlewareStack, which we will place in a new file booktime/auth.py (same folder of settings.py), which adds token authentication on top of all the other ways of authenticating:

```
from urllib.parse import parse_qs
from channels.auth import AuthMiddlewareStack
from rest_framework.authtoken.models import Token

class TokenGetAuthMiddleware:
    def __init__ (self, inner):
        self.inner = inner

    def __call__ (self, scope):
        params = parse_qs(scope["query_string"])
        if b"token" in params:
            try:
```

```
                token_key = params[b"token"][0].decode()
                token = Token.objects.get(key=token_key)
                scope["user"] = token.user
            except Token.DoesNotExist:
                pass
        return self.inner(scope)

TokenGetAuthMiddlewareStack = lambda inner:
TokenGetAuthMiddleware(
    AuthMiddlewareStack(inner)
)
```

We will use this new middleware in our routing files. These are the changes to booktime/routing.py:

```
from .auth import TokenGetAuthMiddlewareStack

...

application = ProtocolTypeRouter(
    {
        "websocket": TokenGetAuthMiddlewareStack(
            URLRouter(main.routing.websocket_urlpatterns)
        ),
        ...
    }
)
```

These are the changes to main/routing.py:

```
from booktime.auth import TokenGetAuthMiddlewareStack

...

http_urlpatterns = [
    ...
```

```
path(
    "mobile-api/my-orders/<int:order_id>/tracker/",
    TokenGetAuthMiddlewareStack(consumers.
    OrderTrackerConsumer),
)
]
```

The last thing we need during development of the mobile app, or any mobile app, is to make sure we can serve requests coming from the network, instead of just our local browser.

To change this, we will add an extra setting to our booktime/settings.py:

```
ALLOWED_HOSTS = ['*']
```

This causes Django to allow requests with any "Host" header. Please make sure this setting is *not* enabled on the production environment (just like DEBUG).

From now on we will launch the dev server with the option to listen to all available network interfaces, not just the local interface. We can do so with the following command:

```
$ ./manage.py runserver 0.0.0.0:8000
Performing system checks...

System check identified no issues (0 silenced).
August 22, 2018 - 15:28:01
Django version 2.1, using settings 'booktime.settings'
Starting ASGI/Channels version 2.1.2 development server at
http://0.0.0.0:8000/
Quit the server with CONTROL-C.
2018-08-22 15:28:01,644 - INFO - server - HTTP/2 support not
                                  enabled (install the
                                  http2 and tls Twisted
                                  extras)
```

```
2018-08-22 15:28:01,644 - INFO - server - Configuring endpoint
                                          tcp:port=8000:
                                          interface=0.0.0.0
2018-08-22 15:28:01,645 - INFO - server - Listening on TCP
                                          address 0.0.0.0:8000
```

This will allow our app (running on a mobile device) to connect to our server through the local network.

Summary

The goal of this chapter was to use Channels, an extension of Django for asynchronous programming, to build a chat backend. Channels introduces many new concepts, consumers, routers, channel layers, and groups, all of which have been explained in this chapter.

In practical terms, we built a chat backend and its dashboard for our company's customer-service representatives. We also had to reach out to Redis directly for some of the more advanced features that we required that Channels does not offer.

In the last sections, we also talked about the necessary infrastructure for a mobile app, which I will present in the next chapter.

CHAPTER 9

Mobile Customer-Service App

In this chapter we are going to build a bare-bones mobile app using React Native. The app we build will be used by customers to retrieve their orders and to chat with customer-service representatives about them.

Both order visualization and chat will use the APIs that we built in Chapter 8. We are going to use this mobile app to explore how can we support API consumers that have different requirements from static HTML pages.

Why React Native

In this book I do not wish to take sides about any technology other than Django. I do not wish to present a polished native app, because that would require more setup work and would move the focus away from integrating with Django. This chapter will be about having just enough of an app to build upon.

Many concepts that will be presented in this chapter can be applied to other technology stacks. There are a number of frameworks to build hybrid apps. Given that you were already introduced to React in the previous chapters, you will not struggle to understand React Native.

© Federico Marani 2019
F. Marani, *Practical Django 2 and Channels 2*,
https://doi.org/10.1007/978-1-4842-4099-1_9

React Native reuses many concepts of React, but it uses native components instead of HTML tags. React Native runs on mobile, a device that is not what we use to develop and run our Django application. It is important to remember this because it will impact the development workflow.

We are going to use React Native in the same way that we used Bootstrap. We will not delve too much into it, but just enough to consume the work we have done in Chapter 8 and demonstrate our use case.

Setting Up React Native

React Native is written in JavaScript. To run the following command, you need a recent version of Node at least 8.x), one that supplies the npx command. We will do the initial setup with `create-react-native-app`:

```
$ npx create-react-native-app booktime_mobile
...
Inside that directory, you can run several commands:

  yarn start
    Starts the development server so you can open your app in
    the Expo app on your phone.

  yarn run ios
    (Mac only, requires Xcode)
    Starts the development server and loads your app in an iOS
    simulator.

  yarn run android
    (Requires Android build tools)
    Starts the development server and loads your app on a
    connected Android device or emulator.
```

```
yarn test
  Starts the test runner.

yarn run eject
  Removes this tool and copies build dependencies,
  configuration files and scripts into the app directory.
  If you do this, you can't go back!
```

We suggest that you begin by typing:

```
cd booktime_mobile
yarn start
```

Happy hacking!

```
$ cd booktime_mobile
```

In the booktime_mobile folder just created, all React Native commands can be launched with yarn. Before launching the suggested command yarn start, be warned that you may have to tweak some system parameters. If that is the case, you will see a warning on the screen.

Components Hierarchy

Before jumping into coding of any complex frontend, you should have an idea of how to divide the various screens of your app into components. Components are reusable pieces of your user interface. They may be the entire screen or only a portion of it.

Each component in React Native is just like a React component: it can have state and props. Props are read-only and passed from the parent, while state is managed internally.

In our case, our simple app will have

- A login screen, with a username/password form. This will be a component on its own.

- An order selection and chat screen. This screen will be divided into two main components.

To help us identify where each component is on the display, we can use some visual cues like setting border colors, as shown in Figures 9-1 and 9-2. Generally, developing for mobile is not as immediate as it is when developing in a browser. You will need some time to get used to it.

Figure 9-1. Mobile login page

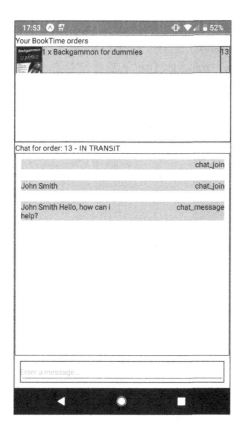

Figure 9-2. *Mobile main page*

API Client Library

Before building anything that is specific to React Native, we will create a JavaScript class that will take care of all communication between the client and server. We are doing so because, by mocking it, it will be easier to test our components.

We will place all code, apart from the initial App.js, inside a src folder. This will be inside src/backend.js (substitute the relevant URLs for the strings 'CHANGETHIS'):

```javascript
export default class BackendApi {
  constructor (envName) {
    if (envName == 'production') {
      this.hostName = 'CHANGETHIS'
    } else {
      this.hostName = 'CHANGETHIS'
    }
    this.baseHttpApi = 'http://' + this.hostName + '/mobile-api'
  }

  auth (username, password) {
    return fetch(this.baseHttpApi + `/auth/`, {
      method: 'POST',
      headers: {
        Accept: 'application/json',
        'Content-Type': 'application/json'
      },
      body: JSON.stringify({
        username: username,
        password: password
      })
    })
      .then(response => response.json())
      .catch(error => {
        console.error(error)
      })
      .then(response => {
        if (response.token) {
          this.loggedInToken = response.token
          return true
        }
```

```
      return false
    })
}

fetchOrders () {
  return fetch(this.baseHttpApi + `/my-orders/`, {
    method: 'GET',
    headers: {
      Accept: 'application/json',
      'Content-Type': 'application/json',
      Authorization: 'Token ' + this.loggedInToken
    }
  })
    .then(response => response.json())
    .catch(error => {
      console.error(error)
    })
}

fetchShipmentStatus (id) {
  let url = this.baseHttpApi + `/my-orders/${id}/tracker` +
    `/?token=` + this.loggedInToken
  return fetch(url, {
    method: 'GET',
    headers: {
      Authorization: 'Token ' + this.loggedInToken
    }
  })
    .then(response=> response.text())
    .catch(error=> {
      console.error(error)
    })
}
```

```
openMessagesStream (id, onMessageCb) {
  var ws_url =
    `ws://` +
    this.hostName +
    `/ws/customer-service/` +
    Id +
    `/?token=` +
    this.loggedInToken

  this.ws = new WebSocket(ws_url)
  this.ws.onmessage = function (event) {
    var data = JSON.parse(event.data)
    onMessageCb(data)
  }
  this.ws.onerror = function (error) {
    console.error('WebSocket error: ', error)
  }
  this.ws.onopen = function () {
    this.heartbeatTimer = setInterval(this.sendHeartbeat.
    bind(this), 10000)
  }.bind(this)
}

closeMessagesStream () {
  clearInterval(this.heartbeatTimer)
  if (this.ws) {
    this.ws.close()
  }
}

sendMessage (message) {
  this.ws.send(
    JSON.stringify({
```

```
      type: 'message',
      message: message
    })
  )
}

sendHeartbeat () {
  this.ws.send(
    JSON.stringify({
      type: 'heartbeat'
    })
  )
}

createAbsUrl (relative_uri) {
  return 'http://' + this.hostName + relative_uri
}
}
```

This basic JavaScript class will take care of all HTTP requests. All requests will be directed to an environment specified when instantiating the class.

The auth() method in the preceding code uses the authentication endpoint we created in the previous chapter and, if successful, stores the returned token inside the BackendApi instance. That token will be used later in every request.

There are several methods for the chat component: openMessagesStream(), closeMessagesStream(), and sendMessage(). The sendHeartbeat() method is used internally to signal the presence of this client to the server.

LoginView

We are going to put all React components in `src/components/`. This is our first component, `LoginView.js`:

```
import React, { Component } from 'react'
import {
  StyleSheet,
  Text,
  View,
  TouchableHighlight,
  TextInput
} from 'react-native'

const styles = StyleSheet.create({
  container: {
    flex: 1,
    justifyContent: 'center',
    alignItems: 'center'
  },

  welcome: {
    fontSize: 20,
    textAlign: 'center',
    margin:10
  },
  instructions: {
    textAlign: 'center',
    color: '#333333',
    marginBottom: 5
  },
  input: {
    height: 40,
```

```
    fontSize: 18,
    width: 150
  },
  button: {
    padding: 10
  }
})
export default class LoginView extends Component {
  constructor (props) {
    super(props)
    this.state = {
      username: '',
      password: ''
    }
    this.handleSubmitLogin = this.handleSubmitLogin.bind(this)
  }

  handleSubmitLogin () {
    if (this.state.username && this.state.password) {
      return this .props.backendApi
        .auth(this.state.username, this.state.password)
        .then(loggedIn => {
          if (loggedIn) {
            this.props.setLoggedIn()
          } else {
            this.setState({
              username: '',
              password: ''
            })
            alert('Login unsuccessful')
          }
        })
```

```
      }
    }
  render () {
    return (
      <View style={styles.container}>
        <Text style={styles.welcome}>BookTime</Text>
        <Text style={styles.instructions}>Please login to see
        your orders</Text>
        <TextInput
          style={styles.input}
          placeholder="Username"
          value={this.state.username}
          onChangeText={text => {
            this.setState({ username: text })
          }}
        />
        <TextInput
          style={styles.input}
          placeholder="Password"
          value={this.state.password}
          secureTextEntry={true}
          onChangeText={text => {
            this.setState({ password: text })
          }}
        />
        <TouchableHighlight
          style={styles.button}
          onPress={this.handleSubmitLogin}
        >
          <Text>Submit</Text>
        </TouchableHighlight>
```

```
        </View>
      )
    }
  }
}
```

React Native is using flexbox as a layout engine, which is a feature that comes from CSS. This is used in the styles variable in the preceding code. Our styles are mostly doing positioning and sizing of the elements, rather than visual styling. It is the bare minimum for us to get going.

In the render() method we build our rendering tree, and that is where we use the React Native built-in components. View is a wrapper for a section of the screen and does not bring additional functionality—it is purely a wrapper around other components.

Text is a label component, used to print text. TextInput, which is the equivalent of <input type="text"> in HTML, is used to input text. TouchableHighlight is a button with touch feedback.

We will include a test for this view. It is pretty basic and it avoids testing event triggering by calling the internal functions directly. As long as we trust the JSX[1] we wrote, it is an acceptable compromise for our purpose.

We will place the following code in src/components/LoginView.test.js:

```
import React from 'react'
import LoginView from './LoginView'

import renderer from 'react-test-renderer'

it('renders without crashing', () => {
  const rendered = renderer.create(<LoginView />)
  expect(rendered).toBeTruthy()
})
```

---

[1]https://reactjs.org/docs/introducing-jsx.html

```
it('logins successfully when backend returns true', () => {
  const setLoggedIn = jest.fn()
  const backendApi = {
    auth: jest.fn(() => new Promise((resolve, reject) => resolve
    (true)))
  }
  const rendered = renderer.create(
    <LoginView backendApi={backendApi} setLoggedIn={setLoggedIn} />
  )
  rendered.root.instance.state.username = 'a'
  rendered.root.instance.state.password = 'b'
  rendered.root.instance
    .handleSubmitLogin()
    .then(() => expect(setLoggedIn.mock.calls.length).toBe(1))
  expect(backendApi.auth.mock.calls.length).toBe(1)
  expect(backendApi.auth.mock.calls[0][0]).toBe('a')
  expect(backendApi.auth.mock.calls[0][1]).toBe('b')
})

it('login fails when backend returns false', () => {
  const setLoggedIn = jest.fn()
  const backendApi = {
    auth: jest.fn(() => new Promise((resolve, reject) => resolve
    (false)))
  }
  const rendered = renderer.create(
    <LoginView backendApi={backendApi} setLoggedIn={setLoggedIn} />
  )
  rendered.root.instance.state.username = 'a'
  rendered.root.instance.state.password = 'b'
  rendered.root.instance
    .handleSubmitLogin()
```

```
  .then(() => expect(setLoggedIn.mock.calls.length).toBe(0))
  expect(backendApi.auth.mock.calls.length).toBe(1)
  expect(backendApi.auth.mock.calls[0][0]).toBe('a')
  expect(backendApi.auth.mock.calls[0][1]).toBe('b')
})

it('login fails when backend fails', () => {
  const setLoggedIn = jest.fn()
  const backendApi = {
    auth: jest.fn(() => new Promise((resolve, reject) => reject()))
  }
  const rendered = renderer.create(
    <LoginView backendApi={backendApi} setLoggedIn={setLoggedIn} />
  )
  rendered.root.instance.state.username = 'a'
  rendered.root.instance.state.password = 'b'
  rendered.root.instance
    .handleSubmitLogin()
    .then(() => expect(setLoggedIn.mock.calls.length).toBe(0))
  expect(backendApi.auth.mock.calls.length).toBe(1)
  expect(backendApi.auth.mock.calls[0][0]).toBe('a')
  expect(backendApi.auth.mock.calls[0][1]).toBe('b')
})
```

I will explain how to run this test later in the chapter.

ChatView

We are going to dedicate this component to all chat interactions, which will be in a section of the main screen (src/components/ChatView.js):

```
import React from 'react'
import {StyleSheet, Text, TextInput, ScrollView, View } from
'react-native'
```

```
const styles = StyleSheet.create({
  chatContainer: {
    borderColor: 'orange',
    borderWidth: 1,
    flex: 1
  },
  chatMessages: {
    borderColor: 'purple',
    borderWidth: 1,
    flex: 1
  },
  chatInput: {
    height: 40,
    margin: 10,
    borderWidth: 1
  },
  chatMessage: {
    backgroundColor: 'lightgrey',
    margin: 10,
    flex: 1,
    flexDirection: 'row',
    alignSelf: 'stretch'
  },
  chatMessageText: {
    flex: 1
  },
  chatMessageType: {
    flex: 1,
    textAlign: 'right'
  }
})
```

```
export default class ChatView extends React.Component {
  constructor (props) {
    super(props)
    this.state = {
      messages: [],
      shipmentStatus: "n/a"
    }
    this.handleSubmit = this.handleSubmit.bind(this)
  }

  componentDidUpdate (prevProps) {
    if (prevProps.orderCurrentId !== this.props.orderCurrentId) {
      this.props.backendApi.closeMessagesStream()
      this.state = {
        messages: []
      }
      this.props.backendApi
        .fetchShipmentStatus(this.props.orderCurrentId)
        .then(result => {
            this.setState({shipmentStatus: result})
        })
      this.props.backendApi.openMessagesStream(
        this.props.orderCurrentId,
        message => {
          this.setState({
            messages: this.state.messages.concat([message])
          })
        }
      )
    }
  }
}
```

```
handleSubmit(event) {
  var text = event.nativeEvent.text
  this.props.backendApi.sendMessage(text)
  this.refs.textInput.setNativeProps({text: '' })
}

render() {
  if (this.props.orderCurrentId) {
    return (
      <View style={styles.chatContainer}>
        <Text>Chat for order: {this.props.orderCurrentId}
        - { this.state.shipmentStatus}</Text>
        <ScrollView
          style={styles.chatMessages}
          showsVerticalScrollIndicator={true}
          ref={ref => (this.scrollView = ref)}
          onContentSizeChange={(contentWidth, contentHeight) => {
            this.scrollView.scrollToEnd({ animated: true })
          }}
        >
          {this.state.messages.map((m, index) => {
          return (
            <View key={index} style={styles.chatMessage}>
              <Text style={styles.chatMessageText}>
                {m.username} {m.message}
              </Text>
              <Text style={styles.chatMessageType}>{m.type}</Text>
            </View>
          )
        })}
        </ScrollView>
        <TextInput
```

```
      style={styles.chatInput}
      ref="textInput"
      placeholder="Enter a message..."
      returnKeyType="send"
      onSubmitEditing={this.handleSubmit}
    />
    </View>
  )
 } else {
   return (
     <View>
       <Text>No order selected for chat</Text>
     </View>
   )
  }
 }
}
```

The method `componentDidUpdate()` in the preceding code will be called when the React component is rendered with a new `prop` passed in[2]. The first render of this component will always be without a book order selected, but when it is selected, this method will receive the new order id and open the corresponding chat.

When an order is selected, the tree of components rendered will make use of `ScrollView`, which is the equivalent of a `<div>` with a fixed size and the inner content set to automatically overflow internally. We also automatically scroll to the bottom of its content by using an event handler.

For the text input in `ChatView.js`, we are using references instead of storing state like we did in the previous component. References allow React code to refer to components directly by using `this.refs` in the code.

---

[2]https://reactjs.org/docs/components-and-props.html

This is the test (`src/components/ChatView.test.js`):

```
import React from 'react'
import ChatView from './ChatView'

import renderer from 'react-test-renderer'

it('renders without orders specified', () => {
  const rendered = renderer.create(<ChatView />).toJSON()
  expect(rendered).toBeTruthy()
})

it('renders with orders specified', () => {
  const backendApi = {
    openMessagesStream: jest.fn(),
    closeMessagesStream: jest.fn(),
    sendMessage: jest.fn(),
    fetchShipmentStatus: jest.fn(
      () => new Promise((resolve, reject) => resolve())
    ),
  }
  const rendered = renderer.create(
    <ChatView backendApi={backendApi} orderCurrentId="1" />
  )
  rendered.root.instance.componentDidUpdate({})
  expect(backendApi.openMessagesStream.mock.calls.length).toBe(1)
  expect(backendApi.openMessagesStream.mock.calls[0][0]).toBe('1')
  expect(backendApi.fetchShipmentStatus.mock.calls.length).toBe(1)
  expect(backendApi.fetchShipmentStatus.mock.calls[0][0]).toBe('1')
  rendered.getInstance().setState({shipmentStatus: 'shipped'})
  backendApi.openMessagesStream.mock.calls[0][1]('initial message')
  expect(rendered.toJSON()).toMatchSnapshot()
```

```
rendered.root.instance.handleSubmit({ nativeEvent:{ text:
'answer back' } })
expect(backendApi.sendMessage.mock.calls.length).toBe(1)
expect(backendApi.sendMessage.mock.calls[0][0]).toBe('answer back')
expect(rendered.toJSON()).toMatchSnapshot()
})
```

OrderView

This component will manage the whole screen after the login screen. It will also load all its subcomponents, including ChatView.

Here is the component (src/components/OrderView.js):

```
import React from 'react'
import{
  StyleSheet,
  Text,
  Image,
  TouchableHighlight,
  TouchableOpacity,
  View
} from 'react-native'

import ChatView from './ChatView'

const styles = StyleSheet.create({
  container: {
    paddingTop: 25,
    flex: 1
  },
  orderContainer: {
    borderColor: 'blue',
    borderWidth: 1,
```

```
    height: 200
  },
  orderRowOut: {
    borderColor: 'yellow',
    borderWidth: 1,
    height: 52
  },
  orderRowIn: {
    flex: 1,
    flexDirection: 'row',
    alignSelf: 'stretch'
  },
  orderSelected: {
    backgroundColor: 'lightgrey'
  },
  orderImage: {
    borderColor: 'green',
    borderWidth: 1,
    width: 50,
    height: 50
  },
  orderSummary: {
    borderColor: 'red',
    borderWidth: 1,
    flex: 1,
    alignSelf: 'stretch'
  },
  orderPrice: {
    borderColor: 'blue',
    borderWidth: 1
  }
})
```

```
function OrderImage (props) {
  if (props.image) {
    return (
      <Image
        style={{ width: 50, height: 50 }}
        source={{ uri: props.backendApi.createAbsUrl(props.image) }}
      />
    )
  } else {
    return <View />
  }
}

function OrderTouchArea (props) {
  return (
    <View
      style={[
        styles.orderRowIn,
        props.order.id == props.orderCurrentId ? styles.
        orderSelected: null
      ]}
    >
      <View style={styles.orderImage}>
        <OrderImage backendApi={props.backendApi} image={props.
        order.image} />
      </View>
      <Text style={styles.orderSummary}>{props.order.summary}</Text>
      <Text style={styles.orderPrice}>{props.order.price}</Text>
    </View>
  )
}
```

```
function OrderSingleView (props) {
  return (
    <TouchableHighlight
      style={styles.orderRowOut}
      onPress={() => props.setOrderId(props.order.id)}
    >
      <OrderTouchArea
        backendApi={props.backendApi}
        order={props.order}
        orderCurrentId={props.orderCurrentId}
      />
    </TouchableHighlight>
  )
}

export default class OrderView extends React.Component {
  constructor (props) {
    super(props)
    this.state = {
      orders: [],
      orderCurrentId: null
    }
  }

  componentDidMount () {
    this.props.backendApi
      .fetchOrders()
      .then(orders => this.setOrders(orders))
      .catch(() => alert('Error fetching orders'))
  }

  setOrders (orders){
      this.setState({
```

```
      orders: orders
   })
 }

 render(){
   return (
     <View style={styles.container}>
       <View style={styles.orderContainer}>
         <Text>Your BookTime orders</Text>
         {this.state.orders.map(m=> (
           <OrderSingleView
             backendApi={this.props.backendApi}
             key={m.id}
             order={m}
             orderCurrentId={this.state.orderCurrentId}
             setOrderId={ordered => this.setState({
             orderCurrentId: orderId })}
           />
         ))}
       </View>
       <ChatView
         backendApi={this.props.backendApi}
         orderCurrentId={this.state.orderCurrentId}
       />
     </View>
   )
 }
}
```

In React Native, like recent versions of React, it is possible to define components as functions or classes. For simple components, functions are sufficient. This is what we used here, to make the code more readable.

Components that are declared as functions do not have internal state. Components declared in the preceding code are pure functions, with their output based purely on the props passed in.

All the state in the earlier components is managed by the main OrderView component.

Orders are fetched as soon as the component is mounted, which means it is displayed on the screen. Order entries can be pressed in the UI, and that will initialize the chat component and open the WebSocket connection to our server.

Here is the test (src/components/OrderView.test.js):

```
import React from 'react'
import OrderView from './OrderView'

import renderer from 'react-test-renderer'

it('renders without crashing', () => {
  const mockOrders = [{ id: 5, image: null, summary: '2xaa',
  price: 22 }]
  const backendApi = {
    fetchOrders: jest.fn(
      () => new Promise((resolve,reject)=>resolve(mockOrders))
    ),
    createAbsUrl: jest.fn(url => 'http://booktime.domain' + url)
  }

  const rendered = renderer.create(<OrderView
  backendApi={backendApi} />)
  expect(rendered).toBeTruthy()
  expect(backendApi.fetchOrders.mock.calls.length).toBe(1)
  rendered.getInstance().setOrders(mockOrders)
  expect(rendered.getInstance().state.orders).toBe(mockOrders)
  expect(rendered.toJSON()).toMatchSnapshot()
})
```

Main Component

We will override the content of the automatically generated App.js in the
main folder with the code that we need to start the app:

```
import React from 'react'
import LoginView from './src/components/LoginView'
import ChatView from './src/components/ChatView'
import OrderView from './src/components/OrderView'
import BackendApi from './src/backend'

export default class App extends React.Component {
  constructor (props) {
    super(props)
    this.backendApi = new BackendApi()
    this.state = {
      loggedIn: false
    }
  }

  render () {
    if (this.state.loggedIn) {
      return <OrderView backendApi={this.backendApi} />
    } else {
      return (
        <LoginView
          backendApi={this.backendApi}
          setLoggedIn={() => this.setState({loggedIn: true })}
        />
      )
    }
  }
}
```

We construct the API object in this class, and optionally pass the environment we want this app to run against, whether that will be production or a less important environment.

The main container has only one state flag, loggedIn, and that is used to visualize either the first screen (login) or the main screen (order view).

We are going to put its test in the same folder and in the file App.test.js:

```
import React from 'react'
import App from './App'

import renderer from 'react-test-renderer'

it('renders without crashing', () => {
  const rendered = renderer.create(<App />).toJSON()
  expect(rendered).toBeTruthy()
})
```

Running, Testing, and Packaging

As mentioned earlier in the chapter, everything is run with yarn. We use yarn start to start our mobile development server (see Figure 9-3). To see the app, we will install a development client called Expo (https://expo.io) on our mobile device. Please download this mobile app from the app store of your mobile device.

We can also run the tests that we wrote earlier in the chapter with Jest. We are using a feature of Jest called snapshot testing, which simplifies a lot of the assertion work for us.

Here is the output of yarn test, which is using Jest behind the scenes:

```
$ yarn test
yarn run v1.7.0
$ jest
 PASS  src/components/OrderView.test.js (6.403s)
 › 1 snapshot written.
```

```
PASS src/components/LoginView.test.js (6.576s)
PASS ./App.test.js
PASS src/components/ChatView.test.js (8.404s)
 - Console

   console.warn node_modules/react-native/jest/setup.js:93
     Calling .setNativeProps() in the test renderer environment
     is not supported. Instead, mock

 - 2 snapshots written.

Snapshot Summary
 - 3 snapshots written in 2 test suites.

Test Suites: 4 passed, 4 total
Tests:       8 passed, 8 total
Snapshots:   3 added,  3 total
Time:        9.967s
Ran all test suites.
Done in 11.87s.
```

In the first run of yarn test, it will generate all the snapshots for us. In all subsequent runs, it will use the generated snapshots as a reference to check against.

Figure 9-3. *yarn start sample output*

Packaging for Android

All the work we have done so far has led us to the point that we have
a potential app, but we still need to package it and distribute it to our
customers, and that is where the following steps become
platform-specific.

I am going to show how to do this for Android, as the distribution of APKs (the packaged apps) does not require you to sign in to Google Play. You can do so after having installed the exp command-line interface with npm install -g exp

The Expo client (exp) will require you to set up an account on their system. Packaging React Native apps does not require this client, but without it we would have to do a lot more setup work. We would have to install the SDK of all the platforms we want to target. Using the Expo client allows us to use their system for compiling our files.

```
$ exp build:android
[16:29:11] Making sure project is set up correctly...
[16:29:13] Your project looks good!
[16:29:13] Checking if current build exists...

[16:29:14] No currently active or previous builds for this project.
[16:29:15] Unable to find an existing exp instance for this
           directory, starting a new one...
[16:29:16] Starting Metro Bundler on port 19001.
[16:29:17] Metro Bundler ready.
[16:29:17] Publishing to channel 'default'...
[16:29:17] Tunnel URL not found, falled back to LAN URL.
[16:29:17] Building iOS bundle
[16:29:37] Tunnel URL not found, falled back to LAN URL.
[16:29:47] Building Android bundle
Building JavaScript bundle [======================] 100%[16:29:47]
[16:29:57] Tunnel URL not found, falled back to LAN URL.
[16:30:14] Analyzing assets
Building JavaScript bundle [======================] 100%[16:30:14]
Finished building JavaScript bundle in 26994ms.
[16:30:17] Tunnel URL not found, falled back to LAN URL.
```

```
Building JavaScript bundle [======================] 100%[16:30:23]
Finished building JavaScript bundle in 9449ms.
[16:30:33] Uploading assets
Building JavaScript bundle [======================] 100%[16:30:33]
Finished building JavaScript bundle in 9853ms.
[16:30:34] No assets changed, skipped.
[16:30:34] Uploading JavaScript bundles
[16:30:37] Tunnel URL not found, falled back to LAN URL.
[16:30:39] Published
[16:30:39] Your URL is

https://exp.host/@flagz/booktime_mobile

[16:30:39] Building...
[16:30:40] Build started, it may take a few minutes to complete.
[16:30:40] You can check the queue length at
 https://expo.io/turtle-status

[16:30:40] You can monitor the build at

https://expo.io/builds/0bcd5ecb-bd99-419d-94fa-44433820be5e

|[16:30:40] Waiting for build to complete. You can press Ctrl+C to exit.
[16:34:42] Successfully built standalone app: https://expo.io/
artifacts/793ffef3-10a2-4803-a791-c659756c3a8b
```

After having successfully run this, you can download the generated
APK in the link presented in your output.

Summary

This chapter presented a simple React Native app that consumes the APIs
we wrote in Chapter 8. You can take the lessons presented here and extend
them, or simply rewrite this app using Java or Swift.

## CHAPTER 10

How to Deploy Django Sites

In this chapter we will take what we have built so far and deploy it to production. Production systems are those whose purpose is to be utilized by end users.

Generally, we can have many environments available on the Internet, depending on their audience. Some commonly used environments are "production" for the live site and "staging" for the upcoming release, normally accessible to only a select number of people.

This chapter presents a way to deploy an environment regardless of its purpose.

Minifying JS/CSS

The first good practice when you deploy a website is to make sure the assets that you serve back to the client are as efficiently packaged as possible (minified and bundled). This ensures that the client browser will need to transfer less data and open fewer connections. Your site will feel more reactive, and the user will thank you for that.

This is one of the operations that Webpack (which we used back in Chapter 5) makes trivial; therefore, there are no excuses to not do it. We will create a new Webpack configuration in `webpack.prod.config.js`, in the top-level folder:

© Federico Marani 2019
F. Marani, *Practical Django 2 and Channels 2*,
https://doi.org/10.1007/978-1-4842-4099-1_10

```
const common = require('./webpack.config')

module.exports = {
  mode: 'production',
  entry: common.entry,
  plugins: common.plugins,
  output: {
    filename: '[name].bundle.js',
    path: common.output.path
  }
};
```

This configuration reuses most settings from the development configuration, with a few changes. It uses production mode, which turns on minifications and other optimizations built into version 4 of Webpack.

We are going to integrate the new Webpack configuration in our package.json, adding a new entry inside the scripts section:

```
...
    "scripts": {
      "test": "jest",
      "build": "webpack",
      "build-prod": "webpack --config webpack.prod.config.js"
    },
...
```

We can now run this with the following command:

```
$ npm run build-prod

> booktime@1.0.0 build-prod /code
> webpack --config webpack.prod.config.js

Hash: 58037a9e18e1cf5c3bac
Version: webpack 4.12.0
```

```
Time: 2430ms
Built at: 08/30/2018 6:40:26 PM

                                    Asset      Size ...
imageswitcher-58037a9e18e1cf5c3bac.bundle.js   100 KiB ...
[14] ./frontend/imageswitcher.js 931 bytes {0} [built]
    + 14 hidden modules
```

Serving Static Assets

Up to this point in the book, we have only used the development server, but that is not what we are going to use in production. The development server has a special way to serve static assets, but in production we cannot rely on this.

Production environments need a more efficient way to serve static assets. Most setups nowadays are using Nginx as a reverse proxy,[1] connected to a server like Gunicorn or uWSGI, to handle the traffic for the application. Static assets in these cases are served directly by Nginx.

Another possible setup is to use an external Django library that takes care of serving static assets in the most efficient way, even though it is hard to beat the efficiency of Nginx.

Yet another way is to not bother serving static assets from your own web server at all, offloading this responsibility to a service like Amazon S3, Google Cloud Storage, or an open source equivalent such as Minio. These services will take care of storing the static assets and serving them through HTTP.

For the BookTime website, we are going to use the second approach, which is to use an external Django library. This approach strikes a good balance between performance and ease of setup. We are going to use a library called WhiteNoise (http://whitenoise.evans.io), so run the following:

```
$ pipenv install whitenoise
```

---

[1]https://en.wikipedia.org/wiki/Reverse_proxy

We will be inserting the WhiteNoise app above all other `INSTALLED_` `APPS`, and its middleware above all other `MIDDLEWARE` directives, except `SecurityMiddleware`.

We are also going to add the `STATIC_ROOT` variable, which specifies where the static assets will be collected, and `STATICFILES_STORAGE`, for some extra optimizations that WhiteNoise can offer.

These are the proposed configuration changes to `booktime/settings.py`:

```
...

INSTALLED_APPS = [
    "whitenoise.runserver_nostatic",
    ...
]

...

MIDDLEWARE = [
    "django.middleware.security.SecurityMiddleware",
    "whitenoise.middleware.WhiteNoiseMiddleware",
    ...
]

...

STATIC_ROOT = os.path.join(BASE_DIR, "staticfiles")
if not DEBUG:
    STATICFILES_STORAGE = 'whitenoise.storage.
    CompressedManifestStaticFilesStorage'

...
```

WhiteNoise's `CompressedManifestStaticFilesStorage` storage backend adds automatic compression behavior to a built-in Django `ManifestStaticFilesStorage` storage backend, which will be used by the command described next.

Executing collectstatic

Any way we choose to serve static assets, whether with WhiteNoise or without, requires the collectstatic Django command to be executed at the deployment stage, which means before running the application server.

This Django command copies all the static assets from all the apps we have, whether built-in or built by us, in one location, specified by STATIC_ROOT:

```
$ ./manage.py collectstatic
197 static files copied to '/.../booktime/staticfiles', 552
post-processed.
```

When running this command in production, ManifestStaticFiles Storage will be used. Besides copying all the static assets, this storage will also append file hashes to all collected files. This is to do "cache busting": making sure that the client does not use an old version of the assets when a new version is available.

Environment-Specific Variables

For this project, we are going to follow the twelve-factor app methodology (https://12factor.net). We are going to externalize all variables that depend on the environment, such as database URLs, whether DEBUG mode is turned on, and some more.

We will use yet another external library for this, which takes care of reading and transforming the content of environment variables in its equivalent Django format:

```
$ pipenv install django-environ
```

This library will be used inside our booktime/settings.py in several places.

Here are the changes; remove the old lines that do not refer to env():

```python
import environ
...
env = environ.Env(
    # set casting, default value
    DEBUG=(bool, False)
)

env.read_env('.env')

DEBUG = env('DEBUG')

REDIS_URL = env('REDIS_URL')
CHANNEL_LAYERS = {
    "default": {
        "BACKEND": "channels_redis.core.RedisChannelLayer",
        "CONFIG": {"hosts": [REDIS_URL]},
    }
}

DATABASES = {
    "default": env.db()
}

EMAIL_CONFIG = env.email_url('EMAIL_URL')
vars().update(EMAIL_CONFIG)

SECRET_KEY = env('SECRET_KEY')

...
```

You can see from this code that we are loading the library and, besides reading from the current environment, also reading from the .env file. The presence of this .env file is not necessary; we will only use it locally to simplify our development workflow.

You will have to create this file with the configuration you need for your machine. You can use the following template, with your own settings, and store it in .env inside your top-level folder:

```
DATABASE_URL=postgres://user:password@localhost/booktime
REDIS_URL=redis://localhost
EMAIL_URL=consolemail://
SECRET_KEY="change-this-$%£4"
```

This file contains some configuration variables with a URL form. django-environ will take care of translating these in the format Django requires. We are also managing SECRET_KEY here. The value of SECRET_KEY needs to be kept safe. If an attacker discovers the value of this key, he may be able to use it to compromise your site. It is good practice to keep this, and all other details, out of the source code repository, which is possible now given that we are using environment variables.

However, do not commit .env to the repository, as this will defeat our purpose.

Ensuring Nothing Is Left Behind

Something that we need to check before deploying our project to environments other than our local machine is whether we have some hard-coded configuration that needs to vary between environments.

In our case, when we used Redis directly in our chat consumers, we left some code that will not work after deployment. We need to fix this in our main/consumers.py:

```
from django.conf import settings

...

class ChatNotifyConsumer(AsyncHttpConsumer):
    ...
```

```
async def stream(self):
    r_conn = await aioredis.create_redis(settings.REDIS_URL)
    ...

class ChatConsumer(AsyncJsonWebsocketConsumer):
    ...

    async def connect(self):
        ...

        if authorized:
            self.r_conn = await aioredis.create_redis(
                settings.REDIS_URL
            )
            ...
```

Having fixed this code, we are now sure that consumers are no longer dependent on Redis running locally.

Deploying on Dokku/Heroku

We are ready to show our work to the world, by deploying it on a real server. We are going to use Dokku for this, an open source platform as a service (PaaS) that is compatible with Heroku and runs on any Linux server. The advantage of using PaaS instead of normal virtual machines (VMs) is that there is much less setup work.

Common Deployment Steps

First of all, our project needs the equivalent of booktime/wsgi.py but for a Django Channels system. Channels does not use WSGI but uses another protocol called ASGI. ASGI allows Channels to decouple the system that receives the request from the system that runs our code. It is similar in purpose to WSGI, but for asynchronous systems.

We need to do this because the development server of Django does this automatically, but it is only for local use. For production, this needs to be done separately.

In the same folder of booktime/wsgi.py, we will create booktime/asgi.py:

```
"""

ASGI entrypoint. Configures Django and then runs the application
defined in the ASGI_APPLICATION setting.
"""

import os
import django
from channels.routing import get_default_application

os.environ.setdefault("DJANGO_SETTINGS_MODULE", "booktime.settings")
django.setup()
application = get_default_application()
```

This file is needed to deploy to any system.

From now on, the steps start to be Heroku/Dokku specific. We need to create a file called Procfile, in the top-level folder, with this content:

```
web: daphne -p $PORT --bind 0.0.0.0 -v2 booktime.asgi:application
```

This file lists all process types that the process supervisor of our PaaS needs to manage. In our case, there is only one (web), but in more complex systems there may be more, such as background queue workers.

daphne is the built-in web server of Django Channels. For standard Django, there are many WSGI servers, such as Gunicorn, uWSGI, and so on. We cannot use those for Django Channels. At the moment, there are fewer ASGI servers, although this will probably change in the future.

Git

Both Dokku and Heroku rely on git to do new deployments. If you are not using it already in your project, you have to start using it. Fortunately, it is really simple to set up. If you are not familiar with this tool, there is a lot of documentation online on how to use it.

In the top folder, you need to initialize the repository:

```
$ git init
```

After having run this, make sure you have the following .gitignore file in your repository:

```
__pycache__/
db.sqlite3
media/
staticfiles/
bundles/
node_modules/
webpack-stats.json
geckodriver.log
.env
```

Commit this file, commit all your project code, and you will be ready to proceed to your first deployment.

Dokku-Specific Commands

You can easily deploy a VM on DigitalOcean, an infrastructure-hosting company, with Dokku preinstalled, if you want to test this[2].

---

[2]https://www.digitalocean.com/products/one-click-apps/dokku/

Once you have a Dokku server running, the first step is to create the application, as follows. Remember that you need to run all the dokku commands from here forward on your new server.

```
$ dokku apps:create booktime
-----> Creating booktime... done
```

You can see the app now coming through in the list of apps running on the server:

```
$ dokku apps:list booktime
=====> My Apps
booktime
...
```

Next step is to attach all the resources that our application will need, starting from PostgreSQL:

```
$ dokku plugin:install https://github.com/dokku/dokku-postgres.
  git postgres
...
$ dokku postgres:create booktime-database
       Waiting for container to be ready
       Creating container database
       Securing connection to database
=====> Postgres container created: booktime-database
       DSN: postgres://xxx:xxx@dokku-postgres-booktime-
       database:5432/booktime_database

$ dokku postgres:link booktime-database booktime
-----> Setting config vars
       DATABASE_URL: postgres://xxx:xxx@dokku-postgres-
       booktime-database:5432/booktime_database
-----> Restarting app booktime
 !     App booktime has not been deployed
```

Then Redis:

```
$ dokku plugin:install https://github.com/dokku/dokku-redis.git redis
$ dokku redis:create booktime-redis
        Waiting for container to be ready
=====> Redis container created: booktime-redis
=====> Container Information
        Config dir:          /var/lib/dokku/services/redis/
                             booktime-redis/config
        Data dir:            /var/lib/dokku/services/redis/
                             booktime-redis/data
...
        Status:              running
        Version:             redis:4.0.8
$ dokku redis:link booktime-redis booktime
-----> Setting config vars
...
!      App booktime has not been deployed
```

The next two commands that we need to launch are about specifying all the environment variables that our booktime/settings.py requires.

We are not going to use an .env file for production because we do not want this critical information to be stored in the source repository. By putting this information on the server itself, we can restrict who has access to this only to the engineers that have server access.

```
$ dokku config:set booktime SECRET_KEY="change this"
-----> Setting config vars
        SECRET_KEY: abcabcabc
-----> Restarting app booktime
!      App booktime has not been deployed
```

```
$ dokku config:set booktime EMAIL_URL="consolemail://"
-----> Setting config vars
       EMAIL_URL: consolemail://
-----> Restarting app booktime
 !     App booktime has not been deployed
```

The value of the SECRET_KEY should be a random string of characters, preferably more than 40 characters. For EMAIL_URL, if you want to use an SMTP server, you can specify this format: smtp://user:pass@server. com:25.

With the following command we are going to instruct npm to install all dependencies during deployment, because we will need to run Webpack:

```
$ dokku config:set booktime NPM_CONFIG_PRODUCTION=false
```

Dokku-Specific Files

Our project will need to be built with two buildpacks because we are using both Node and Django. Node is used by Webpack, which compiles our React files, and we use Django for everything else.

Buildpacks provide support for deploying and running technical stacks. They are responsible for transforming deployed code into an artifact that can be run inside a container.

Buildpacks are a concept that is equally present in Heroku and Dokku, but the dependencies on those by the project are declared differently. Heroku uses an app manifest called app.json, while Dokku uses an extremely simple .buildpacks file.

Here is the content of our .buildpacks file that needs to be committed:

```
https://github.com/heroku/heroku-buildpack-nodejs.git
https://github.com/heroku/heroku-buildpack-python.git
```

Remaining Common Steps

The Python buildpack that we are using executes automatically a collectstatic step, but unfortunately it does not deal with Webpack compilation. We have to change this.

This deployment step is a step that we can add to by creating a new file, bin/post_compile, in our repository, and committing it. This is its content:

```
#!/bin/bash
export PATH=/app/.heroku/node/bin:$PATH
npm run build-prod
./manage.py collectstatic --noinput
./manage.py migrate --noinput
```

Notice that we also added the migrate command. Running this here means that we are trusting that the migrations that our master branch contain have been reviewed and are stable. If you do not feel confident about this, you can run this step manually through the dokku run command on the Dokku server:

```
$ dokku run booktime ./manage.py migrate
```

We now have to configure git. Please make a note of your server address. If you have created a new VM, you may not have a DNS entry for it yet, in which case you will have to use its IP address. Use the value you found and run the following command:

```
$ git remote add dokku dokku@YOUR_DOKKU_FQDN:booktime
```

Finally, we can push our site live:

```
$ git push dokku master
Counting objects: 145, done.
Delta compression using up to 4 threads.
```

Compressing objects: 100% (136/136), done.
Writing objects: 100% (145/145), 678.92 KiB | 7.89 MiB/s, done.
Total 145 (delta 12), reused 0 (delta 0)
-----> Cleaning up...
-----> Building booktime from herokuish...
-----> Injecting apt repositories and packages ...
-----> Adding BUILD_ENV to build environment...
----->   Warning: Multiple default buildpacks reported the
         ability to handle this app. The first buildpack in the
         list below will be used.
         Detected buildpacks: multi nodejs python
-----> Multipack app detected
=====> Downloading Buildpack: https://github.com/heroku/heroku-
       buildpack-nodejs.git
=====> Detected Framework: Node.js

-----> Creating runtime environment

       NPM_CONFIG_LOGLEVEL=error
       NPM_CONFIG_PRODUCTION=false
       NODE_VERBOSE=false
       NODE_ENV=production
       NODE_MODULES_CACHE=true

-----> Installing binaries
       engines.node (package.json): unspecified
       engines.npm (package.json): unspecified (use default)

       Resolving node version 8.x...
       Downloading and installing node 8.11.4...
       Using default npm version: 5.6.0

-----> Restoring cache
       Skipping cache restore (not-found)

```
-----> Building dependencies
       Installing node modules (package.json)
       added 861 packages in 30.635s

-----> Caching build
       Clearing previous node cache
       Saving 2 cacheDirectories (default):
       - node_modules
       - bower_components (nothing to cache)

-----> Pruning devDependencies
       Skipping because NPM_CONFIG_PRODUCTION is 'false'

-----> Build succeeded!
=====> Downloading Buildpack: https://github.com/heroku/heroku-
       buildpack-python.git
=====> Detected Framework: Python
-----> Installing python-3.6.6
-----> Installing pip
-----> Installing dependencies with Pipenv 2018.5.18...
       Installing dependencies from Pipfile.lock (93c72c)...
-----> $ python manage.py collectstatic --noinput
       194 static files copied to '/tmp/build/staticfiles',
       574 post-processed.

       Using release configuration from last framework (Python).
-----> Running post-compile hook

       > booktime@1.0.0 build-prod /tmp/build
       > webpack --config webpack.prod.config.js

       Hash: 116cb912ed906360d169
       Version: webpack 4.17.1
       Time: 3997ms
       Built at: 2018-09-03 09:01:56
```

```
Asset      Size  Chunks           Chunk Names
imageswitcher-116cb912ed906360d169.bundle.js  100 KiB
       0  [emitted]  imageswitcher
Entrypoint imageswitcher = imageswitcher-
116cb912ed906360d169.bundle.js
[5] ./frontend/imageswitcher.js 931 bytes {0} [built]
+ 14 hidden modules

1 static file copied to '/tmp/build/staticfiles', 195
unmodified, 412 post-process Operations to perform:
Apply all migrations: admin, auth, authtoken,
contenttypes, main, sessions
Running migrations:
 Applying contenttypes.0001_initial... OK
 Applying contenttypes.0002_remove_content_type_name... OK
 Applying auth.0001_initial... OK
 Applying auth.0002_alter_permission_name_max_length... OK
 Applying auth.0003_alter_user_email_max_length... OK
 Applying auth.0004_alter_user_username_opts... OK
 Applying auth.0005_alter_user_last_login_null... OK
 Applying auth.0006_require_contenttypes_0002... OK
 Applying auth.0007_alter_validators_add_error_messages... OK
 Applying auth.0008_alter_user_username_max_length...  OK
 Applying auth.0009_alter_user_last_name_max_length...  OK
 Applying main.0001_initial... OK
 Applying admin.0001_initial... OK
 Applying admin.0002_logentry_remove_auto_add...   OK
 Applying admin.0003_logentry_add_action_flag_choices...OK
 Applying authtoken.0001_initial... OK
 Applying authtoken.0002_auto_20160226_1747... OK
 Applying main.0002_address... OK
 Applying main.0003_basket_basketline... OK
```

```
        Applying main.0004_auto_20180524_2143... OK
        Applying main.0005_auto_20180605_1835... OK
        Applying main.0006_auto_20180606_0801... OK
        Applying main.0007_order_last_spoken_to... OK
        Applying sessions.0001_initial... OK
     Using release configuration from last framework (Python).
-----> Discovering process types
        Procfile declares types -> web
-----> Releasing booktime (dokku/booktime:latest)...
-----> Deploying booktime (dokku/booktime:latest)...
-----> Attempting to run scripts.dokku.predeploy from app.json
       (if defined)
-----> App Procfile file found (/home/dokku/booktime/DOKKU_
       PROCFILE)
-----> DOKKU_SCALE file not found in app image. Generating one
       based on Procfile...
-----> New DOKKU_SCALE file generated
=====> web=1
-----> Attempting pre-flight checks
        For more efficient zero downtime deployments, create a
        file CHECKS.
        See http://dokku.viewdocs.io/dokku/deployment/zero-
        downtime-deploys/ for examples
        CHECKS file not found in container: Running simple
        container check...
-----> Waiting for 10 seconds ...
-----> Default container check successful!
-----> Running post-deploy
-----> Creating new /home/dokku/booktime/VHOST...
-----> Setting config vars DOKKU_PROXY_PORT: 80
-----> Setting config vars DOKKU_PROXY_PORT_MAP: http:80:5000
```

```
-----> Configuring booktime....(using built-in template)
-----> Creating http nginx.conf
-----> Running nginx-pre-reload
       Reloading nginx
-----> Setting config vars
       DOKKU_APP_RESTORE: 1
=====> Renaming container (b6d94002989c) elastic_ardinghelli to
       booktime.web.1
-----> Attempting to run scripts.dokku.postdeploy from app.json
       (if defined)
=====> Application deployed:
       http://booktime.YOUR_DOKKU_FQDN
```

If you see similar output, congratulations! You have managed to successfully deploy your first Django app. The final URL of your app is the last thing printed in the deployment output.

You can see the logging output of this app with this command:

```
$ dokku logs booktime -t
```

At this point, if you have not done it already, you would have to add the host URL to your ALLOWED_HOSTS in booktime/settings.py:

```
...

if DEBUG:
    ALLOWED_HOSTS = ['*']
else:
    ALLOWED_HOSTS = ['booktime.YOUR_DOKKU_FQDN', 'localhost']

...
```

Commit and push again. Next time when you browse the URL, you will see a working site.

SSL, WebSockets, and HTTP/2

Because our website is handling e-commerce transactions and managing user data, all connections should be done through a secure channel. It is generally good practice to offer HTTPS nowadays, but it does require some extra setup.

Platforms like Dokku or Heroku make this very easy for us. Heroku offers limited built-in support for SSL certificates, and Dokku, with its Let's Encrypt plug-in, offers automatic management for this.

HTTP/2, unlike HTTP/1.x, has SSL/TLS built in. But HTTP/2 has a lot more than built-in security; it is a vastly more efficient protocol than its predecessor, being able to multiplex all HTTP requests in one single connection and improving on compression rates.

In these Dokku or Heroku, Django runs behind their load balancers, which are managing SSL, its certificates, and HTTP/2. The role of Django in these PaaS environments is minor. Dokku offers HTTP to HTTPS redirection by default, while Heroku does not.

Django can be instructed to use a secure connection by default, whether it is HTTP/2 or HTTPS/1.x. These are the additional settings that we can add to do so:

```
SECURE_PROXY_SSL_HEADER = ('HTTP_X_FORWARDED_PROTO', 'https')
SECURE_SSL_REDIRECT = True
SESSION_COOKIE_SECURE = True
CSRF_COOKIE_SECURE = True
```

These settings will allow Django to detect whether it is running against a secure connection and, if not, trigger a redirect. In our setup with Dokku, however, this is not necessary, as HTTP is always redirected.

WebSockets are an extension of HTTP/1.1, also present in HTTP/2. Different from normal HTTP/1.1 connections, these are long-running connections. They keep their channels open. Dokku, which uses Nginx as a reverse proxy internally, relays these connections properly. Heroku is equally able to do so.

Media Storage on Amazon S3

In a project like ours, where potentially there could be thousands of product images, it is preferable to delegate the storage and serving of those images to a separate system that is optimized for this purpose. With systems like Amazon S3 (or similar), we can do this easily.

Delegating media storage to a dedicated system also frees us from having to manage issues around filesystem scaling and making sure we do not run out of disk space.

When deploying to a PaaS, delegating media storage is also the only way. When developing apps using the twelve-factor app guidelines mentioned earlier, we cannot rely on storing files locally. For every new version of our site that we deploy, a new container will be deployed with a clean filesystem. If we store user uploads locally, they will become unavailable as soon as a new version of our site goes live.

We need to install two libraries for this purpose:

```
$ pipenv install boto3 django-storages
```

This installs Boto 3, which is the S3 library, and django-storages, which is an additional Django library that links Boto 3 to Django. Django-storages offers support for S3, Azure, DigitalOcean, and some other platforms.

First of all, we need to create a bucket on S3 that is publicly readable. We also need to have API access to this by creating the necessary access through Amazon Web Services (AWS) Identity and Access Management (IAM). We will not cover this in detail, as there are many tutorials online on how to do so.

Ultimately, you need an access key ID and a secret access key for your AWS account. It is not recommended you use keys associated with your superuser/main AWS account, which is why IAM lets you make users with more appropriate access restrictions.

Here are some of the configuration changes that need to be added to our `booktime/settings.py`:

```
if env('AWS_ACCESS_KEY_ID', default=None):
    DEFAULT_FILE_STORAGE = "storages.backends.s3boto3.
    S3Boto3Storage"
    # AWS_S3_ENDPOINT_URL = "FQDN of Minio, only if you are
    using it"
    AWS_ACCESS_KEY_ID = env('AWS_ACCESS_KEY_ID')
    AWS_SECRET_ACCESS_KEY = env('AWS_SECRET_ACCESS_KEY')
    AWS_STORAGE_BUCKET_NAME = env('AWS_STORAGE_BUCKET_NAME')
```

This piece of configuration is changing the DEFAULT_FILE_STORAGE if the AWS access key ID is specified in the environment. Access keys and secrets are available through IAM after creating the access. The bucket name is what you created on S3 as a destination for your app's uploaded files.

There are open source cloud storage platforms that are compatible with S3, such as Minio. You can use these as well, but you would need to specify an extra AWS_S3_ENDPOINT_URL to override the default behavior of django-storages.

After having deployed this change, you will need to set these new environment variables. You can do so easily on Heroku through the dashboard or CLI, or using the dokku config:set command on your Dokku server. On your local machine, you should include those lines in your .env file.

Setting Frontend Variables

Django offers an abstraction called context processors, which are used to inject variables at the template-rendering stage. In the past chapters we used the request context processor, but now we are going to create one of our own.

We will use this context processor to inject a couple of simple variables in the base template, to make their value available to anyone that is browsing the site. The variables in question will be

- The revision of the last commit in Git

- The tracker ID that is needed by Google Analytics to bootstrap its JavaScript client

The context processor will be created in the new file main/context_ processors.py:

```
import os
from django.conf import settings
def globals(request):
    data = {}
    data.update({
        'VERSION': os.environ.get("GIT_REV",""),
        'GA_TRACKER_ID': settings.GA_TRACKER_ID,
    })
    return data
```

This code will read from an environment variable called GIT_REV, which is present on every Dokku deployment. The other variable, GA_TRACKER_ID, is read from our settings file. We also need to activate this context processor.

These are the changes that need to be applied to booktime/settings. py file:

```
TEMPLATES = [
    {
        "BACKEND": "django.template.backends.django.DjangoTemplates",
        ...
        "OPTIONS": {
            "context_processors": [
```

```
    ...
        "main.context_processors.globals",
    ]
  },
  }
]

...

GA_TRACKER_ID = "123"
```

Having done all the above, it is now possible to print these variables inside the HTML without having the view explicitly passing this variables in. We are going to do so in `main/templates/base.html`, which is the base used for every page of the site.

```
{% load static %}
<!doctype html>
<html lang="en">
  <head>
    ...
    <!-- Booktime version: {{ VERSION }} -->
    <script charset="utf-8">
      var tracker_id={{ GA_TRACKER_ID }};
    </script>
  </head>
...
```

You can now commit and deploy these two changes. To verify it is working, open any page on the website and view the HTML source.

Customizing Error Pages

Before the site goes public, we want to make sure that the final user will not see any error message that would be too intimidating and unhelpful. If an exception occurs on production, we want to reassure the user that it will be fixed soon, and they should come back to the site sometime later.

We are going to customize the responses for the HTTP statuses 404 and 500, which are triggered when a URL does not map to anything and when an error occurred in our code.

Django makes this very simple. When the DEBUG setting is False, Django automatically renders the templates 404.html and 500.html in case of 404 or 500 code errors.

Place the following inside templates/404.html in the top folder:

```
<!DOCTYPE html>
<html>
    <head>
        <meta charset="UTF-8" />
        <meta name="viewport" content="width=device-width"/>
        <title>404</title>
    </head>
    <body>
        <h1>We could not find this page</h1>
        <p>Please contact our support.</p>
    </body>
</html>
```

And place the following in templates/500.html:

```
<!DOCTYPE html>
<html>
    <head>
        <meta charset="UTF-8" />
```

387

```
    <meta name="viewport" content="width=device-width"/>
    <title>500</title>
  </head>
  <body>
    <h1>An error has occurred</h1>
    <p>Our support team has been notified.</p>
  </body>
</html>
```

These two templates are kept deliberately simple, to minimize the chance of having a rendering error while handling the initial error.

Error Reporting

While it is good practice to hide an error from the final user, we need to make sure that the IT team of BookTime is notified when a problem occurs. Therefore, we are going to configure Django to send e-mails to admins when an error happens. Add this code to booktime/settings.py:

```
...

ADMINS = (
    ('Booktime IT', 'systems@booktime.domain'),
)

EMAIL_SUBJECT_PREFIX = "[Booktime] "
```

In its default configuration, Django will then trigger e-mails to all ADMINS when an error/exception occurs. This happens only for deployments with the DEBUG flag set to False.

This reporting is pretty basic but enough for an initial setup. Later, you might want to use a third-party system that does error aggregation and general management, such as Sentry (https://sentry.io).

Making Sure Tests Are Passing

Every time we deploy our site, we want to make sure that everything works. To do so, we rely on tests. Our tests must be passing. If they are passing, we will be reasonably certain that the new version of the site that we are about to release is working as expected.

At this initial stage of the project we do not have a continuous integration (CI) system yet. This would be the best solution as it will notify engineers of broken tests as soon as they are committed, but setting up a CI system requires more work. A simple stopgap measure for us would be to run the tests during the Heroku/Dokku compilation phase.

We are going to change our bin/post_compile command to this:

```
#!/bin/bash
export PATH=/app/.heroku/node/bin:$PATH
npm run build-prod
./manage.py collectstatic --noinput
./manage.py migrate --noinput
npm test -- frontend
./manage.py test --noinput
```

In this way, if all these commands are successful, we will publish; otherwise, we will not.

Let's go ahead and try it:

```
$ git push dokku master
Counting objects: 39, done.
Delta compression using up to 4 threads.
Compressing objects: 100% (38/38), done.
Writing objects: 100% (39/39), 3.98 KiB | 370.00 KiB/s, done.
Total 39 (delta 25), reused 0 (delta 0)
remote: Preparing /tmp/dokku_git.PJBq (identifier dokku_git.PJBq)
remote: ~/booktime /tmp/dokku_git.PJBq ~/booktime
```

```
remote: /tmp/dokku_git.PJBq ~/booktime
-----> Cleaning up...
-----> Building booktime from herokuish...

...

-----> Running post-compile hook

      > booktime@1.0.0 build-prod /tmp/build
      > webpack --config webpack.prod.config.js

...

      > booktime@1.0.0 test /tmp/build
      > jest "frontend"

remote: PASS frontend/imageswitcher.test.js
remote: - ImageBox switches images correctly (25ms)
remote:
remote: Test Suites: 1 passed, 1 total
remote: Tests:       1 passed, 1 total
remote: Snapshots:   0 total
remote: Time:        2.833s
remote: Ran all test suites matching /frontend/i.
      Creating test database for alias 'default'...
      System check identified no issues (0 silenced).

...

remote: .E
remote: =======================================================
remote: ERROR: setUpClass (main.tests.test_e2e.FrontendTests)
remote: -------------------------------------------------------
remote: Traceback (most recent call last):
remote:   File "/app/.heroku/python/lib/python3.6/site-
          packages/selenium/webdriver/common/service .py",
          line 76, in start
```

```
remote:      stdin=PIPE)
remote:      File "/app/.heroku/python/lib/python3.6/subprocess.py",
             line 709, in __init__
remote:        restore_signals, start_new_session)
remote:      File "/app/.heroku/python/lib/python3.6/subprocess.py",
             line 1344, in _execute_child
remote:        raise child_exception_type(errno_num, err_msg, err_
             filename)
remote:      FileNotFoundError: [Errno 2] No such file or
             directory: 'geckodriver': 'geckodriver'
remote:
remote:      During handling of the above exception, another
             exception occurred:
remote:
remote:      Traceback (most recent call last):
remote:      File "/tmp/build/main/tests/test_e2e.py", line 15, in
             setUpClass
remote:        cls.selenium = WebDriver()
remote:      File "/app/.heroku/python/lib/python3.6/site-
             packages/selenium/webdriver/firefox/webdriver.py",
             line 157, in __init__
remote:        self.service.start()
remote:      File "/app/.heroku/python/lib/python3.6/site-packages/
             selenium/webdriver/common/service.py", line 83, in start
remote:        os.path.basename(self.path), self.start_error_message)
remote:      selenium.common.exceptions.WebDriverException:
             Message: 'geckodriver' executable needs to be in PATH.
remote:
remote:
remote: =========================================================
remote: FAIL: test_invoice_renders_exactly_as_expected (main.
        tests.test_admin.TestAdminViews)
```

391

```
remote: ----------------------------------------------------------
remote: Traceback (most recent call last):
remote:   File "/tmp/build/main/tests/test_admin.py", line 105,
          in test_invoice_renders_exactly_as_expected
remote:     self.assertEqual(content, expected_content)
remote: AssertionError: '\n<![111 chars].min.450fc463b8b1.
        css">\n <title>Invoice</t[1573 chars]tml>' != '\n<![111
        chars].min.css">\n    <title>Invoice</title>\n
        </he[1560 chars]tml>'
remote: Diff is 1919 characters long. Set self.maxDiff to None
to see it.
remote:
remote: ----------------------------------------------------------
remote: Ran 25 tests in 16.839s
remote:
remote: FAILED (failures=1, errors=1)
        Destroying test database for alias 'default'...
To ...:booktime
 ! [remote rejected] master -> master (pre-receive hook declined)
error: failed to push some refs to 'dokku@...:booktime'
```

As you can see, there are a couple of tests that are not working. The first one is the Selenium test. Unfortunately, there is no way to run this test as is, as it is relies on launching Firefox. We have to skip it.

We are going to use the test-tagging feature of Django to mark this test. It is a small change of main/tests/test_e2e.py:

```
from django.test import tag
...

@tag('e2e')
class FrontendTests(StaticLiveServerTestCase):
    ...
```

Having done so, we can now exclude it from the tests to be run pre-deployment, which means changing the last line of bin/post_compile to

```
./manage.py test --noinput --exclude-tag=e2e
```

There is one last broken test, and it is about the invoice. This happened in this chapter, while introducing WhiteNoise in the project. WhiteNoise does not generate the same output for every {% static %} tag evaluation.

We are also going to alter the test on the PDF because, being a low-level format, its binary output depends on too many factors, even though visually might be equal.

We are going to change main/tests/test_admin.py in this way:

```
import re
...

def compare_bodies(content, expected_content):
    c_match = re.search(r '<body>(.*)</body>', content,
    re.DOTALL|re.M)
    e_match = re.search(r '<body>(.*)</body>', expected_content,
    re.DOTALL|re.M)
    if c_match and e_match:
        return c_match.group(1) == e_match.group(1)
    return False

class TestAdminViews(TestCase):
    ...

    def test_invoice_renders_exactly_as_expected(self):
        ...

        response = self.client.get(
            reverse(
                "admin:invoice", kwargs={"order_id": order.id}
            )
        )
```

```python
    self.assertEqual(response.status_code, 200)
    content = response.content.decode("utf8")

    with open(
        "main/fixtures/invoice_test_order.html","r"
    ) as fixture:
        expected_content = fixture.read()

    self.assertTrue(compare_bodies(content, expected_content))

    response = self.client.get(
        reverse(
            "admin:invoice", kwargs={"order_id": order.id}
        ),
        {"format": "pdf"},
    )
    self.assertEqual(response.status_code, 200)
    content = response.content

    with open(
        "main/fixtures/invoice_test_order.pdf", "rb"
    ) as fixture:
        expected_content = fixture.read()

    self.assertEqual(content[:5], expected_content[:5])
```

We changed the assertions to do the following:

- Test the content of the <body> element of the HTML version. This will take away the problem and still give us the benefit of testing.

- Test the PDF by only testing the file signature. We changed this from testing that the PDF is an identical binary to testing that it is a valid PDF. It is an acceptable compromise for now.

Summary

This chapter illustrated many of the common steps that every project must go through when it is time to publish. Scalability, security, and logging are all important things to take care of in a finished product, but they are not of primary concern while in the development phase.

We have seen how to optimize static assets for transmission and execution speed using both JavaScript and Python tools, because I tried to pick the best tools available for the job regardless of the language.

Even though this book is not about deployments and configuring servers, not mentioning how to do this would not give you the full picture. PaaS is not the only way to deploy, but it is certainly one of the easiest, which is why I picked it for the start.

We also explored integration with object stores such as S3. For sites that need to manage a high volume of media files, choosing these tools can save you a lot of troubles down the line. Integrating these with Django is easy.

I hope you enjoyed this book. Now you have the necessary knowledge to tackle most Django projects. Please go ahead and have fun!

Index

© Federico Marani 2019
F. Marani, *Practical Django 2 and Channels 2*,
https://doi.org/10.1007/978-1-4842-4099-1

S

Sass, 180
save() method, registration
  page, 122
SECRET_KEY, 20
Selenium, 191
self.stderr.write, 95
self.stdout.write, 95
Single-page application (SPA), 183
send_mail() function, 46, 128
Sentry, 388
Serialization, 86
Server-sent events (SSE), 303
Serving static assets
  Amazon S3, 365
  collectstatic Django
    command, 367
  Django library, 365
  Google Cloud Storage, 365
  Minio, 365
  Nginx, 365
  WhiteNoise, 366
SessionMiddleware, 17
Shipment tracking
  aiohttp, 322
  aioredis, 322
  asynchronous network
    library, 322
  BookTime, 320
  consumer, 322, 324
  HTTP API, 320
  Pastebin, 321–322, 324
  query_remote_server(), 324, 326

reverse-proxy system, 321
test, 324–325
showmigrations command, 68
show_urls command, 236
Signup page, 126
SingleObjectMixin class, 140
Single-page application (SPA)
  bootstrap page, 184
  drawbacks, 183
  REST APIs, 183
  routing, 183
Single product page
  DetailView, 104, 106, 108
  object.tags.all, 107
  template filters, 106
  urlpattern, 107
SMTP, 20, 46
SQLite, 6, 117
sqlmigrate, 68
SQL queries, 4
Static file, 179–180
StaticLiveServerTestCase, 193
STATIC_ROOT, 16
STATIC_URL, 16
stream() method, 309
Stylus, 181
Support views, 238
SyncConsumer, 283

T

Templates, 18
TransactionTestCase, 65
Twelve-factor app methodology, 367

Printed in the United States
By Bookmasters